When One Wants Out and the Other Doesn't

Doing Therapy with Polarized Couples

When One Wants Out and the Other Doesn't

Doing Therapy with Polarized Couples

Edited by

John F. Crosby, Ph.D.

The University of Kentucky

BRUNNER/MAZEL, *Publishers* • New York

Library of Congress Cataloging-in-Publication Data

When one wants out and the other doesn't.

Includes bibliographies and index.
1. Marital psychotherapy. 2. Family psychotherapy.
3. Polarity (Psychology) I. Crosby, John F.
RC488.5.W47 1989   616.89'156   88-7444
ISBN 0-87630-527-3

Published by
BRUNNER/MAZEL, INC.
19 Union Square
New York, New York 10003

10 9 8 7 6 5 4 3 2

This book is dedicated
to the memory of
Ann Alhadeff

Preface

Probably everyone who practices marriage and family therapy has one kind of client population that seems to be a modal or predominating type. For three decades I have experienced more marital situations where one of the couple wants "out" of the marriage and the other wants to "stay in" than any other type.

The idea for this collection of first-person therapy methodologies came to me after two successive national meetings of the American Association for Marriage and Family Therapy (AAMFT), in New York (1985) and Orlando (1986). The cases that were discussed were characterized by the presence of alcoholism, and drug and other addictions. Oftentimes there was a clear pathology and a diagnostic label. Rarely did I hear a presentation that dealt with a polarized couple wherein the marriage had simply become a devitalized, ho-hum relationship. While I was duly impressed with the programs and the presenters, the scholarship and the theoretical analyses, I kept thinking of several of my own cases of polarized couples. I wondered why these nonpathological, worn-down, and polarized couples were seldom dealt with at professional meetings. In my own practice I often felt that rebuilding the marriage of a polarized couple was almost a hopeless task because already at the first session one of the partners was making a claim for "wanting out." I wondered how other therapists were dealing with this very real problem. How did people like Tony Jurich and Candyce Russell, Laura Singer, Bill Nichols, Craig Everett, Elly Macklin, and Marcia Lasswell handle situations like this?

This small volume is one answer. Add to the above the names of Mike Sporakowski, Wayne Oates, Luciano L'Abate, Barbara Fisher, and Barbara James, together with co-authors Doris Hewitt, Sandy Volgy, Charles Drees, and Robert Calhoun, and we have the thinking and methodology of a considerable group of respected marriage and family therapists, each of whom is bringing his or her mental acuity and therapeutic touch to the same type of situation.

My thanks to the authors for sharing their thinking and their methods. In a very real sense this is their book and I am simply the one who orchestrated it. I hope that young professionals, seasoned professionals, and students preparing for the field will benefit by integrating and selecting from the various methods and procedures contained herein. Of course, this is no "last word" because the authors will keep on changing and reintegrating, rethinking, and revising their theory and their methods of doing therapy with polarized couples. Such activity is the essence of growth. We invite the reader to do the same: to change, to think, to revise, to integrate, to grow.

No book would be complete without noting the work of one's colleagues and support staff. I especially am indebted to Darla Botkin, Ph.D., for her friendly adversary role in helping me decide on the sequencing of the chapters. Mr. Michael Rupured has contributed excellent support via his wordprocessing skills; I am very appreciative of his commitment to this work. My thanks to the support staff at Brunner/Mazel and especially to my editor, Ann Alhadeff. Ann believed in the *promise* and in the *message* of these pages. She gave of herself in the editorial process to such an extent that *When One Wants Out and the Other Doesn't* is also "her" book.

John F. Crosby, Ph.D.

Contents

Contributors

ROBERT W. CALHOUN, Ph.D., is Co-Director of the Rocky
Mountain Marriage and Family Institute in Fort Collins, Colorado, and is in private practice as a licensed psychologist and
marriage and family therapist. He received his doctorate in
counseling psychology from the University of Texas at Austin
after attending Union Theological Seminary in New York
City. Dr. Calhoun has worked in various settings including
community mental health, and residential treatment for children and adolescents. He is a Clinical Member of the American
Association for Marriage and Family Therapy and a member
of the American Psychological Association.

CHARLES M. DREES, M.S., is in private practice in Topeka,
Kansas. He received his master's degree in marriage and family
therapy from Kansas State University. While there, he was
Project Coordinator of a therapy outcome study directed by
Candyce Russell. In addition to private practice, Mr. Drees is
pursuing a degree in Social Work from the University of
Kansas.

CRAIG A. EVERETT, Ph.D., is currently in private practice in
marital and family therapy, and divorce mediation, Tucson,
Arizona. He received his Ph.D. from Florida State University.
He is also Director, Arizona Institute for Family Therapy,
Hospital Corporation of America Sonora Desert Hospital. He
is past President of the American Association for Marriage
and Family Therapy; Editor, *Journal of Divorce*; Fellow and

Approved Supervisor, AAMFT. He has served on the editorial boards of six journals. He was formerly Associate Professor and Director of the accredited graduate programs in family therapy at Florida State University and Auburn University.

BARBARA L. FISHER, Ph.D., is Co-Director of the Rocky Mountain Marriage and Family Institute in Fort Collins, Colorado; and Associate Professor of Human Development and Family Studies and Director of Marriage and Family Therapy at Colorado State University. She received her M.S. and Ph.D. degrees in marriage and family therapy from Brigham Young University. She has taught family therapy at Brigham Young University, Purdue University, Colorado State University, and through the Rocky Mountain Institute. She is a Clinical Member and Approved Supervisor of the American Association for Marriage and Family Therapy. She is also a member of the Commission on Accreditation for Marriage and Family Therapy Education and a past member of the Board of Directors of AAMFT.

DORIS W. HEWITT, Ph.D., is Director of Professional Services for Cross Keys Counseling Center in Atlanta and has practiced marriage and family therapy in Atlanta since 1972. She received her Ph.D. from Florida State University. Dr. Hewitt is a member and Approved Supervisor of the American Association for Marriage and Family Therapy, and has served as both Treasurer and Vice President of the Georgia Association for Marriage and Family Therapy.

BARBARA E. JAMES, Ph.D., is Associate Professor and Acting Director of the Division of Community and Administrative Psychiatry, Department of Psychiatry, School of Medicine, University of North Carolina at Chapel Hill. For 10 years she has been a consultant in the area of marriage and family therapy to the Lee-Harnett Mental Health Center and to the Family Life Center at Fort Bragg, North Carolina. Her clinical work is mostly with couples in which at least one of the spouses is a physician. She is a member of the American Association for Marriage and Family Therapy and President of the North Carolina Association for Marriage and Family Therapists.

ANTHONY P. JURICH, Ph.D., is a Professor of Human Development and Family Studies and Clinical Director of Marriage and Family Therapy at Kansas State University. He is the author of 84 book chapters and journal articles, including *Marriage and Family Therapy: New Perspectives in Theory, Research, and Practice.* He is a Fellow of the American Association for Marriage and Family Therapy and has received Outstanding Teaching Awards from both Kansas State and the National Council on Family Relations.

LUCIANO L'ABATE, Ph.D., is a Diplomate and Examiner of the American Board of Examiners in Professional Psychology, and a Fellow and Approved Supervisor in the American Association for Marriage and Family Therapy. He is a Fellow and Life Member in the American Orthopsychiatric Association, and Charter Member of the American Family Therapy Association. He is also a member of other professional associations including the National Council on Family Relations. He serves on the Editorial Board of seven journals and as a consultant to various publishing houses. He is an author, co-author, and editor of over 20 books, in addition to more than 200 professional papers and chapters.

MARCIA LASSWELL, M.A., is Professor of Psychology, California State University, Pomona, California; Professor of Marriage and Family Therapy, University of Southern California, Los Angeles; and in private practice with her husband, Thomas Lasswell, in Los Angeles and Claremont, California. She has published widely in professional journals and in popular magazines. She has authored and co-authored seven books in the marriage and family field. She is a member of the Board of Directors of the American Association for Marriage and Family Therapy, a past President of the Southern California Association of Marriage and Family Therapy, and a consultant to the State of California Board of Behavioral Science Examiners.

ELEANOR D. MACKLIN, Ph.D., is Associate Professor, Department of Child, Family and Community Studies, and Director, Marriage and Family Therapy Program, at Syracuse University. Dr. Macklin is nationally known for her leadership in the study of nontraditional family forms and in the field of family therapy. She is currently a member of the Steering Committee of the National Training Directors of the American Association for Marriage and Family Therapy, Chair of the AIDS Task Force for Groves Conference on Marriage and the Family, and Co-Chair of the National Coalition on AIDS and Families. She is a Clinical Member, an Approved Supervisor, and a Fellow of the American Association for Marriage and Family Therapy, and a certified sex educator and sex therapist with the American Association of Sex Educators, Counselors, and Therapists.

WILLIAM C. NICHOLS, Ed.D., a Diplomate in Clinical Psychology of The American Board of Professional Psychology, is in private practice in Tallahassee, Florida, and is former President of both the American Association for Marriage and Family Therapy and the National Council on Family Relations. He has been active in the family therapy field for a quarter century. Currently editor of *Contemporary Family Therapy* and the AAMFT's *Family Therapy News,* he founded the *Journal of Marital and Family Therapy,* and also edited *Family Relations* and *Marriage and Family Therapy: A Reader.* Co-author of *Systemic Family Therapy* and author of *Marital Therapy: An Integrative Approach,* he holds a doctorate from Columbia University, and is licensed in Michigan (clinical psychologist and marriage counselor) and Florida (marriage and family therapist).

WAYNE E. OATES, Ph.D., is Professor of Psychiatry and Behavioral Sciences at the School of Medicine of the University of Louisville. He is also Senior Professor of Psychology of Religion and Pastoral Counseling at the Southern Baptist Theological Seminary. He is a member, Approved Supervisor, and

Fellow of the American Association for Marriage and Family Therapy and Diplomate of the American Association of Pastoral Counselors. Dr. Oates is the author of 45 books and over 200 articles. He edited *The Christian Care Series* of the Westminster Press which deals with such family issues as the convalescent mental patient at home, the family survivors of a suicide, the abusing family, grandparenthood, and the family of the homosexual person. His most recent book is *Behind the Masks: Personality Disorders in Religious Behavior.*

CANDYCE S. RUSSELL, Ph.D., is Professor of Marriage and Family Therapy at Kansas State University, an approved Supervisor and Fellow and a former Secretary of the American Association for Marriage and Family Therapy. Along with David Olson and Douglas Sprenkle, she is co-developer of the Circumplex Model of Marital and Family Systems, and co-editor of the two-volume series, *Circumplex Model: Systemic Assessment and Treatment of Families.* She has conducted research on the transition to parenthood, rural families, marital quality, and predictors of family therapy outcome. Dr. Russell holds a doctorate from the University of Minnesota and has taken additional clinical training at the Philadelphia Child Guidance Clinic and the Menninger Foundation.

LAURA J. SINGER-MAGDOFF, Ed.D., is President and Founder of the Interpersonal Development Institute, Inc., and "Save A Marriage" (S.A.M.), and a practicing marital and family psychotherapist. She is a Fellow and past President of the American Association for Marriage and Family Therapy and a charter member of the American Family Therapy Association. Dr. Singer was an adjunct associate professor at Columbia University Teacher's College. She is a fellow and former faculty member of the American Institute for Psychotherapy and Psychoanalysis. She is consulting editor for the *Journal of Sex and Marital Therapy*; the co-author of *Sex Education on Film*; and *Stages: The Crises That Shape Your Marriage,* and has been published in numerous professional publications.

MICHAEL J. SPORAKOWSKI, Ph.D., received his Ph.D. from Florida State University. He is currently Professor; Department of Family and Child Development, at Virginia Polytechnic Institute and State University. He was an NIMH post-doctoral trainee in marriage counseling at the University of Minnesota and has served on the faculties of Florida State University and the University of Illinois. Dr. Sporakowski is former Editor of *Family Relations: Journal of Applied Family and Child Studies.* He has served as President of the Southeastern Council on Family Relations and the Virginia Association of Marital and Family Therapists. He is a Fellow and Approved Supervisor of the American Association for Marriage and Family Therapy.

SANDRA S. VOLGY, Ph.D., is currently in private practice in clinical and child psychology, family therapy and divorce mediation, Tucson, Arizona. She received her Ph.D. from the University of Arizona. She is an Approved Supervisor of the American Association for Marriage and Family Therapy and consultant in child therapy, Hospital Corporation of America Sonora Desert Hospital. Dr. Volgy was formerly in private practice, Southeast Family Institute, and adjunct clinical faculty, Florida State University, Tallahassee; formerly, Director, Child Advocacy Services, Pima County Conciliation Court, Tucson; formerly Chief Psychologist, Tucson Child Guidance Clinic.

Introduction

The literature on marriage and family theory and therapy has proliferated in the 1970s and 1980s. Theoretical methodologies, ranging from insight-oriented approaches to behavioral to systems frameworks, are given major attention in the literature. A plethora of therapeutic methods, themes, and modalities are presented: structural, strategic, experiential, extended, communication, functional, contextual, neurolinguistic programming, integrative, and object relations. Cognitive restructuring, the use of many kinds and types of paradox, directives, and genograms are often practiced as techniques. Sometimes these techniques are utilized quite apart from their respective theoretical bases.

In the decade of the 1960s a marriage therapist had to choose between doing work with only one partner, or both partners together, or both partners separately, or with one partner while the other partner worked with another therapist. Today the marital therapist is still faced with these choices. However, today the therapist is also expected to define his or her epistemology and to clarify his or her cybernetic orientation as first order or second order. Today's marital therapist is expected to be on the cutting edge of theory while remaining ever the practical tactician.

Additionally, the literature is concerned with specific disorders, such as anorexia, bulimia, alcohol addiction, drug addiction, sexual addictions, and schizophrenia. Amidst this abundance of pathological categories there remains the nonpathological marriage, which is perhaps best described in earlier literature as the "devitalized marriage" (Cuber & Haroff, 1965) and more recently as "ambivalent" by two of the authors in this volume (Nichols & Everett, 1986). I am referring to the marriage where "ho hum" rules the day. Emotional divorce is either just around the corner or is a fact. The partners go through the motions, but what appears to an outsider to be intimacy is nothing more than pseudomutuality and/or parallel living. Scholars, including empirical researchers, theorists, and demographers, have yet to agree on what proportion of marriages ending in divorce are of the more severe pathological type or the self-destructing, ambivalent/devitalized type.

This volume is concerned exclusively with the ambivalent/ devitalized type, which includes, but is not necessarily limited to, ho-hum marriages, with parallel-living couples. Love has died for at least one partner and the couple is often emotionally, if not legally, divorced. These marriages do not present huge problems, such as alcoholism, drug addiction, or major or tragic catastrophes. Sometimes there is an affair, or perhaps rebellious and/or unappreciative offspring.

Having asked the authors to address their chapter to the polarized marriage, I wanted to be more specific in spelling out the focus and style of the chapter. I wanted the chapter to illustrate how the author(s) integrated his or her theory with its corresponding methodology. Often it is only with difficulty, if at all, that we can see how theory and method are integrated, that is, how our theory informs our methodology and procedures in actual cases. In order to guide the authors in this endeavor, I gave them a series of questions and a directive. These questions and the directive are as follows:

> How do you handle couples like this?
> What do you do with them in therapy?
> What is your theoretical framework?
> Do you use working hypotheses?
> Do you diagnose in any formal way?
> How do you avoid being triangled?
> Are you strategic, structural, extended, functional, integrated, eclectic, etc.?
> How do you deal with the likely outcome where one still persists in filing for divorce and the other becomes angry and bitter?

Illustrate your method and style: Through the medium of print, let the reader *see* how you work.

The 12 chapters that follow are "grass roots" literature. The chapters represent a wide range of theory and method. Perhaps the reader will identify more readily with some authors than others, because we usually tend to look for confirmation and validation of our own theory and method. However, there is much to be learned and much to be gleaned by careful consideration of each of the authors' positions. The reader will bring his or her own theoretical and applied background to each of the chapters and may well see patterns and nuances of procedure and method that many of the rest of us fail to recognize. In the *Afterword* I attempt to pull together what I see in terms of consensuality and commonality. In this respect the *Afterword* really should not be read until one has had sufficient time to digest each of the 12 accounts. Indeed, a good exercise would be to write one's own *Afterword* to this volume.

As a final thought prior to reading the 12 chapters, I would like to introduce the reader to my version of the four basic errors related to marriage, divorce, and remarriage (Crosby, 1985): type I error—marrying too early and too quickly and for the wrong reasons; type II error—remaining married for the wrong reasons; type III error—divorcing prematurely and too hastily; type IV error—remarrying too quickly and for the wrong reasons. Suffice it to say that the authors of this volume are addressing the type II and type III errors, and by implication the type IV error.

The antidote for a type II error lies in helping people discover the right reasons for them to remain together. This collection of 12 accounts of doing therapy with polarized couples is targeted most specifically at this antidote. In order to do this, the type III error must be avoided, that is, ending the relationship prematurely and too hastily. Therefore, I find it axiomatic that when we do therapy with polarized couples where one wants out and the other doesn't, we are presented with a unique opportunity. We can help the couple reconnect and rebuild and stay together for the right reasons, or we can help the couple disconnect for the right reasons by establishing a mutually beneficial therapeutic relationship in which neither partner acts hastily or prematurely in a unilateral attempt to end the marriage. And if divorce is the final disposition in a case, at the same time implicit within the therapeutic endeavor is the reeducation opportunity to guard against remarriage too quickly and for the wrong reasons.

As Robert Anderson, the playwright, has said: "In every marriage more than a week old, there are grounds for divorce. The trick is to find, and continue to find, grounds for marriage" (1972, p. 39).

John F. Crosby, Ph.D.

REFERENCES

Anderson, R. W. (1972). *Solitaire and double solitaire* (p. 39). New York: Random House.

Crosby, J. F. (1985). *Illusion and disillusion: The self in love and marriage* (3rd Ed.) (pp. 299–300). Belmont, CA: Wadsworth Publishing Co.

Cuber, J. F., & Haroff, P. B. (1965). *Sex and the significant Americans* (pp. 46–50). New York: Appleton-Century.

Nichols, W. C., & Everett, C. A. (1986). *Systemic family therapy* (pp. 287–288). New York: Guilford Press.

When One Wants Out and the Other Doesn't

*Doing Therapy with
Polarized Couples*

1

Polarized Couples: Behind the Facade

William C. Nichols

Some marriages ostensibly are in good condition. Judged by the absence of major disruptive factors such as alcoholism, drug addiction, or catastrophic stresses, they appear on the surface to be functioning adequately. Nevertheless, participants in such marriages sometimes appear in the therapist's office with one spouse expressing a desire to divorce and the other pushing hard for reconciliation and continuation of the relationship. The calm surface has been disturbed, the misleading facade penetrated. What does the therapist find and what can be done with it?

One day an attorney colleague asked me, "Will you see a client of mine? She and her husband have been seeing a pair of marriage counselors for six or seven months. The other day she brought in a four-page, single-spaced joint custody agreement that the counselors are trying to get them to accept. She wants to marry a fellow who lives halfway across the country, and this agreement would have the kids moving back and forth between

Mrs. White and her current husband several times a year. They're stuck; he doesn't want a divorce and she's adamant about leaving."

A second case involved a socially prominent middle-aged couple. Mrs. West called for an appointment for herself and her dentist husband. She indicated that he had left for a weekend a couple of months earlier and was still saying that he wanted a divorce, although he had agreed to seeing a therapist. Mrs. West reported that she was reasonably happy with life as it was, that things were "on the rise" for her personally, and that she definitely did not want to divorce.

Both Mrs. White and Dr. and Mrs. West were seen in therapy. We shall return to both cases after a look at some of the general issues in dealing therapeutically with polarized couples.

THE COMMITMENT ISSUE

"It takes two to make, one to break." Marriage, as the lone voluntary relationship in families, can be broken by either one or both of the partners. Polarized couples thus raise immediately the issue of commitment. This kind of case strikes at something fundamentally different from marital cases that involve primarily communication difficulties, disagreements, and so on. The very relationship itself is at stake here.

Assessment of the nature of the commitment, therefore, is a top priority. What commitment do they have to each other and the marriage? What do they want out of treatment? The initial assessment, therefore, has both practical and ethical concerns. Is there anything to work with? Will the therapist's interventions tip the scales? If so, in what direction? This is not a place where a responsible therapist will seek to demonstrate his or her ability to employ dazzling interventions, but rather, will proceed with a clear understanding that the clients have the responsibility for determining where they wish to go with their lives. The therapist is not neutral, but impartial.

I have described individuals as being preambivalent, ambivalent, or postambivalent with regard to their commitment to the spouse and the marriage (Nichols & Everett, 1986). Those who are preambivalent have not considered the possibility of breaking the marriage. Ambivalent spouses regard their mate and marriage with mixed negative and positive feelings and fluctuate between the positive-negative, love-hate extremes. Postambivalent individuals have resolved their conflict and decided either to end or to continue the marriage.

Clarifying the nature of the partner's commitment to their spouse and personal willingness to work on the relationship thus becomes an issue whenever the possibility of marital breakup is raised. Sometimes both partners come into therapy with their minds made up as to what they are going to do about the marriage. Sometimes one has reached a decision regarding the marriage and the other is undecided or ambivalent.

One very important factor to assess is whether or not the spouse who claims to wish a divorce actually has reached the point of "crossing the Rubicon" so that he or she will go ahead with the divorcing process. Has that person reached the point of no return? Occasionally, one sees a case where that point is reached after the couple come in for treatment. One spouse may decide that the other "is not a nice person," after seeing that he or she is behaving in ways that show a lack of caring. When evidence of betrayal and lack of caring are solidly manifested, the offended spouse crosses the Rubicon and decides that the marriage is over, that there is no point in trying any longer.

When the Luckeys made their first appointment, George Luckey was living out of the marital home. At that time he wished to maintain a separation, but did not desire a divorce. Jean Luckey wanted a reconciliation. Within a month, Jean began to change her mind. George dropped out of treatment after three or four sessions and broke a number of promises to Jean. When she encountered George with his girlfriend at his apartment on a couple of occasions, witnessed his "lack of caring and lack of responsibility for the children," and found that he had been untruthful on several matters, she became convinced that George had "really changed" and that he could not be trusted any longer, that he "lies and lies and lies and cares only about himself, not the children or me." Jean filed for divorce and set about putting a new life in order for herself and their two children. This did not appear to be a case in which George "really wanted a divorce and maneuvered" Jean into filing, because there were some practical financial reasons why he did not wish to divorce. More important from a therapeutic point of view was the fact that Jean made some significant gains in self-esteem and self-confidence by "accepting the reality of the situation" and "taking control of my life," as she put it.

The manner of presentation certainly affects the way in which I try to clarify the commitment question. Three broad approaches are used when the partners come in together. One involves asking direct questions of the individuals. This includes exploring with them their feelings and motivations as effectively as possible. Indirect or projective types of questions also may be used. A second and related approach involves assessing descriptions and observations of their behaviors: What do the spouses say and do? What do I observe them doing in the sessions? Third, how do they handle any tasks or assignments that I give them to perform?

One of the crucial things that I look for in assessment is the object relations capacity of each partner. What seem to be the emotional bases on which they relate to and need the other person? To what extent, for example, do they appear to be functioning at a "need gratification" level in which the partner is viewed primarily as a source of gratification for them, a kind of emotional service station? Or are they functioning essentially at a level of "object constancy" in which the partner is viewed more as a whole person who has needs and wishes of his or her own as well as being a source of gratification? What seems to be the capacity of each to give emotionally to their partner?

Feedback and sharing with the partner or partners of some of my impressions and questions provide opportunity to test the validity of my hypotheses. How do they respond? Also, how do they react when I push on the boundaries of the relationship by asking questions that challenge their joint defenses? For example, I may say, "It seems to me from what you have described that you have been doing a lot of talking about divorce. Have you seriously considered or talked about separation? What you will do regarding the children if you should divorce? How you will relate to each other if you divorce?"

Another aspect of commitment pertains to forming a therapeutic alliance and a therapeutic contract or bargain. Can the therapist and clients form a working relationship? Can they formulate a working agreement concerning the goals of the therapeutic work?

Precipitating factors that brought about the decision to seek out a therapist, the stage of the partners in their marital life cycle, any pertinent difficulties and problems of one partner, and unresolved issues in communication and in the conflict/compromise areas also get early attention in the ongoing assessment process.

The marital complementarity—how the partners "fit together"—is a matter of concern both at the beginning of contact with the partners and in treatment subsequently. Is it possible to reestablish a workable complementarity? Or is the marriage headed for divorce because, for whatever reasons, it is not possible to bring about a situation in which both partners secure an acceptable level of satisfaction in the relationship?

COMMON CLINICAL TYPES AND CAUSATIVE FACTORS

What do we find when we dig into the situations that present under the rubric of "one wants out and the other doesn't?" The presenting complaint and the genuine problems frequently are not the same. Often there are combinations of individual and interactive problems behind the complaint that "I want a divorce and my mate doesn't." The descriptions that follow are only a partial listing of the kinds of difficulties encountered clinically.

Faulty Original "Contract"

The marriage turns out to be different than expected. Passage of time exposes the fact that the original set of expectations was not the same for both spouses or that one mate is unable or unwilling to hold up her or his end of the bargain. On the surface the marriage may look all right and outsiders may not be aware that there is anything deficient in the relationship.

Douglas was startled, for example, a few months after the wedding to find that Kathleen had married him in order to escape her family and small town. Her caring about him was minimal and her commitment to being married was nonexistent. Now living in a city with a job and a few friends, she had no further need for him as a partner. In terms of social exchange theory, Kathleen had secured what she desired and no longer found that being married to Douglas provided more benefits than not being married to him. All she wanted was a divorce, as much money as she could get, and to be able to retain her married name. Kathleen did not come in but made it clear by telephone that those were her feelings, that any therapy in that case would be with Douglas, if he wanted it, and that she had no need or intention of seeing anybody other than her attorney.

The marriage of Tom and Joanne lasted two years. Superficially, it appeared to be all right, but the original marital "contract" was thrown together in the midst of a rebound situation. Tom, who operated at a need gratification level, had spotted someone (almost literally, something) he wanted, and had moved in with a huge rush, playing on Joanne's needs, insecurities, and upset over the breaking of a previous engagement. Once married, he failed to uphold the promises that Joanne could continue her education while she worked and replaced his egalitarian behaviors of the courtship with demands that she do things the way he insisted was "right." Joanne left three times during the brief marriage, but was persuaded to return twice by Tom's promises to "get some help" for their marriage. With two different therapists he essentially tried to enlist the clinicians in the cause of getting his wife to do what he wished. Despite his protestations of love and commitment, once he was convinced that Joanne was not coming back a third time, he rapidly replaced her with a live-in mate whom he married as soon as the divorce was final.

In neither of these cases was there anything substantial to work with regarding the marriage. Kathleen was never seen by the therapist. Forming a therapeutic relationship with Tom was not possible for either of two therapists. Divorce followed in both cases.

Differential Development

Some couples had an original contract and complementarity that were workable. Neither partner has a conscious or deliberate intent to sabotage the marital "contract," but the development of different needs eventually makes them incompatible. Changes in one but not in the other partner or growth in different directions bring them to the point that one wants out of the marriage. This kind of marriage does not appear to be in trouble to outsiders and evokes a "What a shame" kind of reaction from friends and acquaintances.

The Allisons had been married for more than 25 years and had grown children. Originally their relationship had been based firmly on a conservative religio-social foundation. Mrs. Allison had not changed her beliefs and still went to church for at least three services weekly. Mr. Allison had loosened up considerably and enjoyed "taking a drink" socially and wanted to be able to drink beer and wine at home. He complained that he could no longer let his behaviors be bound by the strictures of conservative religion. In terms of commitment, Mrs. Allison was preambivalent and would not consider divorce. She wanted her husband to "be like he used to be" and things to be as they had been in the early years of marriage. This was "not possible" for her husband, who was moving toward a postambivalent stance.

Life-Cycle Transitions

New expectations and demands arise as a couple moves through the family life cycle, their individual life cycles, and the marital life cycle. The birth of a child can be a traumatic event that disrupts the marital complementarity, for example. Hitting the middle years similarly may call for changes that affect the marriage, although the concept of "a midlife crisis" frequently is used too facilely as an explanation for behavioral changes.

Mrs. East sought therapeutic help to deal with her reactions to her husband's departure from the home and his statements that he wanted a divorce. He was not available for therapy, refusing to come in even for a single session focused on child-rearing. Ostensibly, the addition of a second child had caused the marital difficulty. An examination of the situation with Mrs. East, however, disclosed that it was not the birth of their son as such, but an illness that she had during the pregnancy that precipitated Mr. East's departure. From descriptions of his re-actions, it appeared that her inability to give him the attention that she had previously provided led to the departure. The issue was that she had become emotionally and physically unavailable to her husband for a period of several weeks and that he had found this unforgivable. There were additional indications during subsequent months that he regarded her in object relations terms as a "bad mother" to him.

Treatment was conducted only with Mrs. East. She required help in dealing with the loss and coping with life alone with the children. She also needed help with clarification/confrontation until she got to the point when she recognized, following the divorce, that the house was hers, that her former husband no longer had any claims there, that his visits were solely for the purpose of picking up and returning the children, and that he had no proprietary rights to go into her bedroom, use a bathroom for shaving, and so forth. Treatment focused in part on helping Mrs. East get over the hurt, bewilderment, and guilt feelings, learn to be appropriately assertive and firm with her former husband. She also worked out some unresolved issues with her family of origin that had contributed to her past acceptance of a subservient role in the marriage.

External/Situational Factors

By this, I mean that one partner does not wish to get a divorce because it will cost him money or cause difficulty and embar-rassment in some other way. The Hills, a social register type of couple, furnish an illustration.

Mrs. Hill wanted a divorce and contacted me because her attorney recommended that she do so in order to make certain that she knew what she wanted. The husband did not want a divorce, ostensibly because his wife "just doesn't know what she wants. She's into women's lib and that sort of thing." It quickly became evident that he was not in a posture to make personal changes or to work on the marriage. Rather, he would point out to his wife what a great lifestyle she had and make threats that if she persisted with the divorce he would hide his money so that she and her attorney would never find it. Also, it became clear very early that he feared his powerful father's disapproval. The elder Mr. Hill was very fond of his daughter-in-law and especially his two grandchildren.

Mrs. Hill reached the final-straw stage when her husband gave her genital herpes, although he continued to deny that he had any involvement in extramarital sex. She also was at a point that she knew that if she were to divorce, her father and father-in-law would see that she and the children were well cared for economically. She and the children could continue to live in the style to which they were accustomed. Additionally, she was gaining her own identity through going to school and preparing for a career, something that her husband had initially supported but subsequently fought every step of the way. At the same time her husband was still without his own identity, being known as "the son of . . . ," his socially prominent attorney father.

Mr. Hill left treatment after a few sessions. What eventually emerged was that he did not wish to risk having his financial situation come into the open. He feared that going to court would expose a financial situation that would lead to jail for him. Eventually he did go to jail, although exposure came from an auditor's discovery of his embezzlement of funds from the bank where he worked.

Individual Problems

Burt and Sarah were a "model young couple" insofar as their families, friends, and members of their church were concerned.

Married nearly three years, they were doing well financially, with both working and progressing in their jobs. They were childless by choice and had acquired a nice suburban home. Hence, it was a shock to Sarah and all who knew them when Burt suddenly moved out of the house and moved in with a young divorcée with one child whom he met in the course of his work.

After several weeks, Burt agreed to go with Sarah to see a clinician, although he was reluctant and went "only because you want to go." When I asked him, "Why are you here?" he could respond only that Sarah wished to come and that their clergyman recommended it. After some exploration, he could acknowledge that he was somewhat confused about doing things that were against his consciously held values. I pointed out to him that he owed it to himself, to his wife, and to the woman he was living with to try and answer a few questions before taking the step of divorce, that he could always divorce later if that were his choice, but that he needed to know what he was doing. Since he could not deal with these issues in his wife's presence, and there was no basis for conjoint work at that time, I saw him alone for a couple of sessions.

Burt talked rather freely in those sessions as I explored with him his past heterosexual relationships, learning about his first love, a high-school romance with a pregnancy, followed by an abortion against his wishes that he was compelled by his father to pay for. I gave him strong support for the meaning that the attachment had for him, validation for the depth and painfulness of his feelings, and some interpretation of what I perceived to be his conflicts. These included his feelings of helplessness, loss, and guilt in the high-school love affair and his ambivalent feelings toward his powerful and highly moral/moralistic father. The struggles were close enough to the surface for Burt to be able to acknowledge the possible presence of ties between the old conflicts and the present situation. The need to oppose his father at the same time that he sought his father's approval as part of establishing his own power and identity and the need to deal with old guilt feelings by staying with and taking care of a substitute for the "abandoned" high-school sweetheart were presented to Burt as a possible explanation for what was happening. This was laid before him as something that "seems to make sense," with the request that he think about it and see if it helped with his puzzlement and conflict.

Following those meetings I saw Burt and Sarah together once again. I sketched the situation: At that time Sarah still wished to work on the marriage and Burt still planned to continue living with the other woman. Then there was no contact with the couple for a few months. During that hiatus Burt broke up with his girlfriend—although there was some ambivalence and wavering initially—and went home. Sarah gave him support for staying home and helped him with his resolution to stay out of the other relationship. Eventually, the partners returned for therapy.

The individual problems that emerge in such cases can range from unconscious conflicts carried over from earlier life and various family-of-origin difficulties to specific, unresolved grief situations. Burt's case, as others, illustrates the client's attempt to use "a neurotic solution," which actually is an attempted solution because neurotic symptoms and solutions focus on substitute matters and thus do not solve the actual problem.

As most clinicians and citizens know, extramarital sexual involvement by one partner does not automatically mean that the marriage is over. When the attempted solution of personal conflicts through an extramarital relationship or affair does not work, the spouse with the outside involvement frequently returns to the original object relations choice—the marital partner—as Burt did.

With Burt, the relationship with his wife was a mixed one in which the splits in object relations were a significant factor. He was attracted to the exciting part of his wife and frightened of the powerful part of her. She appeared to be an ally against his powerful father, but this also frightened him because of the largely unconscious fear of what would happen if he did what she urged him to do and opposed the father, cutting loose from working for his father in his manufacturing business. There were other relationship issues for Burt and Sarah that were addressed when they came back into therapy with the jointly expressed desire to work on their marriage and personal problems.

There were some similar issues in the Bass case, although they came into treatment at a later stage in the process than did Burt and Sarah. Dr. Bass, a psychiatric resident, had lived with a coworker for three months, having left home after the birth of a son. Propinquity and the fact that he had the girl friend all alone and did not have to share her had been part of the original attraction. Eventually he returned home and came with his wife to see me in "a last ditch effort to save our marriage." Mrs. Bass had wished to salvage the relationship all along.

In this case, the husband's efforts with intimacy were a significant issue. He could not get past the anxiety that gripped him in sex with his wife, and this had moved outward so that he generally avoided her except in dealing with mundane matters. Evidently, he had initially been able to function adequately with the girl friend because of the allure and excitement that propelled him in the early stages until it became clear that he had her, that she was committed. Then it became frightening to him and he backed off. Behind this were early and continued rejections by his mother which left him needy and ambivalent, capped off by rejection from his first true love when he was 15, and issues of differentiation from his family of origin. This case thus had several similarities to Burt and Sarah's situation, although the Basses essentially had moved out of their previously polarized positions before consulting a therapist.

Extramarital Affairs

When extramarital affairs are involved in polarized cases, therefore, it is not so much a question of whether there is such involvement, but of what it means and what the therapist does in regard to it. Careful, sensitive work on the part of the clinician often is crucial in enabling the partners to get back together or to get apart in nondestructive ways.

Midwiving or bridging work by the therapist often is a vital factor in the couple's and the individuals' actions and future.

The extramaritally involved person sometimes will leave the outside relationship on her or his own, after it has been eroded by the passage of time, but will not work out the situation with the spouse without bridging work by the therapist. Pride, apprehension over losing "face," and fear often prevent the person from making a move toward reconciliation on her or his own. Even if the person does go back, it often takes the intervention of an outsider to clean up the residue, clear out scar tissue, and help the partners to form as much of a new relationship of trust as possible. The same often holds true for getting out of an unproductive extramarital relationship and ending an unsatisfactory marriage without dragging along unresolved emotional conflicts.

THERAPEUTIC INTERVENTION

Therapeutic tasks and goals with polarized couples who reconcile and whose marriages last involve, broadly speaking, four parts: clarification, bridging, rebuilding, and pioneering. Clarification of commitment and other significant issues is partly done during the early assessment. There may be, of course, other elucidation of issues during subsequent treatment. Assessment and therapy generally blend together in a recursive fashion so that it is virtually impossible to distinguish between them.

Bridging misunderstandings between the partners is both an early therapeutic task and one that reappears at various points later in treatment. It involves not only an exploration of what they were expecting but also a reworking of differences and establishment of appropriate appreciation of their "good faith efforts" in the past. To the extent that it is true that "nobody set out to mess things up" or to deprive the other of marital satisfaction, this fact needs to be recognized and acknowledged by both partners. Whether the marriage continues or there is a divorce, this kind of establishment of a common ground of understanding between the partners is important to their future growth and development.

Rebuilding of trust following a rupture of the original relationship is essential if the spouses are to live in a marriage with a reasonable degree of security and comfort. If there has been a breaching of the boundaries through extramarital involvement on the part of one or both partners or the threat of divorce for any reason, it is impossible to return to a condition of naive trust. At least one of the partners has reached, for a time, a position of ambivalence regarding the marriage. Never again will it be possible for divorce or other threats to the solidity of the relationship to be "unthinkable." Frankly facing the reality that innocence is gone and establishing patterns of "good faith" behavior and clear communication between the partners so that they can strive for a relationship of realistic trust is an exceedingly important phase and goal of restorative work.

Pioneering into new relationship areas or "breaking new ground" also is vitally important in such work. The inability or failure of the couple to do this earlier in their marriage is a significant factor in reaching the polarization crisis in some cases. Whether this involves establishing a new complementarity of needs and interaction between them or simply pertains to jointly entering new stages of the life cycle and trying new behaviors, it is likely to engender anxiety in many couples. By the time the therapist gets to this stage of working with formerly polarized couples, he or she has moved into a stage of general therapeutic work that appears in the majority of marital cases. That is, the case is no longer concerned with commitment issues and the need to determine what is beneath or behind the polarization; it has become like any other marital therapy case.

At this point, we return to the two cases mentioned at the beginning of the chapter—Mrs. White and Dr. and Mrs. West.

Therapy with One Partner

When my attorney colleague asked me to see Mrs. White, who was at an impasse in her work with other clinicians, I agreed to see her for one session on a consultative basis. The most striking aspects of the 32-year-old woman were her frozen affect and evident depression. After she told me briefly that her husband had dropped out of the conjoint therapeutic work and found his own individual therapist, she showed me the four-page proposed joint custody agreement. I asked her, "What's happened with you in the last year or so?"

Briefly, what emerged was that her best friend had died some 10 months earlier. Three months after that, Mrs. White and the friend's widower decided that they were in love—they had "always been attracted, but had never even thought about doing anything about it before"—and would get married. Mr. White, objecting that it had been a happy marriage for more than 10 years, said that he did not want a divorce and would not let her take the children out of state. The Whites began their conjoint work with a cotherapy team shortly after that confrontation and had been, as her attorney indicated, at an impasse for four months.

I explored with Mrs. White what the friend had meant to her. Mrs. White, an only child, had not been close to her parents. The friend, she said, "was the sister I never had and just about the only close female friend that I have ever had." After we talked about the other significant losses that she had experienced, I began to talk about bereavement and grief and explained normal loss reactions. Then I sat quietly as Mrs. White cried softly for nearly 10 minutes. Afterwards, we dealt with some of her reactions. I suggested that she had undergone a major loss and had been "frozen" emotionally as a way of protecting herself against the pain of the loss, but that I was glad that she had cried and that she did not have to continue to be frozen. When she asked if we could continue, I agreed to see her after she terminated appropriately with the cotherapists, which she did.

One of several dramatic turning points came in the third session when she asked, "Is it possible that I have transferred my feelings for my friend over to her husband?" My response was simply, "I think it's not only possible but probable that that's what's happened." Another significant occurrence came a few sessions later when she reported a dream which, with her associations, indicated that she was "letting go" and letting her friend die. By that time, she was deciding on her own that she did not wish to continue with the divorce-remarriage plans. I gave her some help with regard to how she breaks off with the man, after she had determined that that was the course she would follow.

After the grief began to be resolved, we moved on to deal with some family-of-origin issues. Primarily we tried to rework her current relationships with her parents. I attempted to help her accept them as they were, with both their strengths and blemishes. As she became able to accept their limitations, Mrs. White began to report positive changes in the relationship with her parents. Although we spent very little time on the marriage itself, things began to improve and to return "to normal, only better." Mrs. White terminated after about 12 sessions, reporting that things were fine in the marriage and that she was taking steps to form friendships with other women and other new social relationships.

I never saw Mr. White. Why not? He was not readily available. By the time that I saw his wife, he had his own therapist and evidently needed to protect himself against the possibility of further frustration and hurt. They had seen therapists together for nearly six months, and it had not worked out well for him or the marital relationship. There also were indications that the Whites' marriage had been a relatively solid one for approximately a decade before the interruption and that the significant therapeutic issues did not reside in the marital relationship but in Mrs. White's unresolved grief and family-of-origin relationships. The clinical judgment that she was ready for a direct confrontation of her unresolved grief fortunately was sustained.

Three years after termination, when I spoke to an organization to which she belonged, Mrs. White was in the audience and came up to let me know that she and the marriage were still doing very well. Reports from persons referred by the Whites in subsequent years and other indirect sources have indicated that the Whites have continued to fare well in their marriage.

A More Typical Case

Is what the therapist discovers beneath the ostensibly calm surface, behind the deceptively solid facade, serious enough to lead to a breakup of the polarized marriage? That question typically cannot be answered as quickly or easily as it could in the case of the Whites. In the polarized marriage where differences are resolved, there frequently is a period of several weeks— sometimes shorter, sometimes longer—before both partners are reasonably certain that the relationship will continue. Even after a solid commitment to working on the marriage has been gained, there may be ambivalence and uncertainty. With Dr. and Mrs. West, the commitment to work on the marriage was established rather quickly. The couple's apprehensions about whether they could "make it work" and could establish a marriage that was satisfactory continued to be an issue for some months.

What precipitated Dr. West's brief absence from home and request for a divorce? The immediate factor was the announcement by his dental assistant that she was getting married and leaving her position in his office. The assistant looked up to Dr. West with a kind of "hero worship" that provided him with an emotional boost that he did not receive from his wife. Dr. West, who had served as a mentor for the young woman for five or six years and had become emotionally invested in furthering her career, went into a depression when she decided to get married and stop working. The Wests agreed that the changes with the assistant, the overt transfer of her dependence and emotional responses to her fiancée, were what provoked the dentist's decision to leave home and seek a divorce.

During the initial assessment it became evident that the original marital complementarity between the partners had shifted across the years. They had formed patterns in which they derived significant amounts of their emotional gratification from sources other than the marriage. During early years the husband had focused on his career. Economically he had done well and was continuing to produce income at a high level. He had attained a high degree of technical proficiency and professional recognition, and was spending large amounts of time in professional, political, and organizational activities. Those new interests were providing some gratification, but not enough and not the right kind. Work and profession, in brief, were no longer a major source of gratification as they had been in the past. As work had provided fewer satisfactions and his wife had been absorbed first with their children and then with other activities, he had shifted to the young assistant where his "fathering" and "mentoring" roles had provided some of the emotional gratification that he desired. This need deepened and the focus moved back to his wife more intensely as he lost the emotional gratifications provided when he "took care of" the young assistant.

Mrs. West had been doing some shifting of her own. As the children left home, she moved rather steadily out into the work world and into community activity that provided her with high visibility and a considerable amount of recognition and gratification. Her community social contacts were varied, while those of her husband were largely limited to patients—who could not talk with him while he had his hands in their mouth—and to other dentists with whom he came into contact in their professional-political activities. Thus, while his wife came into contact with a rather wide variety of people, female and male, his contacts were somewhat restricted and consisted primarily of professional peers, many of whom were likely to be in competition with him for both clientele and recognition. When her husband turned his expectations for emotional nurturance on her and "began to need her" as he had not previously, Mrs. West did not know how to respond. Our exploration disclosed that she did not feel adequate to provide all of the time and attention that her husband was suddenly demanding. She made it clear, as I strove to open up a safe arena for communication between them, that she felt inadequate, blamed, and somewhat resentful. By this time Dr. West was making it clear that he did not feel gratified in the marriage, that he felt neglected and resentful.

Concurrently giving some support for their feelings and remarking that both the anxiety and consequent resentment were understandable, I began to explore with them what they would wish to have changed in the marriage. What would make them feel that they were getting what they needed? This involved working with their expectations piece by piece for a short time. I asked for their expectations in the abstract (e.g., What does a good husband do? a good wife?), using this approach as a kind of simple projective device.

The process that was transpiring was as significant as the content of the sessions, and perhaps more important. Not only were the Wests being heard, beginning to hear each other more clearly and having their misunderstandings corrected, but also the rudiments of trust were being reestablished. They could work together on their relationship in a "good faith" fashion. Most of the resentments began to disappear without being directly addressed.

With respect to the past, we spent little time rehashing what had or had not been, doing only the amount that seemed essential in order for one or both of them to drop something and move on. They were able to accept my statement, "It doesn't look like anybody deliberately set out to make anybody else unhappy. Most people most of the time are doing the best that they can, and for better or worse, this seems to have been the case with you." The main issue became not what had been but what could be done now.

This case was spread out. The couple went on vacation after the first three sessions. On their return attention was focused on how they dealt with one another while they were away from their usual environment. Both expressed satisfaction with what had happened; they had concentrated on each other and their relationship and had found that they still liked and loved each other. Outside things had not interfered. They decided that the amount and kind of time they spent together was important and they looked at how they could be assured of their significance to their partner in their everyday life.

After deciding to stay together, the Wests got involved in selling their large house and subsequently in buying and refurnishing a smaller home. The sharing and mutual involvement in those activities was satisfying to both and especially to the husband, but he voiced his apprehension that this "good situation" would not last. At that juncture we looked once again at the reciprocal, circular nature of their interaction. In present-tense terms, as he becomes more satisfied and, therefore, less blame and resentment flow toward his wife, she gives more. As she gives more, he becomes less apprehensive and less resentful, gives more, and expresses more satisfaction. And so on.

We recognized the ability of both partners to affect their interaction. In view of Dr. West's initial strong feeling that he did not have much power in the relationship, efforts were made to help him perceive his genuine ability to change what occurred. We established, for example, that Mrs. West loved and respected him, but resisted being the object of his resentments and disapproval because she was not in his estimation giving him the time, attention, and nurturance that he desired. We noted that when he began to relax, she began to relax. Help was also given Dr. West in recognizing how he could get his message across much more directly and effectively when he expressed his needs rather than his complaints and other reactions to not getting his needs met. Conversely, efforts were made to help Mrs. West become less frightened of his disapproval and more capable of taking the initiative in stating her own wishes.

Dr. West, who had operated somewhat at a need-gratification level at some points, began to question whether he was expecting too much from his wife. One conversation went essentially as follows:

Dr. West: Am I expecting too much?
Therapist: (No verbal response, simply a nod to indicate that the statement/question had been heard.)
Dr. West: Sometimes I wonder if I am expecting too much?
Therapist: Are you? What do you think?
Dr. West: I don't know. Maybe I am.
Therapist: Perhaps. *(to Mrs. West)* What do you feel about it?

This simple kind of interchange was repeated several times as therapy moved toward a conclusion. The partners assumed more readily the task of addressing their own issues and solving their own problems as the commitment to the marriage became established, misunderstandings corrected, trust rebuilt, and pioneering and the breaking of new ground proceeded. In this instance, attention was kept deliberately on the general expectations rather than placed on specifics of the Wests' behaviors. They were aided once again in exploring what they could realistically expect as primary emotional objects for one another and how they could communicate and negotiate.

A major goal with the Wests was to restore a complementarity that would provide an adequate amount and kind of emotional sustenance for both partners. This case represented an increased balance in marital complementarity, as well as progress in several object relations issues that have been mentioned only briefly in this presentation. At termination the Wests seemed to be growing in their ability to deal more adequately and realistically with one another. As we ended I had the feeling that they well might need some additional help somewhere down the road to keep an appropriate balance in their relationship, although we had done what could be done at that time and they had improved markedly.

CODA

The approach used in dealing with polarized marriages is an integrative one that involves systemic, broad psychodynamic, and social learning theory elements. In terms of technique, my work is pragmatic. That is, I use what I think will work best with a particular couple or individual at a given time, fitting the techniques to the case rather than the case to the techniques. Although I do not hesitate to take stands and make suggestions, assign tasks, and make interpretations and be confrontive regarding reality as I perceive it, I try to be mindful at all times of the voluntary nature of the marital relationship and the rights of the clients to make their own determinations and to take their own responsibility for the outcome of their life and marriage.

Once again, it is essential to penetrate the facade with a polarized couple in order to determine whether they need no therapy, marital therapy, divorce therapy, or a period of benign neglect until they are ready to make their commitments and deal with the issues that cause them to be polarized.

REFERENCE

Nichols, W. C., & Everett, C. A. (1986). *Systemic family therapy*. New York: Guilford Press.

2

"I Do and I Don't": Treating Systemic Ambivalence

Barbara L. Fisher and
Robert W. Calhoun

Phil and Diane faithfully attended weekly couple therapy sessions. They were "good" clients in that they expressed their feelings openly, processed their concerns and problems, occasionally did their assignments, attentively listened to their therapist's wisdom and directives, and paid their bill for therapy. In what seemed to be a sudden decision, Phil announced in a routine session that he planned to obtain a divorce. A devastated Diane curled into a ball in a corner of the therapist's office and sobbed. Later in the session, as she threatened suicide, Phil left to find a suitable apartment. Phil never reconsidered the marriage; his wife of 20 years has continued to struggle for the past 16 months to view herself as separate and worthwhile without Phil.

Ron and Nancy dated for six years before entering couples therapy. Nancy was extremely dissatisfied with Ron and did not disguise her agenda of wanting him "fixed." Ron wanted the relationship to continue but her complaints did not make sense to him. He clarified in the first session that he was satisfied with himself and had no interest in changing to meet her expectations. Nancy then demanded that he "go to hell" and never see her again. He agreed to both requests. After a sleepless night, each called the therapist and requested further conjoint sessions to clarify whether they should split up or not.

Leigh scheduled an "emergency" therapy session for herself, indicating that marital therapy might be appropriate at a later time. In spite of the usual first session discomfort, Leigh, a beautiful woman of 40, unloaded her dilemma, desperately hoping for an answer. She loved her husband of 17 years, Gary, and their two children but was "in love" with another man. Within a week, Gary "discovered" Leigh's affair, confronted her, and entered marital therapy with her. Within three months, Leigh decided to leave the marriage; Gary decided he wanted the marriage to work more than ever.

Cases like these, in which one partner wants to end the relationship and the other wants to continue it, are multidimensionally perplexing for couple therapists. On a conceptual level, those of us who operate from a systemic perspective are baffled by a system not striving to maintain itself. Someone trying, ostensibly, to rid himself or herself of a system does not fit the theory without some stretching and bending of homeostatic concepts. On another level, there is not a mutually agreed-upon goal for therapy, which, in our opinion, is vital for effective therapy. In fact, the goals of each partner usually compete as each seeks for validation from the therapist for his or her own goal. Additionally, the dilemma of one spouse wanting to leave and the other wanting to stay almost always involves ongoing issues of power, hurt, abandonment, and unilateral decision making, which can leave the therapist feeling overwhelmed, triangulated, and helpless. Finally, many of these cases involve rampant ambivalence about the relationship which creates havoc for maintaining consistency of goals and treatment.

This chapter will examine our approach for conceptualizing, assessing, and treating couples presenting with this dilemma. We will begin with a presentation of a process model and a clarification of the goals possible in this situation. Next we will examine treatment recommendations and considerations. Our focus will be primarily on couples who either present with ambivalence about the relationship (one wants to leave but is not quite sure) or who have reached a final decision but would benefit from working together to understand the relationship failure.

TREATMENT MODEL

Therapy for couples in which one partner wants to leave may proceed in several directions depending upon the couple and the nature of the request to leave. Figure 1 shows a model for understanding the complex process of treatment for polarized couples which begins with a "crisis" or "dilemma," that is, one partner verbalizes that he or she wants to end the relationship and the other partner disagrees. Some couples enter therapy when this dilemma occurs. The therapist knows little about the relationship and individual needs, making it more difficult to address the issue at the level the couple is ready for. For other couples, the issue arises during couple therapy. In these cases, the therapist has some background and experience with the couple which aids in addressing the couple's needs.

The model shows that after a therapist has been contacted, three levels of treatment are possible, depending upon the couple's or individual's goals. If the couple (or one partner) chooses to not work on the dilemma together, no couple contract is developed. In these cases, therapy may end (or never begin), or one or both partners may begin individual therapy to adjust to the divorce*—*Level I.* Individual therapy may also be offered to a partner with ambivalence about the relationship to facilitate decision making.

---

* We use the term divorce to refer to the dissolution of any intimate relationship.

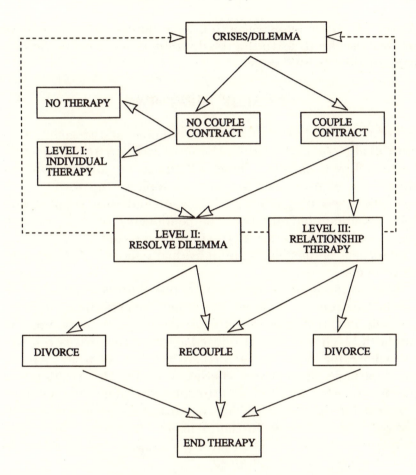

Figure 1. A model of the treatment process for polarized couples.

If a couple agrees to resolve the dilemma together, a couple contract is developed which may focus on (1) working toward a decision to maintain or dissolve the relationship or understand the relationship failure—*Level II*; or (2) improving the relationship through couple therapy on a trial basis—*Level III*. Treatment ends when the couple decides to either stay together or end the relationship. Couples may move between the three levels of goals. For example, they may begin with a couple contract to resolve the dilemma together (Level II) and shift to relationship therapy

(Level III). If a couple is working on a mutual contract and one partner decides to leave the relationship, this moves the process back to the "Crisis" stage.

GOALS OF TREATMENT

Treatment begins with the establishment of the couple's or individual's goals. In couple therapy, each partner frequently has a different agenda. These differences are never more incompatible than in cases that are the topic of this text.

Three levels of goals may be negotiated with couples who have disparate opinions about the continuance of their relationship. *Level I* goals are those when no couple contract is possible. The focus is on facilitating an individual's decision making and/or recovery.

Often a therapist is contacted by one partner requesting individual treatment to clarify his or her feelings about the relationship and to decide whether to stay or leave. Such was the case with Leigh who was introduced above. If the partner resolves to explore the relationship further, a couple contract may be developed. If the partner chooses to leave the relationship, therapy focuses on divorce adjustment. Other times, the therapist is contacted when one partner has made the final decision to divorce and wants no further contact. Obviously, no couple contract is possible. Contact with a therapist may be made by the "dumper" or the "dumpee."

> Bill came home from work one afternoon and found that his wife had moved precisely one-half of everything out of the house—furniture, kitchen supplies, towels, etc. She never called or returned. His only contact with her was through her attorney. Bill sought therapy to recover from the abruptness of the loss.

At other times, a therapist continues to work with one partner after couple therapy ends in a divorce. Such was the case with Diane, introduced earlier. Recovery is the goal, which includes, at minimum, resolution of feelings, identity adjustments, and rebuilding self-esteem. If the partner is the "leaver," specific focus is on resolution of guilt, confusion, ambivalence, and so on. If the partner is the "leavee," the specific focus is on resolution of abandonment, betrayal, anger, and acceptance of the divorce.

Level II goals are directed at resolving the couple's dilemma. The couple enters therapy together because one wants out and the other does not. Often, the final decision has not been made. At other times, the decision is final but the couple is seeking understanding, information, and/or help for their situation. The couple, as a whole, has ambivalence about the relationship, with the partners polarized on either side of the issue. Level II goals focus on resolving this ambivalence, clarifying options, and facilitating decision making. A minimum of three solutions are possible: (1) the couple may stay together and rebuild the marriage; (2) the couple may pursue divorce; or (3) the couple may stay ambivalent.

Optimally, Level II goals are directed at resolving the dilemma from the vantage point of colleagueship. The couple agrees to work together toward the resolution of the relationship dilemma. Together, they focus on understanding the relationship and themselves and why they are currently wrestling with this dilemma.

Level III goals are designed to improve the relationship before a decision is reached. This may be a temporary solution, but couples often find it helpful to try "one more time" to fix the relationship.

CONTRACT

Therapy begins with the establishment of a contract to work on articulated and mutual goals. This contract may be with the couple or with one member individually. For couples in this "crisis" it is critical to establish an agreement on how to proceed. That is, at what level to focus treatment.

It is important for the therapist to understand each partner's agenda early in the treatment process. Often one partner "drags" the other into the therapist's office hoping the therapist will convince him or her to be "fixed" or to not leave the marriage. Other times, a partner's covert agenda in starting therapy is to "dump" their partner onto a caring therapist to support them through the process of divorce.

Frequently, the couple arrives in therapy feeling hopeless about possible change as well as disagreeing about what needs to be changed. Conflicting goals for therapy do not preclude a couple from working toward the resolution of their dilemma together. However, if one of the partners is simply not willing to work toward resolution in the context of therapy, couple treatment ends. Two dangers are possible at this point. First, the therapist may assume too quickly that a contract exists to proceed in therapy. In so doing, the therapist runs the risk of aligning himself or herself with the partner desiring the relationship and therapy and may polarize the other partner even further. Second, the therapist may assume too quickly that no contract can be reached. Ambivalence or dogma about divorce may merely reflect the partner's current anger with the spouse, stress level, or emotional state.

> Brenda and Ralph started couples therapy at her initiation. During the first session, she was furious and demanded a divorce. This appeared nonnegotiable. The therapist helped her express her feelings in a productive way and helped Ralph respond without defensiveness. Brenda calmed down and admitted she was premenstrual and had overreacted. The divorce crises passed for another month.

While Brenda had legitimate complaints, her physical/emotional state created bipolar reactions. If not kept in perspective, the therapist might have pursued the question of divorce prematurely.

Facilitating the couple's decision about their goals is the major task for the therapist at this stage of therapy. At times, the goals are obvious. For example, if one partner leaves the relationship and refuses to participate in further interactions with the ex-partner, divorce adjustment is the only possible goal. However, couples frequently need assistance in determining a course of action. Ambivalence about the relationship is common. Some partners want to leave the relationship but do not believe they have "tried hard enough" to justify divorce. Others are hurt and angry and would stay if their partner would change. Still others want to leave but genuinely want to continue a relationship with the partner and/or be assured that the other is okay. There are those who vacillate about the relationship depending upon the issue "du jour." Guidance toward goals is necessary in these cases. We prefer to work with the couple together as much as possible whether the goal is recoupling, deciding, or divorcing. Establishing a goal can be facilitated by insisting upon a time line to the pursuit of that goal. For example, a couple may agree to work on their relationship for three months without the threat of divorce if there is a time limit to this endeavor. This relieves the pressure of making a decision and allows for exploration of the relationship. It also restricts the couples from "pulling the rug out" if the exploration becomes difficult. Knowing they have a limited time, couples frequently work more efficiently. Re-evaluation of the relationship occurs at the end of the agreed-upon time.

TREATMENT

Based on the therapy goals, treatment contract, interactions around establishing the goals and identified problems in the relationship, the therapist formulates working hypotheses about the problem, the couple's relationship, and possible treatment strategies. Rather than collecting random data and intervening haphazardly, the therapist gathers information and intervenes in an organized fashion to test his or her hypotheses. Using tested hypotheses, the therapist then develops a congruent treatment strategy which is aimed at achieving the therapy goals.

The majority of this section will focus on treatment of Level II goals, i.e., to work toward a decision to either separate or stay together. We have found little that guides the therapist through the process of facilitating this dilemma's resolution. But first, we will briefly summarize our approach to Level I.

Treatment of Level I Goals

Individuals presenting this dilemma enter therapy at various degrees of polarization. At one extreme is the couple in which the decision to divorce has been made. The role of the therapist, in this case, generally speaking, is divorce adjustment counseling. We encourage treatment to provide the individual with a deliberate process with which to cope with this transition. Individuals frequently find divorce adjustment groups helpful at this time. Groups provide support and new social networks, as well as help with identity adjustments, feelings, and grief. Bibliotherapy is also valuable. Reading articles or books written for the lay person such as Bruce Fisher's *Rebuilding* (1981) can be both validating and encouraging.

Individuals also enter therapy to resolve their ambivalence about a relationship. We then focus on processing information about the relationship, value clarification, and decision making. The specific areas of information are similar to those covered with couples in Level II, the difference being that in Level I, the individual covers these areas alone.

Treatment of Level II Goals

Level II goals are unique—they are neither divorce adjustment nor couple therapy. Instead, Level II goals focus on resolving the dilemma of only one partner wanting to leave a relationship. Resolution may mean: (1) facilitating a decision regarding continuing the relationship; or (2) processing information related to the occurrence of the dilemma at this time. As stated earlier, our preference is to create a couple contract when this particular dilemma occurs. We believe this generally reduces the trauma and pain attached to this experience and promotes greater individual insight and emotional health. We also prefer to establish a time frame for therapy. Setting limits for the length of treatment not only helps engage some reluctant participants but also forces couples to work on their goals more conscientiously, knowing they "don't have forever."

There are many benefits of directing a couple toward Level II. First, each partner gains new insights about his or her behavior in this relationship and can work toward change for future relationships (which may include the current one). Second, Level II goals are directed at building a perspective about oneself, one's partner, and the relationship. Partners frequently have biased theories about their contribution to the relationship and what they may legitimately expect. If asked who contributes the most, both will say "I do!"; if asked who criticizes the most, both will say "I don't." Building realistic expectations of a relationship is another aspect of Level II goals.

> Tammy and Jim separated at Tammy's initiation after several months of therapy. She wanted to leave the marriage but was willing to try a six-month separation. The trauma of the separation forced both to look at their marriage more honestly than before. Both had fostered a mutually dependent relationship for the first eight years of their marriage. Without realizing her dissatisfaction with the dependence, Tammy began building relationships outside the marriage. Jim was hurt and uncomfortable with the changes in the rules and became less supportive and more argumentative and defensive. This drove Tammy further away until she decided to separate. With the separation, both realized that their dependence was no longer working for them. Tammy gained a perspective on her needs, some of which needed to be met outside the marriage by female friends. Jim gained a perspective on his dependence and its impact on Tammy and began to build outside relationships too.

A final benefit of working through Level II is the increased possibility of a mutual agreement to stay or leave the relationship. One of the most devastating aspects of divorce for both partners is the impact of a unilateral decision. The deciding partner frequently experiences guilt and confusion regarding the hurt and anger of the partner who is not part of the decision.

We have found that working with the couple together also facilitates each partner's recovery in the case of a divorce. If one partner decides to leave the relationship but is willing to resolve the dilemma with the other, focus may then be placed on understanding the breakdown of the relationship, each person's contribution, and subsequently, areas for further personal growth (with or without the partner).

Ellen decided to leave her four-year nonmarital relationship to Al. He entered treatment to understand "what went wrong." After a few sessions, it was clear he did not have enough information to reach his therapy goals. Ellen was invited and agreed to enter treatment with him. At the beginning of the first of several conjoint sessions, all agreed that therapy would not focus on reconciling the relationship but on exploring the contributions each made to the relationship failure. This time was invaluable to Al as he recovered from the loss of Ellen and learned enhanced ways to build new relationships.

In achieving Level II goals, it may be necessary to split the couple for separate therapy sessions. This is frequently the case when one partner is excessively angry about the other's desire to leave or confused by his or her own feelings about the relationship.

Sue was furious with Jack's confusion about their marriage. Her fury was pushing Jack further away from the relationship. Continuing couple therapy was accelerating the movement toward divorce. Both partners were sent to individual therapists— Sue to address her anger in less destructive ways, and Jack to decide about continuing the relationship.

We arrange for each partner to see a new therapist, forming a therapeutic team of three. The original therapist does not engage in individual therapy with one or both partners in order to maintain neutrality in working on the relationship/divorce. The two individual therapists maintain close contact with the couple therapist who helps establish and monitor the goals of the individuals. After several individual sessions for both partners, a couple session is arranged with all therapists and the couple. We use a one-way mirror for the individual therapists. During the couple session, progress in individual therapy is reviewed and the three therapists develop a team message regarding the direction for future treatment.

> Janet and Jerry were "stuck" in marital therapy. Janet wanted a divorce but did not think she had "tried everything" to make her marriage work. However, she was too angry with Jerry to try anything that had the slightest chance of improving the relationship. She blamed him for *all* marital and family difficulties. Jerry tended to accept this responsibility. He completed every therapy assignment but was hurt when she did little to improve their relationship. The therapist asked both to see separate therapists, explaining that Janet needed to resolve her historical anger and examine how she contributed to the marital discord and Jerry needed to build his self-confidence, learn how to share feelings without being hurtful, and come to terms with only half of the responsibility for the marriage. After three months of individual therapy, a meeting with the three therapists, Janet, and Jerry was held. When asked what each had learned in individual therapy, Jerry shared many insights about his behavior in the relationship and his self-esteem. Much to the disconcerted surprise of her therapist, Janet replied that she learned that "Jerry is a jerk." She acknowledged that he had changed but realized that no amount of change on his part would move her closer to him. Although she never acknowledged her role in the marital problems, the individual sessions helped her clarify that she would not allow the relationship to improve. She soon filed for divorce.

While the couple is working on resolving the dilemma, our goal is to provide new information and alternate frames for understanding their relationship and current situation. This process is facilitated by exploring the following areas:

1. Timing. It is important to identify the developmental stage of each individual, the relationship, and the larger system (e.g., family). Development crises may provoke strong negative feelings about a primary relationship. For example, research indicates that couples are least satisfied with marriage during the teenage stage of the family life cycle (Rollins & Feldman, 1970). This stage frequently corresponds with midlife for the individuals—a time for reevaluating one's life and, consequently, one's primary relationship.

Another issue of timing is "Why now?" What has changed for whom in the marriage that has created the incompatible directions? Why is the relationship in this dilemma at this time?

> Janet and Jerry had survived 20 years of marriage. Both were in their forties. Their oldest child was leaving for college within a few months when they entered therapy. Janet claimed she came to therapy to try "one more thing" before pursuing divorce so she would feel good about the decision. She reported living with years of abuse—emotional and physical. When asked for specifics, she admitted the "attacks" were reciprocal, infrequent and mild, and had ended after the birth of their 15-year-old son. However, she was still harboring deep resentments toward Jerry. She had withdrawn emotionally and became verbally abusive herself to counter his behavior. In the opinions of three therapists who worked with them as a team, they had lived with mutual abuse for at least 15 years. Why were they pursuing therapy at this time? Both anticipated a change in the family structure and were concerned about living together post children. Eventually, Janet asked Jerry to move and proceeded with divorce. At age 45, she returned to college to pursue a master's degree.

2. *Family of origin.* It is useful to connect the current situation with the family-of-origin legacies. For example, did one partner's parents divorce at a similar life stage? Is there loyalty to family of origin that must be maintained at the cost of the relationship? Has one or both partners excessive dependence on parents or siblings?

> Lynn, a therapist in his early thirties, wanted to leave his wife, Angie. They had only been married six months when he began individual therapy to understand his feelings of dissatisfaction. It soon became clear that he felt extremely disloyal to his mother when he was happy, satisfied, and comfortable with Angie. He fantasized that his mom was in the room when they made love

(and she disapproved!). He realized that his mom had been unhappy since her first husband of six months died in combat. In fact, she had never resolved her grief. Lynn worked to separate his feelings from hers and to separate his role as husband from his role as son. He began pacing his mother with regard to her unhappiness, asking her during their weekly phone calls what had she done to make herself happy. At first, she was taken aback but soon learned to please her son by reporting many positive things in her life. Lynn soon was free to be satisfied with his wife and marriage without the sense of disloyalty that was disguised as anger toward Angie.

3. Unresolved grief. Unresolved grief from the family of origin or previous relationship may impinge upon current relationships.

Tex and Justine dated for a year before entering premarital therapy to find healthier ways of resolving conflict. In the first few sessions, Tex, acting as couple cheerleader, tried to convince Justine they should and could have a closer relationship. Justine, grieving over the recent death of her mother, seemed invested in fighting to escape her own pain. Just as Justine began to invest in the relationship, Tex found the conflict unbearable and announced, in session, his decision to leave the relationship. Justine was shocked and overwhelmed by the abandonment and loss. She stayed in therapy for three months to focus on recovering from the loss of her mother and Tex.

4. Rationale. It is important to explore the theory each partner has developed about the current dilemma. This includes each person's ideas about why the leaver wants to leave and the leavee wants to stay. Their theories are rich sources of relationship patterns, roles, and rules.

Donna thought Steve wanted to leave their three-year marriage because of mutual disrespect with her parents. Steve acknowledged this stressor but revealed, for the first time, that he wanted to leave because of her sexual inexpressiveness. Unknowingly, Donna had been working on the wrong issue!

5. *Values.* Central to the confusion and ambivalence surrounding this dilemma are individual and shared values. It therefore becomes crucial for the therapist to assist the couple in clarifying their values about marriage, commitment, intimacy, divorce, and infidelity and the comparative importance each places upon these values. This process will lead to a more measured (less reactive) resolution for the couple.

> After a second miscarriage, Joe threw himself into his career, leaving his wife, Bonnie, to seek emotional support elsewhere. Over the next six months, Bonnie's friendship with Larry developed into a love relationship as the distance in the marriage widened. Joe learned of Bonnie's other relationship and called for an appointment in a panic. Bonnie felt she had no choice but to leave the marriage. She was in love with another man and felt too guilty to return to Joe. Both Joe and Bonnie shared a deep commitment to a religious faith that spoke strongly against divorce and for marriage. By exploring in therapy the conflict between her belief system and her behavior, Bonnie was able to clarify herself that her allegiance to her religious values was stronger than her love for Larry. Bonnie then made a commitment to improve the marriage with Joe.

6. *History.* The history of this particular dilemma in this relationship may provide valuable perspective on the current situation. For example, is this a chronic pattern or is it a first-time crisis? How long has the potential leaver wanted to leave? How long has the potential leavee been aware of the other's desires? Have the roles been reversed?

7. *Meaning.* We believe that relationship problems have a function or purpose and the meaning placed upon the problem by the couple should be explored. For example, what is being communicated by the dilemma? Is the polarity a metaphor for the rest of the relationship? That is, does the dilemma represent relationship themes of seeking attention, reassurance, abandonment, or power struggles? Often when a partner says he or she wants a divorce, it is a cry for attention and/or reassurance that the spouse wants and needs them. At times, a partner may use

a threat of divorce to test the other's commitment to the relationship—"Just talk me out of this" is the agenda. Other times a divorce is used to balance power in the system. A partner may feel very "one-down" and that divorce is the only way to gain power. Therefore, threats of divorce are part of the couple's dance. The degree to which this is occurring is important to assess.

The threat of divorce can also be an attempt to get the other to change. This was the case of Ron and Nancy, introduced at the beginning of the chapter.

> Nancy demanded that Ron change or she would leave the relationship. Ron, who did not want to be in therapy, was very uncomfortable with the position he was in. In an effort to join Ron and "hook" him into treatment, the therapist commented on the "blackmail" nature of this demand. Ron then clearly told Nancy that he did not want to change and she told him to move his things out of her house. The session ended and both partners thanked the therapist for helping them clarify what they wanted. However, they went home and discussed their decision at length and requested another session to further clarify what it is that needed to be changed in their relationship. The deliberate joining with Ron increased the chance he would return to therapy to explore Nancy's complaints and his needs.

8. Burnout. It is possible that one partner is experiencing "burnout" with the marriage. Burnout was conceptualized by Herbert Freudenberger in the 1970s to account for decrease in effective functioning or productivity at a professional activity. The effects of burnout have been described as exhaustion, cynicism, negative feelings, decreased empathy, and physical symptoms. Burnout is caused by stress, perceived lack of support, decrease in trust and satisfaction, disappointment over unmet expectations, and role ambiguity (Freudenberger, 1974). Prognosis for recovery from burnout is related to the progression of the symptoms of this syndrome (Rogers, 1987). Maslach (1978) classified three phases of burnout: Phase 1 includes emotional and physical exhaustion; Phase 2 involves negative attitudes, avoidance behavior, and withdrawal with decrease in work accomplishments; and Phase 3 represents terminal burnout. There is no recovery from Phase 3. People suffer from burnout in relationships as well as professional activities. The same symptoms are evident in relationships and are caused by stress, disappointment, and decreased trust and satisfaction. The prevention of burnout is preferable over treatment, but recovery from burnout is possible (Rogers, 1987). The earlier burnout is caught, the better the chances of rebuilding (Maslach, 1978).

9. Other person. One partner may have an emotionally or physically intimate relationship with another person that impinges on the primary relationship and this can be a serious detriment to building a satisfying relationship. The partner not involved in the relationship may be jealous and hurt, while the partner in the outside relationship may be confused by the closeness of the other person. As in the case of Bonnie and Joe above, Bonnie was clearly confused by her strong emotional involvement with Larry. Critical to the resolution of the couple dilemma was Bonnie's decision about Larry and her religion. Understanding the meaning of an outsider (e.g., a cry for attention, an expression of anger or hurt) can open the opportunity for couples to reconsider their relationship.

10. Cost/benefit ratio. Important to explore are the cost and benefits of leaving and staying in the relationship. Partners may be slanting their decision by ignoring all data. Exploring these areas will provide the couple with valuable information with which they can make a clear and informed choice about their relationship.

11. Larger systems. The interface between the primary relationship and work, family, friends, church, and culture may create stress and problems for the relationship. For example, couples are strongly impacted by each partner's career issues.

Doug was having difficulty at work. He had been given several unfavorable evaluations. His home life was eroding concurrently. When he decided upon a linear explanation for his troubles—

the home problems caused the work problems—he wanted a divorce! Trudy convinced him to try a few sessions of therapy. Doug explored his work stresses and soon realized the reciprocity between his two worlds. He decided to divorce his employer rather than his wife.

Exploration of the above areas significantly impact the couple and their perspective about their relationship. Information is the basis of feelings, thoughts, and actions and therefore influences the decisions each partner makes. We have found that honest discussion of these areas helps the couple decide whether to work on their relationship or pursue divorce.

Managing the Pragmatics

A couple agreeing to Level II goals may have difficulty managing the pragmatics of life together. A pressing agenda for the therapist is assisting the couple in decisions around day-to-day living arrangements while they work in therapy to resolve their dilemma. Polarized couples present a crisis of intimacy and are in need of some kind of map (guide). Specifically, issues include whether or not to share a bedroom or even the same house; whether to have sex or not; how much daily communication to have; whether communication should be structured and time-limited. In addition to issues of intimacy, couples must make decisions around finances, children, house maintenance, pet care, and so forth.

Kim, after a number of months in individual therapy related to depression, was referred to couple therapy with her husband, John. She soon announced that she wanted a separation to help sort out her many conflicting feelings about herself and her marriage. John, although extremely concerned for his wife, did not think it was right for him to have to leave the family home and the two children for whom he assumed much of the responsibility and care. Much of the initial phase of therapy was focused on working through the details of the family living arrangements and related emotions. This couple was able to sell the family home (which had been on th market), buy a smaller home and lease a second home near by. This allowed for creative involvement of both parents with the children. It also provided the space Kim needed to clarify her conflicting feelings. In fact, soon after the separation, Kim was able to share in therapy past childhood sexual abuses which were at the core of her current marital dilemma.

In some cases, couples will have already designed arrangements of managing intimacy and the pragmatics of their relationship before entering therapy. In other cases, the couple will bring their concerns to the therapist. In all cases, it is important for the therapist to help the couple develop a temporary solution to managing their relationship while resolving their dilemma. A structural separation agreement (Granvold, 1983) is very helpful. The couple agrees to parameters around finances, child care, outside relationships, privacy, sex, and so forth. This helps reduce conflict over day-to-day living.

Treatment of Level III Goals

If the couple has resolved their dilemma in the direction of maintaining the relationship, therapy shifts to resolving couple conflicts and working toward a healthier and more satisfying relationship. Because of the recent crisis, it is important for the therapist to offer some structure to the work in order to eliminate (as much as possible) feelings of mistrust and overcautiousness. First, it is helpful to establish a time frame that provides parameters for the couple. At the end of the time, the couple can reevaluate the commitment.

Leslie wanted to leave her one-year marriage to Tom. She was angry that he did not support her in her educational goals and that he did not attach to her daughter by a previous marriage. However, her ambivalence, fear of being alone, financial dependence, and love for Tom prevented her from actually leaving. Tom was angry that she had so many complaints about him and that she did not acknowledge his support. When they began couple therapy, the therapist asked for a 10-week commitment to work on the relationship. Both agreed. Through the course of the 10 weeks both felt strongly inclined to leave the relationship but stayed because of the commitment made during the first session. During the 10 weeks, they began to communicate about their dissatisfactions without arguing since the therapist was working as a referee. With coaching, they began to learn how to express empathy in lieu of defensiveness. They became aware of how negative they were with one another and started more positive exchanges. At the end of 10 weeks, they renegotiated for another 10 weeks of working toward a more satisfying, intimate relationship.

Several strategies are useful in helping couples rebuild their relationship. "Caring Days" or "Love Days" (Liberman, 1970; Stuart, 1980) may be implemented to create positive energy. Communication and/or problem-solving training helps the couple relate in more effective and positive ways. Books to read aloud are valuable not only for the information provided but also for the experience of reading together and discussing the information. Excellent books for this experience include Maggie Scarf's *Intimate Partners* (1987) and Bach and Wyden's *The Intimate Enemy* (1968).

At this level, couples work to negotiate their needs, communicate feelings, explore what each needs from the relationship, and create realistic goals and expectations.

One important area to consider is the fallout of trust a couple may experience after one partner has announced a desire to leave. If the couple is trying to rebuild the relationship, this could play a significant role in the risk taking the partners engage in. We believe in confronting this issue directly by predicting the fallout and providing positive connotations for both the mistrust and the ambivalence about the relationship.

AFTERTHOUGHTS

Working with polarized couples presents a number of dilemmas for the therapist. Of major concern is the potential for the therapist to be triangulated into the couple's dilemma. These cases present the therapist with an emotionally charged system in which the levels of pain, frustration, and mistrust can be very high. The very fact that the couple is in treatment suggests that at least one of the pair is pulling strongly on the therapist to offer some stability to the struggle and to the system in general and, most likely, to offer support for his or her position. The therapist's urge to be "helpful" can quickly place the therapist in a position of the pawn in the continuing struggle between the partners. The therapist must find ways to join with each partner, viewing the dilemma as both a systemic struggle (a struggle for equilibrium at either the old level or at a new level of interaction), as well as individual struggles (a crisis for each partner—developmental, existential, spiritual, etc.). Becoming triangulated into the couple dilemma decreases the therapist's power, maneuverability, and effectiveness with the system. Referring each partner to an individual therapist may be a strategy to retain (or regain) one's power as a couple therapist.

In our view it is important that the therapist initially position himself or herself on neutral footing with each partner in order to retain effectiveness in working with the system. Out of frustration and desperation, couples often request the expert's opinion about whether to continue their relationship. Our commitment is to help relieve the suffering and confusion but we try not to influence the direction the relief takes. Paradoxically, the therapist is most powerful in being "helpless" at solving the dilemma for the couple.

A second dilemma has to do with the therapist's own value system as it relates to relationship integrity and divorce and the extent to which these values may infiltrate the therapy process. Most of us have been trained to somehow keep our values out of the therapy setting. However, this type of case has the potential of bringing to the foreground our own beliefs and myths about relationships (especially marriage). It may also elicit the therapist's feelings (e.g., insecurities, anger) about his or her own intimate relationships. Suffice it to say, these cases challenge the therapist's ability to separate his or her own feelings and values from those of the couple being treated. It is our position that the therapist role is primarily to assist the couple in solving their dilemma using their values and their definitions, and helping them sort out their options.

Finally, it is important for the therapist to represent realistically to the couple what therapy can and cannot offer. This can be helpful to the therapist's survival, keeping him or her from getting too emotionally drained by a sense of overresponsibility for the outcome of treatment. One strategy is for the therapist to keep in mind that successful therapy is the resolution of the dilemma and clarification of relationship issues. It is not a "happily-ever-after" ending for the relationship.

SUMMARY

Participating in a volume devoted entirely to the treatment of polarized couples is exciting for these two believers in the field of marriage and family therapy. This book is a statement that the field has progressed beyond generalist knowledge (i.e., generic couple's therapy texts) and focus on treatment of specific debilatating problems (e.g., alcoholic marriages) to treatment of a "core" process of a relationship: systemic ambivalence. We work with these couples every day but have read little in the literature to enlighten our treatment. Like these couples, the literature is polarized—treat relationships or treat divorce. It is valuable for us to articulate that in-between gray area—our Level II—in which treatment focuses on resolving this dilemma.

REFERENCES

Bach, G. R., & Wyden, P. (1968). *The intimate enemy: How to fight fair in love and marriage.* New York: William Morrow.

Fisher, B. (1981). *Rebuilding: When your relationship ends.* San Luis Obispo, CA: Impact Publishers.

Freudenberger, H. J. (1974). Staff burn-out. *Journal of Social Issues, 30* (1), 159–165.

Granvold, D. K. (1983). Structured separation for marital treatment and decision making. *Journal of Marriage and Family Therapy, 9,* 403–412.

Liberman, R. P. (1970). Behavioral approaches to family and couple therapy. *American Journal of Orthopsychiatry, 40,* 106–118.

Maslach, C. (1978). Job burnout—How people cope. *Public Welfare, 36,* 56.

Rollins, B. C., & Feldman, H. (1970). Marital satisfaction over the family life cycle. *Journal of Marriage and the Family, 32,* 20–28.

Rogers, E. R. (1987). Professional burnout: A review of concepts. *The Clinical Supervisor, 5,* 91–106.

Scarf, M. (1987). *Intimate partners.* New York: Random House.

Stuart, R. B. (1980). *Helping couples change.* New York: Guilford Press.

3

The Art of Depolarization

Anthony P. Jurich

You can tell a lot about a couple coming for marital counseling, before they ever start talking to you, by the way in which they come into your office and sit down. If they come into the room and both sit down together on the couch, you can pretty much figure that you have a couple who are still in love and will at least make the attempt to work together on a solution to their problems. If they come in and sit in two chairs on opposite sides of the room, not saying a word to each other, you probably have a disengaged or fairly hostile couple who have agreed that disagreement is the order of the day. If, however, one spouse sits down, the other spouse sits right next to him or her, only to have the first spouse proceed to get up and change chairs to gain more distance, you have a "dance of polarization." In its most extreme form it means "one spouse wants out and the other one doesn't."

DIFFERENT AGENDA—DIFFERENT DIRECTIONS

As a therapist, such polarized couples are very difficult people with whom to do marital therapy. When couples are willing to work together, the therapist can harness that energy for the common goal of working toward a happier, better-functioning relationship. Even when couples are disengaged or conflict-habituated, the spouses at least agree to a common ground—either little contact or lots of competitive contact. Although neither stance is conducive toward building a good relationship, the therapist can at least build upon the fact that each spouse is cooperating with the other spouse in viewing the problem similarly and attempting to solve their marital problems in a similar way. The therapist can address the couple as a unit, which may serve as the foundation for a team effort toward the solution of a problem. When a polarized couple arrive at the office, the therapist must realize, from the outset, that each spouse has a different agenda and that these agendas are conflicting and competing.

The different agendas of a polarized couple, simply stated, are "one wants out" and "one wants to stay together." The energies of one spouse are directed in a centrifugal fashion. The energy flows from the center of the relationship outside to the things on the periphery or outside of the relationship. This spouse focuses time and energy on things outside of the relationship such as work, another romantic relationship, or "palling around with friends." Within the relationship this centrifugal spouse may spend his or her relationship time on trivial or mundane matters, such as formal social events or scheduling activities for the children. The couple's children are often the repository for this centrifugal spousal energy. Although parenting is an activity central to the family's quality of life, it can be quite centrifugal to the spousal relationship and, therefore, be used to draw time and energy away from the conjugal couple. Because of our societal sex role expectations, a woman will often bury herself in her mothering role in an effort to distance herself from a marriage which she would like to leave. In this way, this spouse achieves a tacit divorce from her spouse. In either case, the centrifugal spouse comes to therapy with an agenda to enlist either therapy or the therapist to support his or her efforts in distancing the other spouse and/or ending the relationship.

The energies of the spouse who "wants to stay together" are directed in a centripetal fashion, with the direction of that spouse's energies being toward the center of the marriage, the other spouse, and the spousal dyad. For this spouse, the focal point of his or her entire life is the maintenance and survival of the conjugal dyad. All other matters are secondary or even ignored. This centripetal flow of energy is exacerbated by the increasingly dawning realization that the centrifugal spouse is making efforts to minimize spousal contact and possibly even end the relationship. In such a case, the centripetal spouse's response may be to increase the spousal focus to the point of neglect of job, friends, extended family, and even children, in an effort to convince the centrifugal spouse that "the marriage is worth saving." Sometimes this tactic works and the centrifugal spouse becomes more centripetal or at least less centrifugal in his or her stance. Sometimes this strategy works temporarily, with the centrifugal spouse drawing closer for a time but then pulling away again because the reasons for his or her centrifugal pattern remain unexplored and unchanged, leading to a resurfacing of the same issues. Most often, the centrifugal spouse's response to his or her spouse's "push for closeness" is to run away even further and become even more centrifugal. In trying to be closer, the centripetal spouse often simply exaggerates the very sequence of relationship behavior that motivated the centrifugal spouse to get out in the first place. As the centrifugal spouse attempts to pull away even further, the centripetal spouse can become obsessed with keeping the relationship vibrant. The comment most typically made at this time is "I can't live without him or her." The extremity of this message sends the centrifugal spouse running out the door to "avoid being sucked into the quicksand of a marriage from which I want out."

This escalation of incompatible motivations is often what brings the couple into the therapist's office. The centrifugal spouse wants to get the therapist to align himself or herself with the position that "everybody would be better off if the marriage ended," in an effort to minimize his or her own responsibility and guilt. The centripetal spouse wants to coalign with the therapist to convince the other spouse that he or she "is being unreasonable and, therefore, the marriage is worth saving," in order to gain allies in fighting what the centripetal spouse feels to be a losing battle. They now arrive at the therapist's office saying, "Side with me, my spouse is wrong."

TRIANGULATION VERSUS DETRIANGULATION

Any situation in marital therapy where the agendas are so contrary to each other produces a situation that is ripe for triangulation. Each spouse is attempting to enlist the aid of the therapist in inducing change in the other spouse. The therapist must be on guard against being placed in the middle of this argument and being fought over in an attempt by both spouses to form a coalition with the therapist against the other spouse's position. I believe that, if a therapist is to avoid this triangulated position, there are several things that must happen.

First, the therapist needs to be overt and explicit about the "ground rules of therapy." The easiest way to keep from being manipulated by clients is to try to structure the rules so that it is hard for manipulation to take place. When a polarized couple comes to me for marital therapy, one of the first things I do is spell out the rules. I tell them that I prefer to see both of them in therapy together and remind them that little can be done in therapy if the spouse isn't present also. However, I am also aware that such a request does not prohibit some moments in therapy where one spouse may be in my presence without the other being present also. One spouse may show up earlier than the other or attempt to leave a therapy session later. One spouse may have to go to the bathroom in the middle of a session, leaving me with the other spouse. I may run into one spouse at the supermarket without the other spouse's being present.

Most often, these situations are accidental and are not planned. However, never underestimate the manipulative abilities of a desperate spouse. I had a spouse confess to me that she was having an affair, while we were both standing in a checkout line at the grocery store. To make matters worse, there was a poor innocent bystander in line between us who was obviously uncomfortably trapped in the middle of my client's confession. This client later explained to me that it was the only time she had seen me alone without her husband. Lest I seem too callous, let me say that I have the greatest compassion for my clients in these circumstances. They are manipulating because they are desperate. Their pain is paramount. However, I believe that the best thing I can do for them is to take a clear, explicit stance and stay with it, even if it appears to my clients to be too hard and rigid at the time. I tell polarized couples, "Everything you say to me you say to your spouse, whether that spouse is present or not. Everything you say to me is food for therapy. So don't tell me things you don't want your spouse to know." Such a strict rule of communication may not be important in all marital therapy cases but, with polarized couples, I consider it a necessity.

Many therapists consider it a necessity to see both spouses in the same session. Although I consider it very important to do so, I will make exceptions and see a spouse separately if it is understood by all that my first rule of sharing *all* communication is *always* in effect. Some spouses find it easier to "sound out" their problems with the therapist alone before telling a spouse themselves. This is fine with me, as long as they have no expectations of my keeping secrets. I also make my expectation known to them that I expect them to tell their spouse what we discussed. I make it clear that I will not be their "switchboard operator" or "hit man." However, I consider keeping secrets more harmful. Therefore, if I am forced to reveal a piece of information in order to keep it from becoming a "shared secret," I will do so. However, I will hold no further individual sessions with either party. I believe that it is important to achieve a sense of balance when working with polarized couples. I will not see one individual alone without making an offer to see the other spouse alone also. Obviously, all this could be avoided if I just saw the couples together. This is my preference and I would make it a "hard-and-fast rule," except that I have seen many polarized marriages where the centrifugal spouse leaves therapy fairly rapidly. In such a case, I consider it unethical to terminate therapy, leaving the centripetal spouse with no support system. Still, whenever possible, my rule of thumb is to see spouses together.

Other rules of therapy should be stated explicitly. I try to hold to a strict one-hour time limit on a therapy session with a polarized couple in order to convince them that manipulation will not work. Frequently, in a polarized marriage, the centrifugal member will do much of the talking and the centripetal spouse will offer no responses, even if asked to do so by the therapist, until the last five minutes, in which case the centripetal spouse bursts forth in anguish. Likewise, the centripetal spouse may spend the whole session complaining about the centrifugal spouse's lack of effort, which the centrifugal spouse attempts to defend at great length with two minutes to go in the session. In either case, the prolongation of the session will be seen as a victory of the spouse who delayed his or her responses to the end. I tend to deal with this strategically by interrupting the "tardy spouse" and asking him or her why he or she waited until the end. If I have made sure that he or she had the opportunity to speak earlier, I will tell the "tardy spouse" that I will prolong the session another five minutes to discuss why he or she waited but not to discuss his or her agenda. I explain to the "tardy spouse," "Next week, we will begin with your *very* important points, and since they are so important, you should take the time until the next session to think about them, but for now I have to end the session."

I take a similar stance on between-session contacts. If there is a legitimate emergency, I will allow a between-session phone call or visit. However, I determine whether it is an emergency and, if it is not, I explain to the couple, "It is important to spend some time thinking about that so that you will be better able to articulate it in the next session." This may seem cruel but, if clear boundaries aren't established, the therapist becomes ripe for triangulation.

One rule for avoiding triangulation also doubles as a highly effective therapeutic rule for polarized couples: Always make the covert overt. Polarized couples who are aware of their spouses' agendas are at least knowledgeable about the nature of the marital battle they are waging. However, seldom is the case that both or either spouse is willing to be completely "up front" and explicit about his or her expectations. Most of these spouses prefer to wage the battle covertly, which gives rise to hidden agendas.

Polarized spouses use hidden agendas to trap either the therapist, the other spouse, or both into agreeing with their point of view. In most cases, the other spouse is too defensive and caught up in his or her own point of view to recognize this manipulation. The therapist, in a more objective and distant position, needs to be aware of such a ploy. Such an awareness keeps the therapist from being triangulated and making such a covert manipulation overt lets both spouses know that covert agendas will be brought out into the light of day and overtly discussed. In addition, making the covert overt allows both spouses to understand the full range of thoughts and feelings that have brought them into therapy. For example, either spouse may use the children as a ploy to strengthen his or her position. The centripetal spouse may plead a case of staying together "for the sake of the kids," when it is really his or her fear of losing the spouse that is the predominant factor. Likewise, the centrifugal spouse may insist that "the kids would be better off if I weren't here because we fight so much," when that spouse is really having an affair. In either case, there may be a great deal of validity to the position overtly stated. The therapist should validate that position. However, it may not be the only reason for the spouse's actions, nor may it be the most important one.

Often, spouses hint or state sarcastically what their true feelings are. As a therapist, I find it very useful to obviate these feelings and make them part of the overt agenda. If faced with a covert agenda, I typically state, "I understand what you're saying but I get the feeling that you're saying something else at the same time." I try to give the client a chance to unveil his or her hidden agenda first. However, if no exploration of that covert agenda is forthcoming, I will speculate that what I'm feeling might be some "other messages" the spouse is sending. If the client becomes defensive, I become more strategic in meeting that resistance. I typically accomplish this by overinterpreting the client's stated position to the extreme and exaggerating the lack of what I truly believe to be the case.

For example, a client may hint at feeling jealous about his or her spouse's friendships outside the marital dyad. After giving him or her the chance to speak to that feeling and the client's refusing to do so, I might say, "There's something in what you say that makes me feel like you might be a little apprehensive about your spouse's friends." If I still get a denial or defensive statements in response, I answer, "You're right, you wouldn't be the type of person who would ever be apprehensive about his spouse. As a matter of fact, if your spouse admitted to having an affair right now, you probably wouldn't bat an eye." Hyperbolizing, or drawing extreme conclusions, about the client's feelings is specifically intended to force the client into a denial of my extreme statement. Once that is accomplished and the client admits that he or she may have some apprehensions in such an extreme case, I then normalize that apprehension in my extreme example and go on to normalize the same feeling in my original inquiry of the spouse's feelings. This both exposes the hidden agenda and validates that the spouse's feelings are legitimate and, at least to the therapist, acceptable.

One area in which I insist upon being overt is the level of commitment each spouse has in keeping the marriage viable. I have found that when spouses speak in vague generalities, this increases the anxiety of their partners and clouds the issue that is at the very core of a polarized couple. Therefore, I very specifically ask each spouse to rate his or her commitment to keeping the marriage going on a scale of 1 to 10, with 1 being "I want a divorce yesterday," 10 being "I'll do *anything* to keep it going," and 5 being "I've thought about divorce but would also like to see it work." Despite some initial feelings of reluctance, I've never had a client who was unable to, at least temporarily, give me a number. I also tell the couple that fact in order to normalize the very abnormal assignment of putting a number on their marriage. If a spouse chooses a number that is at either extreme (1 or 10), I once again try to hyperbolize the choice as previously described so that he or she doesn't feel so absolute and inflexible. I then launch into a discussion about why both spouses feel as they have expressed and whether they feel surprised at their partner's response. This goes a long way in opening up the discussion of specific details of the couple's major issue.

The last rule in coping with triangulation is for the therapist to take a specific, overt, nontriangulated stance. If we are going to ask a client to take an overt stance, we should follow the same rules. I accomplish this by telling the clients:

> It makes no difference to me if you stay married or get a divorce. It is *your* decision. I have no right to make that decision for you. If I were married to either of you, I would have a right to make such a decision in consultation with you. Since I'm not, I don't have that right. *You* will make that decision, *both of you*. It doesn't seem, now, that you can agree on such a decision. You may not be able to. However, it is my job to help you make a joint decision, if possible, or a temporary decision, if necessary, even if it is not mutual. I'm on neither side, yet on both sides. If you decide to stay married, I'll try to help you create the best marriage you can make. If you decide to divorce, I'll try to help you make the best divorce you can, one in which you can still be civil and work together and one in which you learn from your mistakes in this marriage so that you won't repeat them.

Because of my belief system and the fact that I really do believe that, ethically, the couple does have the right to choose their own destiny, this is an easy stance for me to take. However, either a personal ethical stance (such as one against divorce), a personal emotional problem (overidentification with one of the spouses), or an institutional prohibition (working for a church that does not recognize divorce as proper), all could cause a therapist problems with the stance I have chosen to take. I believe that each therapist must make his or her decisions about the ethical choices which he or she makes as a therapist. However, I also believe that when trying to do therapy with a polarized couple, such a stand as the one I have explained is a necessity. If the therapist's own personal problems force him or her to "take sides" in therapy, the therapist will be working on self-solutions, rather than solutions for his or her clients. This type of countertransference is counterproductive and the case should be referred as soon as the therapist realizes his or her motivation. A therapist with a personal ethical stance toward either eliminating or promoting divorce as an option is under ethical obligation to reveal that stance to the clients so that they can decide, as a couple, about continuing therapy with that therapist. The therapist, working under an institutional prohibition, should explain that prohibition to the clients and the clients should make the choice whether or not to continue therapy with the therapist in that institution. Not informing the clients of such predispositions on the part of the therapist or institution not only restricts the clients' rights to informed consent, but also sets up a double standard for honesty within the session, which is extremely detrimental to the process of therapy.

DIAGNOSIS

I diagnose couples along three dimensions. The first two dimensions are provided by Levinger (1979). Levinger conceptualizes the factors in divorce as falling within two categories: *attractions* and *alternative attractions*. *Attractions* are the rewards within the marriage. A spouse may feel positive attractions and wish to stay in the relationship. He or she may feel negative attraction and feel pushed out of the marriage. Finally, a spouse may feel neither negative nor positive attractions and feel quite ambivalent. *Alternative attractions* are the rewards the spouse perceives outside the marriage. If the alternative attractions are high, the spouse will feel less committed to the marriage and will be more likely to leave it. If the alternative attractions are negative, or few positive, the spouse may or may not want to leave the marriage but will probably remain committed because he or she perceives no or few other options. *Barriers* are the internal and external rules that prohibit divorce. If barriers are low, a couple will be more likely to divorce, regardless of the relative internal and external attractions. If barriers are high, couples will tend to remain together despite the fact that internal attractions are negative and external attractions are positive.

These dimensions of influence on divorcing couples give me a framework to start classifying couples considering divorce.

The third dimension that I consider to be important is the degree to which each couple's perceptions of each of Levinger's categories is based in reality or fantasy. Some couples are very realistic in their assessment of their attractions and alternative attractions. Other couples are mired in unrealistic expectations, misperceptions, and fantasy. They see themselves as far better or much worse than they actually are in their internal attractions (appearance, resources, abilities to cope) and alternative attractions (potential spouses, opportunities, recreational endeavors). Unfortunately, the use of this dimension further complicates things because one spouse may be very realistic while the other is not. The therapist cannot rely upon any objective measure of realism to determine this. Nor can the therapist rely upon an unrealistic client to realistically evaluate his or her realism. Therefore, the therapist will have to utilize his or her subjective opinion as to the degree of realism that the clients have in guiding their perceptions. This is not very scientific and introduces a strong therapist bias into the diagnosis. However, it is unavoidable because of the importance of the reality component with polarized couples. The therapist should exercise caution in his or her assessment of the client's level of reality. These three dimensions—Levinger's factors of attraction, his concept of boundaries, and the level of reality of the clients—comprise the categories of my diagnosis model for polarized couples.

Figure 1 represents a visualization of my diagnostic schema along with three axes: the degree of realism (realist or unrealistic); the predominant attraction (either internal within the marriage or alternative attractions outside the relationship); and the strength of the barriers against divorce (either high or low). This schema yields eight diagnostic categories distinguished by three dimensions.

1. Bound Realists

This group of spouses have a realistic appraisal of the attractions within their marriage. They realistically see both the good

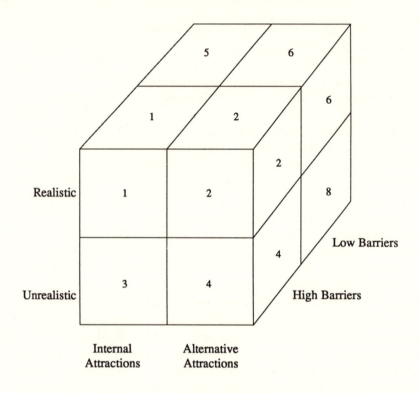

1.	Bound Realists	Realistic,	Internal Attractions,	High Barriers
2.	Stable Well-Grounded	Realistic,	Alternative Attractions,	High Barriers
3.	Caught Overidealists	Unrealistic,	Internal Attractions,	High Barriers
4.	Dreamers	Unrealistic,	Alternative Attractions,	High Barriers
5.	Realistic Shoppers	Realistic,	Internal Attractions,	Low Barriers
6.	Reality Roamers	Realistic,	Alternative Attractions,	Low Barriers
7.	Runners	Unrealistic,	Internal Attractions,	Low Barriers
8.	Emotional Butterflies	Unrealistic,	Alternative Attractions,	Low Barriers

Figure 1. Visualization of diagnostic schema along three axes.

points and bad points of their spouses. They have high barriers
to divorce. Centripetal spouses in this category can realistically
assess their relationship, want to remain committed to the marriage, and have high barriers which strengthen their centripetal
commitment. Centrifugal spouses are realistic about the problems

they see within their marriages but feel trapped in their relationships because of high barriers to divorce. Their predominant feeling is often bitterness.

2. Stable, Well-Grounded

These spouses have a realistic appraisal of the alternative attractions they have to their marriages. They can assess their alternatives well and have a realistic view of their "fair market value" as a potential spouse, should their relationship end. However, they are prevented from taking advantage of these alternatives by a set of highly restrictive barriers. Centripetal spouses in this category most often assess their alternatives as being less desirable than their present relationship. Their realistic appraisal of their alternatives, plus the high barriers to divorce, led them to believe that their present relationship is best for them. Such a position may be based upon a realistic assessment of any number of different criteria (physical attractiveness, the liability of having children, poor financial prospects). The centrifugal spouses realistically judge their alternative attractions to be good but are kept in the marriage by a set of high barriers against divorce. Their predominant emotional state is often frustration.

3. Caught Overidealists

These spouses are overidealistic about either their spouses or their marriage and marital attractions. However, high barriers to divorce restrict them to their present relationship. The centripetal spouses tend to overidealize their spouses and see only the good things about them. They frequently have an image of their spouses that nobody could even approximate. They are frequently overinvolved with a spouse who does not exist in reality. Centrifugal spouses are often guilty of unrealistic expectations of their spouse because they naively believe that a fulfillment of these expectations is possible. They idealistically believe that they should be in the perfect relationship and, therefore, there is no possibility of divorce. They often become disillusioned idealists who feel trapped in their marriage by their own ideals. These couples are often young, naive couples who have had little dating experience except their own present relationship. Such couples may suffer from the Lost Adolescence Syndrome (Jurich & Jurich, 1975), in which the young married couple become disillusioned with married life because they have never dated anyone else and yet their spouses are not living up to their ideals.

4. Dreamers

The Dreamers are spouses with unrealistic evaluations of their alternative attractions who have high barriers against divorce. Centripetal Dreamers downgrade their alternatives and undervalue themselves and their "fair market value." This is most often caused by inordinately high expectations of themselves, based upon a distorted idea of the perfection of everyone else. This results in a low self-concept and a belief that, despite any and all evidence to the contrary, there are and can be no alternative attractions for them outside the marriage. Therefore, even if there are no or negative attractions within the marriage, centripetal Dreamers will hold onto the marriage because they see it as "the only game in town." The centrifugal Dreamers have an unrealistic image of their alternative attractions but a strong barrier against divorce. They derive this unrealistic image from many sources but most frequently from the mass media. They believe the *Playboy, Penthouse Forum, True Romance* and Harlequinn novel views of life and, therefore, imagine that the "grass is greener on the other side of the fence." However, they also see the fence between them and their imagined paradise as too high to cross. Therefore, they resign themselves to dreaming about the "good life" they don't think they have.

5. Realistic Shoppers

These spouses have a realistic view of their assets and liabilities as couples and do not have very high barriers to divorce. The centrifugal spouses assess the relative strengths and weaknesses of their marriage and realistically determine that the weaknesses outweigh the strengths. Because they have few restrictions against divorce, these spouses feel free to follow other pursuits and relationships which are often predicated upon the ending of their present relationship. The centripetal spouses realistically assess their relationship as good but still realize that, even for them, divorce may be an option. Although they desire to work toward the improvement of their present relationships, they do not hold onto these relationships in desperate fashion. In some cases, depending on to whom they are married (e.g., a centrifugal Dreamer), a centripetal Realistic Shopper may actually be the one who files for a divorce, despite the fact that he or she may still want to save the marriage. Such centripetal Realistic Shoppers may realize that, despite their wishes, they will never get what they want from their spouse and they may decide to "cut their losses and leave."

6. Reality Roamers

The Reality Roamers have a realistic view of their alternative attractions and have few barriers to prohibit them from seeking out these alternatives. Centrifugal Reality Roamers focus much of their energies on things outside the marital dyad. These may be affairs, friendships, work, or a number of other endeavors that are rewarding to them. Such spouses, according to Waller's Principle of Least Interest (1937), have a lot of power in their marriages. These spouses have other alternatives to their present relationship and few barriers to divorce. Therefore, they have less interest in continuing the relationship and can utilize the ultimate bargaining chip, the relationship, with greater impunity than spouses who desire the continuation of the relationship. Their stay in the marriage is determined by the realistic assessment of the alternative attractions as compared to their powerful role within their present relationship. The centripetal spouses in this category also realistically assess their alternative attractions. However, because they realistically assess themselves at a disadvantage (e.g., a middle-aged spouse who will probably have the custody of the kids) or not enough of an advantage over their present spousal situation, despite having few barriers to divorce, these centripetal spouses desire to work on their present relationship. However, they are aware of their possibilities, if they should divorce, and have few external barriers to their divorce if it should occur.

7. Runners

Runners have unrealistic views of their internal attractions and have low barriers against divorce. As similar to the Caught Overidealists, the Runners have unrealistic expectations of themselves and their spouses. However, they do not feel trapped by barriers against divorce and feel the freedom to run away from the problems if they so desire. Centrifugal Runners have inordinately high spousal expectations and when their spouse cannot fulfill these often impossible expectations, they run for a divorce and run into another marriage. Such spouses are often "newness junkies." They are most excited by the newness of a relationship and once the initial glitter is gone, they seek to find that excitement with a new relationship. These spouses solve their troubles by running out of their present relationship: "When the going gets tough, the Runners get gone." The centripetal Runners also have unreasonably high expectations of themselves and their spouses. When something goes wrong, they likewise feel a need to run. However, because of a low self-concept, caused by their not being able to meet their own inordinately high spousal expectations of themselves, they fear running outside the marriage. The fact that they recognize their barriers to divorce as low exacerbates this fear of losing their spouse. Therefore, the centripetal Runners run toward their spouse unrealistically. They paint an image of marital perfection, focusing on superficial details and denying any serious problems. They run into a fantasy world of their own creation which may have little to do with reality, yet they are very resistive to changes, since their world rests upon this fragile illusion.

8. Emotional Butterflies

These spouses have very unrealistic perceptions of their alternative attractions and have low barriers to divorce. Such spouses either greatly overestimate or underestimate their attractions outside of their marriage and, therefore, are in a poor position to judge their own resources. The centrifugal Emotional Butterflies believe media images of relationships and, therefore, constantly try to live up to those distorted images of relationships in their own life. Because there are few barriers to divorce and their focus is centrifugal, such spouses often risk their marriage by engaging in a multitude of relationships in order to fulfill that unrealistic ideal. These relationships may vary from business ventures to sexual encounters. However, their chief component will be their compartmentalized nature and their relatively short duration. The centripetal Social Butterfly also has a distorted image of alternative attractions. This image may be very negative (e.g., a good-looking spouse who believes that he or she is ugly, despite all evidence to the contrary) or a spouse who overestimates his or her alternative attractions and utilizes his or her spouse as a trophy for show-and-tell in order to gain more status among his or her external attractions. The former kind of centripetal spouse will cling onto his or her spouse as a way of making up what he or she imagines is a deficit of others. The latter type of centripetal spouse will cling to his or her spouse as a means to further enhance what is perceived to be an important social resource. In either case, the low barriers for divorce will force the centripetal spouse to tighten his or her grip upon the centrifugal spouse.

The above diagnostic scheme allows the therapist to categorize, along three key dimensions, the polarized couple who have come for therapy. If both spouses fall into the same category, there are eight different types of dynamics that may be operative. However, this is not always the case. In most cases, the couple before the therapist is a "mixed bag." For example, the centrifugal spouse may be a Runner, while the centripetal spouse is a Stable Well-Grounded spouse. This blending of types of spouses produces a further 27 possible combinations added to the original eight.

TREATMENT

It would obviously be impossible to describe 35 possible treatment regimens in one chapter. That is the problem of having a multidimensional diagnostic scheme and an eclectic approach to therapy. However, several comments can be made about a therapist's approach to key dimensions as explicated by the above diagnostic scheme.

First, treasure the couples who are both coming from the same orientation. Although in a polarized couple, one will be centrifugal and one centripetal, at least they will both understand the other spouse's point of view because the same combination of factors created both viewpoints. In therapy, I try to build upon that commonality, demonstrating how similar they are to each other and framing both sets of behavior, both centrifugal and centripetal, as opposite sides of the same coin. This increases spousal empathy and understanding and, regardless of whether the couple stay married or divorce, helps each spouse better understand his or her mate and his or her motivations and needs.

If the therapist is not so lucky as to have a couple in the same schematic category, the task of mutual understanding is much more difficult. In such cases, I ask each spouse to explain his or her position along each dimension: realism, attractions, and barriers. I try to facilitate each spouse's understanding of these factors in his and her own and each other's marital perceptions. I also have them rate each other on each of these three dimensions and we discuss the differences as perceived by each of them. This is both time-consuming and arduous work for both the therapist and the clients, but it is a necessary foundation for the action-oriented phase of therapy.

Of the dimensions of polarized couples, the therapist has the least power in trying to maneuver around the area of barriers. For the most part, these barriers have been learned throughout the client's life and are not subject to much alteration. Low barriers will heighten the possibility of flight for the centrifugal spouse. Likewise, low barriers will heighten the fears of the centripetal spouse. High boundaries to divorce will increase the security of the centripetal spouse, while at the same time inducing feelings of entrapment and frustration in the centrifugal spouse. Once he or she understands these dynamics, there is not much the therapist can do about them. If I feel that the boundaries are minimized or blown out of proportion, I might suggest that observation to the client, but there is little else I can do. If, however, I believe that a client is hiding behind these barriers in an attempt to avoid responsibility, I explore with the client the origin of these boundaries along the lines of a Bowen family-of-origin therapist (Kerr, 1981). I work with the client toward a greater differentiation of self so that the boundaries he or she is experiencing can be owned as his or her own and not dredged up from the family of origin to avoid responsibility. Once the client owns the barriers he or she defines as his or her own, the therapist can only take them as a given.

Perhaps the key to my approach to working with polarized couples rests in my emphasis upon the realistic perceptions and expectations of the spouses. I believe that much of the polarization is caused by inflated or distorted expectations that couples learn from the media, their friends, and their families. This is especially true of young couples. The most naive couples on the face of the earth are the couples about to get married. Their visions of marriage are *so* overromanticized that unless they come down to reality, they are often doomed to failure. The most disillusioned couples on the face of the earth are those same couples shortly after the honeymoon. Sometimes they both become disillusioned at the same time. More typically, one spouse crashes while the other still rides high on illusion. Another polarized couple is born! When you have overidealization about marriage and spouses, a Caught Overidealist or a Runner is created. If the overidealism is focused upon the "wonderful things everybody else does," a Dreamer or Emotional Butterfly emerges from its cocoon.

Although I ask each client to assess both his or her own and the partner's level of reality, final judgment of reality has to be mine as therapist. If I judge one or both spouses to be unrealistic, I switch into a teaching modality and try to help each spouse teach the other their view of reality, while I talk about theory and research findings in an effort to help each client become more "grounded in reality." If that works, most of the problems can be realistically addressed, often with dramatic success. Sometimes the therapist can set up an experience that will help bring reality home. In my article on the Lost Adolescence Syndrome (Jurich & Jurich, 1975), I mentioned exposing a spouse, who was overidealistically "pining away" for his lost adolescence, to a group therapy group of single adolescents who reminded him that his retrospective view of adolescence wasn't all it was cracked up to be when compared with the harshness of their reality. If the client does not alter his or her views to a more reality-based framework, the prognosis for the polarized couple is not good. It is rare that they will stay together. Sometimes they will separate or divorce and reunite on a more realistic plane but that is rare and at best is a hit-or-miss solution. Most often, the couple divorces and, if they're lucky, they learn enough in the divorce process and afterward to become less extreme in their distortions of reality before they try marriage again. I try to help this along by strategically making apocalyptic predictions if they don't base their decisions in reality but, after that, I can do little else.

It is with the couples who are grounded in reality that true therapy can take place. When both spouses are reality-based and focusing on internal attractions, either Bound Realists or Realistic Shoppers, I can work directly with the relationship. I typically help the couple to talk out issues and, once we have explored mutual definitions and perceptions, we can work on quid pro quo arrangements (Lederer & Jackson, 1968) and even negotiate behavioral exchange contracts (Jacobson, 1981). If I encounter any resistance, I shift into a strategic modality and try to utilize the couple's leverage points to help induce change and break down old recursive patterns of interaction which are dysfunctional. I carry out much of this along the lines of Haley's *Problem Solving Therapy* (1976) and Madanes's *Strategic Family Therapy* (1981). Strategic therapy is needed even more if I have a polarized couple whose spouses are not in the "realistic" categories. A Bounded Realist and a Runner have very little common ground for direct negotiation. Strategic therapy, especially through the use of well-placed metaphors, can accomplish more than any attempt at direct negotiation.

Couples focusing from a reality base upon alternative attractions can benefit from some direct cognitive approaches, as well as some strategic interventions. The first step I take with couples focusing upon alternative attractions is to take an inventory of the assets and liabilities of the present marriage with the single lifestyle or, if an affair is involved, with the rival relationship. I use this not only as a basis for direct comparison but also as a foundation for strategically pointing up any flaws in the logic presented by the couple. In doing so, I redirect the energy away from the client's vying with me or his or her spouse to the client's trying to resolve his or her internal inconsistencies within him- or herself. It is through these carefully orchestrated little battles that the client learns most about him- or herself. It is this knowledge that will serve him or her best, regardless of whether the couple stay married or divorce.

SUMMARY

This chapter is an attempt at putting down some of my ideas of doing therapy with polarized couples. Obviously, with a diagnosis schema that has 35 possibilities, one chapter does not have the room for all possible diagnoses, much less all therapeutic interventions. However, even if it could be done, I would refrain from going into such detail. Each case is unique. Each therapist is unique. It is that magic combination of the two that gives birth to the process of therapy. Polarized couples have similarities and commonalities. I have pointed out some of them. I believe that there are certain rules governing therapy with polarized couples. However, the true work of therapy is an art that unites the finest efforts of clients and therapist. I have painted my canvas. It is up to the reader to interpret and make it his or her own.

REFERENCES

Haley, J. (1976). *Problem solving therapy.* San Francisco: Jossey-Bass.

Jacobson, N. S. (1981). Behavioral marital therapy. In A. S. Gurman & D. P. Kniskern (Eds.), *Handbook of family therapy* (pp. 556–591). New York: Brunner/Mazel.

Jurich, A. P., & Jurich, J. A. (1975). The lost adolescence syndrome. *Family Coordinator, 24,* 357–361.

Kerr, M. E. (1981). Family systems theory and therapy. In A. S. Gurman & D. P. Kniskern (Eds.), *Handbook of family therapy* (pp. 226–264). New York: Brunner/Mazel.

Lederer, W. J., & Jackson, D. D. (1968). *The mirages of marriage.* New York: W. W. Norton.

Levinger, G. (1979). A social psychological perspective on marital dissolution. In G. Levinger & A. C. Moles (Eds.), *Divorce and separation* (pp. 37–60). New York: Basic Books.

Madanes, C. (1981). *Strategic family therapy.* San Francisco: Jossey-Bass.

Waller, W. W. (1937). The rating and dating complex. *American Sociological Review, 2,* 727–734.

4

The Assessment and Treatment of Polarizing Couples

Craig A. Everett and
Sandra S. Volgy

The drama of polarizing couples who are struggling with the future of their relationships may represent one of the most difficult, as well as challenging, of clinical situations for the family therapist. These cases are characterized by one spouse who is pulling away from the relationship and the other who is wanting to maintain the relationship. These cases lack the clear focus of an identified scapegoated child or a presenting depressive family member. Their presenting problems may range across a broad spectrum of issues from vague dissatisfactions involving communication or sexual dysfunctions, to perceived inadequacies in a spouse, to more severe acting-out episodes by one or both spouses. Often, they involve the expressed intentions, typically by only one spouse, to terminate the relationship.

While the presenting issues may vary from case to case, the underlying clinical dynamic within the relationship system is an apparent imbalance of emotional bonding and attachment. This clinical phenomenon is most easily identified by the therapist in the growing level of ambivalence toward the marriage experienced typically by one spouse. This spouse may report complex fluctuations in feelings from day to day, ranging from wishing to leave the relationship, to fears of separation, to wishes for reconciliation.

Systemically, it is important to recognize that even though this ambivalence may be reported by one spouse, ramifications of the ambivalence will be experienced throughout the intergenerational system. Thus, the spouse pulling away from the relationship may direct anger and dissatisfaction about the other spouse, but the ambivalence and reduction of emotional bonding will be experienced by all other family members as a threat to the cohesion and continuity of the entire system.

It has been our experience over the years that the most effective treatment for such polarizing family cases evolves out of a broadly integrative systemic approach which can identify issues and intervene within various subsystems and locations throughout both the nuclear and intergenerational systems. We have observed elsewhere that the potential or fact of divorce does not occur simply between the two marital partners, nor can its effect be measured in the children's response to parental loss: "If we consider the form of family relationships to be circular and reciprocal, the 'victim' of the divorce is never simply the children, the loss is of the viability and organization of the family's process" (Everett & Volgy, 1983, p. 344).

Thus, polarizing marital cases, which must be viewed by the therapist as a predivorce clinical situation, need to be assessed and treated within the broad intergenerational system. Where the clinical focus remains on the distancing spouse or the immediate marital conflict, the therapist risks being potentially ineffective at two levels. The assessment may be incomplete because the therapist has not searched for reinforcing coalitions and loyalties that may affect the growing relationship imbalance across the family system's broader relationship patterns (e.g., parent-child, family of origin). The actual role of the therapist and the treatment process itself may come to a standstill because the polarizing dynamics of the system tend to trap and triangulate the therapist in the tug-of-war between the spouses or in coalitions with one or the other of the spouses. Here the therapist may end up at best an ineffective "mediator" between the committed spouse and the distancing one. The therapeutic involvement of other relevant family members (e.g., children or family of origin members) allows the therapist to diffuse the triangulating process of the relationship system by incorporating the resources and dynamics of additional relationship patterns.

In this chapter, we share with the reader our observations regarding etiological and assessment features of polarizing cases and pursue specific treatment strategies. From our systemic orientation, we attempt to provide practical and applied management and treatment procedures that are utilized routinely in our own practices.

ETIOLOGICAL AND ASSESSMENT FEATURES

We refer to these cases as *polarizing* rather than *polarized* because we have observed that this process of balancing patterns of separateness and connectedness occurs normatively in all relationship systems. This means that every close relationship is faced with the task of defining degrees of closeness and distance between the members. This involves a process of marking boundaries of both individual space and needs, as well as interactional proximity. Some relationships may require and tolerate more closeness and connectedness (e.g., enmeshing systems), while others may function better with more distance and separateness (e.g., disengaging systems).

Even with these broad systemic patterns, the themes of separateness and connectedness may fluctuate or require adjustments and changes over time due to developmental or external events. For example, the birth of a child in some systems may result in greater separateness within the marital subsystem as both spouses involve themselves emotionally with the new child. In other systems, the death of a family-of-origin parent may reduce prior vertical (intergenerational) loyalties for a spouse and allow for and perhaps even require a new level of emotional connectedness (horizontal loyalty, see Boszormenyi-Nagy & Spark, 1973) to evolve within the spousal relationship.

A clinical expectation of all relationship systems is that there exists a continuing and normative homeostatic process of balancing, adjusting, and rebalancing the patterns that define attachment. For most functional couples, this process is rarely recognized. Expectable levels of ambivalence will, of course, be attached to this ongoing process of balancing separateness and connectedness in relationships. Thus, the initial assessment question for the therapist in understanding the dynamics of the polarizing couple is: What circumstances have caused this system to reach such an imbalanced state that one spouse is clinging to the relationship while the other is distancing him- or herself? Or, What dynamics are present in the family *now* that have rendered the system's typical homeostatic balancing procedures ineffective?

In attempting to answer these questions and develop clinical hypotheses, we typically look at the following potentially causative systemic dynamics (see Everett, in press): expectable developmental occurrences and resultant role shifts, externally induced crises, shifts in intergenerational loyalties and/or coalitions, changes in marital complementarity, and patterns of individual emotional development. For a systemic approach, we have found that it is usually more effective to proceed in assessment first from the externally unpredictable events and the broader developmental issues along a continuum to dyadic and individual factors. This allows the therapist to capture underlying or reinforcing dynamics associated with external events or broad relationship patterns and not become trapped by the drama of the dyadic conflict or individual symptomatology. Often therapists working solely with individuals or couples fail to recognize the influence of these broader relationship dynamics. In these types of cases, where the crisis of divorce may be imminent, the power of loyalties and coalitions that exist throughout the system cannot be overlooked.

Assessing Collusion and Ambivalence

Before we examine the range of etiological conditions that might create the apparently unresolvable imbalance in polarizing couples, there are two underlying dynamics that serve as useful assessment clues for the therapist: marital collusion and the ambivalence continuum. Dicks (1967), in his pioneering clinical studies of marital dynamics at Tavistock, identified the crucial role of marital collusion in sustaining marital attachment. He observed that even at the mate selection stage, potential couples implemented a "mutual signaling system" through which they could unconsciously test the range of needs and vulnerabilities of one another.

Couples who proceed into marriage enter into an emotional pact or collusive agreement that each will protect, and even defend, the vulnerabilities of the other. This often takes the form of an emotional bargain which says: "I will not reveal nor attack your deepest fears or vulnerabilities *if* you agree not to reveal nor attack my deepest fears or vulnerabilities." This bargain provides a protective foundation for the survival of intimate relationships.

The dynamic can be observed, for example, by clinicians in case situations where the therapist inadvertently becomes pulled into conflict between two spouses and appears to be overly critical or even attacking toward one of the spouses. It can usually be observed that the other spouse, who may have just finished cursing at the partner, will now come to their rescue. When therapists unintentionally push too hard on one spouse, this underlying relationship collusion is triggered and the couple pulls together in a defensive posture. The degree to which this collusive dynamic can be triggered in a couple is a direct indicator of the level of continuing emotional attachment and commitment in the relationship. The working clinical hypothesis here is that among polarizing couples some event or process has seriously diminished this collusive bond.

The concept of ambivalence, which denotes seriously mixed or opposing feelings within an individual, can be applied usefully to the assessment of attachment patterns in relationships (Nichols & Everett, 1986). Polarizing couples can be assessed along a continuum from preambivalent to ambivalent and postambivalent. This involves recognizing the presence and degree of ambivalence in each spouse. However, as we have indicated, the polarizing process is experienced by other family members throughout the intergenerational system. So, we apply the same assessment continuum to all relevant members of the system.

Preambivalence characterizes family members who feel that the family is functioning satisfactorily and continuing to meet their basic needs. These members are not concerned about the family's future viability. *Ambivalence* characterizes members who display a mixture or fluctuation of feelings from at times caring to other times disappointment and despair regarding either specific relationships (i.e., the marriage) or the family experience in general. These members may at times work hard on the problematic relationship and then begin to experience more resentment and hopelessness. Degrees of collusion and loyalty to the family continue even though they may be camouflaged by the swings in the ambivalence. In polarizing couples, this ambivalence includes growing fantasies of leaving the marriage and pursuing other relationships. These fantasies are not typically acted upon at this stage except in brief experimental affairs or impulsive separations. *Postambivalence* characterizes members who have moved through their ambivalence of clinging and doubting to an emotional place where they are prepared to withdraw their loyalty from the marriage and the family. The former dynamics of collusion no longer have a binding effect and the clinician can observe a withdrawal of affect and attachment.

While this assessment continuum has a developmental feature of progressing from preambivalence to postambivalence, the actual patterns within polarizing couples are case-specific. In other words, individuals in some cases may move clearly across this continuum and on to divorce, while others may find a homeostatic balance with one member preambivalent and the other ambivalent, or even both ambivalent. This latter pattern is found in chronically polarizing couples who take turns pushing their relationship to the limits and then backing off to preserve some semblance of attachment.

It should be apparent that the prognosis for the continuation of the marriage and the family will diminish as one spouse enters the postambivalent range. However, such spouses may move back and forth across this continuum. Occasionally the crisis produced by a postambivalent spouse will shock the other spouse into a new level of responsiveness, or entry into therapy, such that the postambivalent spouse may renew loyalties to the relationship in an effort to rebuild the marriage. Another example of the influence of this range of ambivalence is seen in the couples who may divorce and remarry the same partner several times.

This clinical feature of ambivalence must also be applied to other family members within the system. It has been our observation that the movement of a spouse into either ambivalence or postambivalence is not simply a subjective or intrapsychic experience. It is typically supported and reinforced by underlying coalitions with other family members, or significant friendships or sexual liaisons within an individual's social network. Thus a spouse whose family-of-origin parents never approved of their marriage may be pulled, gradually, toward ambivalence by the parents' continuing disapproval and intensification of family-of-origin loyalties.

In blended families, the natural children's disapproval of a new stepparent forms an insidious coalition to cause the parent to question their reentry into marriage. As the inevitable parent-child-marital conflict ensues, this coalition may pull the natural parent into a postambivalent stance. The spouse who pursues an extramarital affair for sexual experimentation during ambivalence may be vulnerable to that "causal" relationship moving toward serious attachment. Thus, the extrafamilial liaison may form a new coalition to further pull this spouse into postambivalence.

Several cases will illustrate the usefulness of the ambivalence continuum for the therapist in assessment. In a rather dramatic situation, a couple presented themselves for the initial therapy session which had been arranged by the husband regarding reported "marital conflict." The therapist was a beginning-level graduate student and apparently accepted this statement of the problem at face value over the phone. As soon as brief pleasantries were exchanged at the beginning of the session, the husband stated to the therapist that he was filing for a divorce that day, that there was nothing he wished to deal with in therapy, and that he would pay for the therapy which was needed to "take care of my wife and children." After this statement, he stood up abruptly, handed both his wife and the therapist his attorney's card, and left the room. The wife was stunned and reported having no awareness of either his level of dissatisfaction or his intention to end the marriage.

For this couple the polarization had apparently evolved covertly over a number of years. It was learned later that the husband had been involved with another woman for nearly two years. The general distance that had existed for many years in the marriage and the wife's excessive involvement with the two children seemed to mask the husband's disengagement from the relationship, and his movement through ambivalence and postambivalence while the wife remained at a preambivalent stage. He married the other woman a week after the divorce was finalized.

Another case, which illustrates the more classic polarizing process in a highly ambivalent marriage, involved a childless couple in their mid-twenties who had been married only three years. They reported six months of frustration and discouragement with ambivalence in the relationship, and the husband indicated that he was ready for a divorce but he could not bring himself to leave. An error here in assessment would be to assume that the intense ambivalence and lack of apparent movement in the relationship signaled the end of the marriage. In fact, if the husband had decided on divorce at this point, it would have been due more to the frustration of ambivalence rather than because of the explicit marital conflicts.

It soon became apparent to the therapist that the husband had not yet moved into a postambivalent stance. As the broader systemic reinforcers were identified, an interesting crossover pattern of intergenerational loyalties became apparent. Both spouses were quite immature and dependent for their ages. The wife, an only child, had little social experience in college and remained emotionally tied to her family of origin. Her parents, who lived in the same community, objected strenuously when she decided to marry the "college guy" she had dated during her senior year rather than pursuing her graduate studies. She soon transferred her dependence on her parents to dependence on the marital relationship.

However, the husband, equally immature and undifferentiated from his family of origin, used a macho, athletic prowess to suggest independence and strength. Throughout the marriage he remained intensely identified with his predominantly male peer group from college and high school. Many marital disputes involved his casual absences from home to go "out with the guys" for softball, golf, or a beer. Most of the members of his social network were either already divorced or never married. His parents were supportive of the marriage but had a chronically conflicted relationship themselves. Their message to him was that even though they had been unhappy for years and often thought of divorce, they "never gave up."

These underlying reinforcers helped define the "stuck" and ambivalent place of the marriage. The wife clung dependently to the marriage while her parents tried to pull her toward divorce and back home so she could continue her education. The husband was pulled intensely away from the marriage by his identification with the peers of his social network, while at the same time he was made to feel a failure by his parents if he "gave up" on the marriage. The underlying collusive thread that continued to bind them together was a need to protect, and even deny in one another, their own shared immaturity, fear of responsibility and growing-up, and lack of separation from their respective families of origin. Their dependence was not truly on one another, which was of course the secret under the collusion, because neither was strong enough to sustain the other. Rather, their dependence was on the symbolic value of the marriage itself to pretend adulthood and ward off the powers of their parents.

As this assessment evolved in the marital therapy process, clinical work focused on the interface between their personal maturity and internal struggles with the broader social network (for the husband) and family-of-origin loyalty concerns. This couple made good progress, their respective parents were involved at a later stage of the treatment process, and the relationship remained intact as the various influences on their ambivalence were removed.

Assessing Developmental Factors

The critical early assessment question for therapists working with polarizing couples is: What factors have so imbalanced this system that its homeostatic resources have been ineffective and it is approaching dissolution? Even if the distancing spouse is genuinely postambivalent and ready to file for divorce, it has been our experience that couples need to explore some answers to this question in order to objectify the dissolution process and work through some closure regarding the disappointment and anger of a failed relationship. Thus, in the first couple of therapy sessions, we sort through aspects of the following systemic dynamics which seem to have the power to unbalance a system and deteriorate the relationship's collusive bond. What the therapist is looking for here are clinical factors that may have upset the balance and complementarity of the marital relationship such that the system was forced to accommodate in what became a continuing dysfunctional pattern.

Expectable developmental occurrences and resultant role shifts identify the broad range of life events from family formation and parenthood to geographical relocations and career patterns. These experiences challenge the homeostatic mechanisms of a system by requiring accommodation, flexibility, and redefinition of roles. The developmental event that we most commonly look at, for example, is the marital and intergenerational systems' accommodation to the birth of a child (most therapists tend to look at the drama of the birth of the first child, but systemic dysfunctions may occur after the introduction of any child). This event requires major systemic accommodations involving a shift in boundaries around the marital subsystem, the introduction of a parent-child subsystem, the definition of new parental roles vis-à-vis the marital role, and the potential involvement of grandparents. Many polarizing couples can look back to events such as this and identify the loss of marital intimacy, the onset of child-focused behaviors by one or both spouses, or the decline of communication. Any of these may become insidious threads that perpetuate a marital imbalance that is never corrected until the imbalance causes one partner to pull away from the loyalties and bonds of the relationship.

Shifts in intergenerational loyalties and/or coalitions may have dramatic influences on the emotional commitment of a spouse to his or her marriage. The shifts that we look for in assessment involve the dramatic movement into new roles with parents, such as the caretaker with aged parents or the mediator with divorcing parents, or the sudden loss of a former family-of-origin role, such as that of continuing adult-parentified child to parents and siblings for many years. In the development of a genogram in the first session with polarizing couples (we do this with all of our cases), we look for the recent death of a parent, significant grandparent, or other relevant caretaker. We have observed that such a loss either forces or allows an adult child to redefine roles and loyalties. These intergenerational role shifts may create imbalances in the marital relationship and the onset of a polarizing process. In a preliminary investigation with a clinical population, it was found that a separation or divorce was initiated in over 50% of the cases within one year after the death of a parent (Strange, 1987).

Changes in marital complementarity represent shifts in the emotional balancing of the dyadic relationship. The complementarity of a relationship defines multiple levels of emotional need patterns, both past and present, that become balanced for mutual need gratification in an ongoing relationship (see Winch, 1971, for the original definition of complementarity). An example of complementarity in a marital relationship would be where one spouse performs the role of caretaker to the other spouse and family. The latter spouse's relative dependency is supported by the other spouse's caretaking role, which in turn allows that spouse to meet his or her own caretaking needs for control. Thus, complementarity is a circular and reciprocal pattern that provides stabilizing bonds in a close relationship. Potential changes in the complementary roles may occur, for example, when time or circumstances allow one spouse to outgrow or shift the previously balancing role. In the above example, a dependent husband may no longer require or desire the level of caretaking provided by his wife. As he strives for more independent activities, the wife begins to feel deprived of her ability and need to be caretaker. Thus, the original complementarity of the relationship becomes unbalanced. The relationship system must now accommodate to this shift or face a crisis. If a new level of complementarity is not achieved in this example, a polarizing process may begin, with the husband pulling away into an ambivalent stance and the wife redirecting her caretaking needs toward the children or family-of-origin members.

Patterns of individual emotional development may underlie shifts in the marital complementarity. The therapist needs to assess patterns of personal growth and ego development for each spouse across the history of the relationship. Many young adult marriages fail in the first couple of years because the emotional needs present at marriage may have involved issues of separation and leaving home. Within the first couple of years the romantic idealization fades and the original needs to escape family of origin are replaced by more adult behaviors. When this spouse looks at the other partner, the original attraction, complementarity, and bonding may seem foreign. This polarization then moves this spouse out of the relationship, leaving the other partner still at the original emotional place.

The review of these factors is intended to identify a clinical framework from which the therapist can organize assessment and begin to objectify the influences that may have unbalanced the relationship and caused one partner to move toward divorce. (These developmental factors and other precursors to divorce are elaborated further in Everett, in press.) The usefulness of recognizing these dynamics can be seen in the actual therapy process.

CONDUCTING FAMILY THERAPY

Developing a Clinical Assessment

We treat polarizing couples as presenting a *family problem,* and never focus exclusively on either the distancing spouse or the marital relationship itself. Typically in these cases, the initial contact with the therapist will be made either by the distancing spouse or by the other spouse who becomes fearful that he or she is losing the partner. The distancing spouse seeks therapy because of the discomfort of his or her increasing ambivalence, the pain of guilt associated with leaving, and occasionally because of the fantasy that the therapist will provide support for the other spouse and children should divorce occur. This spouse may also have a secret agenda (common among highly ambivalent individuals) which expects that the therapist will either tell him or her whether or not to stay in the marriage or confirm his or her tentative decision to leave the relationship and divorce.

The spouse who fears being left is, in our experience, the one who more often makes the initial contact for therapy. This individual seeks therapy at one level to alleviate anxiety and fears of the marriage ending. However, this spouse also may have a secret agenda that the therapist will be powerful enough to talk the other spouse into staying in the relationship and working on the marriage. This spouse has often rejected requests earlier in the relationship to seek marital therapy with the partner. It has been our observation that this spouse often needs to make the first contact in order to test the therapist's potential power and support for his or her position of the "one being left." This spouse's entry into therapy carries the unspoken expectation of triangulating the therapist into a secret, collusive attempt to "save the marriage."

These dynamics set the stage for the beginning of therapy. However, we need to point out that many cases may present themselves for therapy where polarizing is present in the marital relationship but the presenting problem is focused on another family member. While this is beyond the scope of this chapter, therapists should recognize that either scapegoated or parentified children, caught in the polarizing process, may present for therapy, or that other symptoms, such as depression, may present in either of the polarizing spouses.

The earliest task for the therapist is to maintain his or her own balancing act between the polarizing spouses. Given the above presenting dynamics for each spouse, their respective agendas for therapy and expectations of the therapist in particular are, for the most part, contradictory and opposing. Thus the therapist must move to the edge of their system, maintaining objectivity, not yet crossing into their relationship boundaries, and offering support to each spouse without crossing the invisible line of being perceived by either spouse as supporting the other. In addition to these difficult tasks, the early therapy sessions are also often punctuated by resentment and fears which will require careful therapeutic management and clinical objectivity.

The traps for the less experienced therapist here typically involve getting pulled into the dyadic system prematurely, before trust and control have been established. The result is that the distancing spouse may perceive the therapist as trying to "save the marriage" and not recognizing the spouse's ambivalence or desire to leave the relationship. On the other hand, the other spouse may perceive the therapist's "neutrality" as support for the exit of the partner and, thus, that this therapist does not possess the power to talk the spouse into staying. If the therapist falls into either of these traps, the result is escalation of the polarizing dynamics and the potential that the "offended" spouse will not return to therapy.

If the therapist more successfully maintains objectivity but is still pulled into the relationship boundaries prematurely, his or her role will deteriorate into that of a harassed mediator being pulled mercilessly back and forth between each spouse seeking to tell the more dramatic story and win the therapist into a coalition with them. Thus, the therapist becomes involved in his or her own balancing act between initiating the therapy process and responding to the needs and emotional climate of the spouses.

The bottom line in beginning therapy with polarizing couples is that the therapist has to "buy some time" to establish rapport and to gain necessary assessment data. We have found it effective to begin therapy with a clinical sequence that moves from one or two initial conjoint sessions with the spouses together, to one, but not more than two, concurrent individual sessions with each spouse separately. These are then followed by conjoint sessions. While we do not believe in circumscribing therapy by establishing arbitrary time limits (i.e., eight sessions), we have found that in highly polarizing couples it is useful to define the initial three to five sessions as an assessment period. We say to the couple that since it has taken so many years for them to reach this place in their relationship, we want to provide them with some understanding and "handles" on how and why they have become stuck. They are told that at the completion of this assessment period specific feedback will be provided to them regarding the issues and dynamics that will need to be explored if they continue in therapy. They are also told that if they decide to pursue a divorce, this process will still provide them with an awareness of how this relationship failed and help them explore concerns that will need to be considered for their children before divorcing. Thus, we explain that the process will enhance their chances of not carrying the same issues into their next relationship.

We are always careful to continue our own balancing of the therapy process by making available to the spouses the opportunity to work on the relationship, while at the same time acknowledging the potential for divorce. This stance confirms objectivity and neutrality. The assessment period provides a settled period for the couple during which we ask that no major decisions (e.g., filing for divorce) be made without discussing them in therapy. This period also tends to dissipate any former urgency toward reactive or impulsive actions leading to premature separation.

In the initial conjoint sessions we simply try to hear each spouse's perspective and issues without letting the emotional drama or threat of divorce escalate. To test patterns of collusion and boundaries, we will observe some of their anger toward one another as a clue to their continuing attachment and the levels of ambivalence. When the intensity begins to escalate into nasty accusations or belligerence, we will suddenly change the focus by inquiring about their children or surprising them by asking them to recall their first date. These are therapeutic ploys to divert them from their interpersonal conflict into, for example, the broader family dynamics of their children. Here we will talk about parent-child roles, developmental and school patterns, and the extent to which the children are aware of the depth of their conflict. Inquiring about the spouses' mate selection process is particularly useful for highly conflicted couples because the surprise allows the therapist to regain control of the therapy process. Here we are looking for evidence of early attachment and experimenting with rekindling the romantic idealization that is present for most couples during their courtship.

The concurrent individual sessions that follow have both pragmatic and strategic functions. They are scheduled for each spouse within the following week, but never back to back. First, they allow for a more relaxed session, involving each spouse's reflections on the issues and needs of the relationship, without the continual sparring and balancing of the conjoint sessions. Second, these sessions provide a structured way for the therapist to cross each spouse's respective boundaries and enter into their system. This creates a confused emotional scenario for each spouse. At one level they look forward to "seducing" the therapist onto their side against the other spouse. However, they also recognize that the other spouse will have an independent session which triggers an immediate concern over their protective collusive bonds. In other words, a spouse must deal with the choice of either "attacking" or "protecting" the other spouse, while at the same time trying to triangulate the therapist.

The goal of these individual sessions is to establish rapport with each spouse, gather family assessment data, and explore perceptions of the relationship that might not be shared readily in the conjoint sessions. Of course, the value of therapeutically entering another's individual system is often offset by potential liabilities. The most common difficulty that a therapist will encounter here is whether to offer confidentiality regarding information discussed in each individual session. Many family therapists believe that confidentiality should not be offered to individual members of a family system because it reinforces secret keeping within the family and triangulates the therapist into a potential coalition with that member.

However, we have observed that polarizing cases typically withhold information and/or secrets from the therapist, as well as from one another, due to their distancing and anger, and because of the potential threat of divorce and adversarial litigation. Often, important information that would significantly affect the assessment of ambivalence, such as extramarital affairs, secret illnesses, or child-related issues, may not emerge in the process of conjoint therapy for months, if ever. We believe that the value of gaining access to such data, most of which is considerably less dramatic than affairs, early in the therapy process far outweighs the potential risks of disruptive triangulation.

We have found that the most effective approach is to offer a "limited confidentiality," or more accurately from the therapist's perspective, a voluntary and limited triangulation. The individual session structures this limited triangulation opportunity for each spouse in which they can be more candid about their dissatisfaction and fears, and risk bypassing their protective collusion by revealing more private data or even secrets. However, this individual session cannot be allowed to evolve into a focused coalition that could be used against the other spouse.

We begin the individual sessions with the statement: "I want you to know that what we talk about here will be private and that I will not report it to your spouse. However, if as we progress in therapy, there is important information or secrets which we discussed that I believe are critical to the therapy, I will privately discuss them with you and how they might be shared in therapy with your spouse. There is the possibility that if we were to disagree about the sharing of certain secrets that I might have to withdraw as therapist in order to protect your spouse from being hurt by the therapy process. I will offer the same relationship to your spouse. Is this acceptable to you?"

Most spouses will accept such a statement. We never use the term "confidentiality" because of the potential confusion with legal issues. The most complex repercussion is learning of an ongoing affair, usually from the distancing ambivalent or post-ambivalent spouse. We handle this straightforwardly by identifying the energy that may be invested in the affair and that is unavailable to the therapy process of looking at the marriage. We indicate our unwillingness to conduct conjoint therapy while the extramarital relationship is active and give the spouse the choice of suspending the relationship during therapy, ending it within a reasonable amount of time, or withdrawing from therapy. We are very clear that our ethical commitment to both spouses will not allow us to conduct therapy while the affair is active.

Of course, this stance puts considerable pressure on the spouse. Typically, the affair for the ambivalent spouse is more casual and more easily given up. However, for the postambivalent spouse, the affair carries more fantasies of "escape" and/or permanence. Thus, the choice of the affair or working on the marriage helps to focus for this spouse his or her genuine degree of ambivalence and may result in a decision to move back toward the marriage or to file for divorce. If the spouse chooses the latter, we will help him or her plan to take the decision back into the therapy process to share with the other spouse. This can be a tough clinical session, but it is necessary in allowing the couple to deal with one another and to identify the therapist's continuing role with them.

The third stage of completing the assessment sequence involves returning to the conjoint session and providing feedback to the couple. Typically, only one, and on occasion two, individual concurrent sessions are held. More than this would reinforce individual attachments and potential coalitions with the therapist and serve to shift the focus from the process of working together in conjoint therapy.

The offer to provide feedback here was given in the first session to define some therapeutic structure and diffuse hostilities. However, we never begin this conjoint session with the feedback itself. We have found that the prior individual sessions may trigger a variety of dynamics in the relationship and even dramatic movement, in either direction, during the ensuing week. Thus, we begin by asking for the spouses' reflections on their individual sessions and about any discussion they may have had during the week. In some cases the couple may move right into identifying and working on new or critical aspects of their relationship, and therapy is clearly underway.

Those couples who are more rigidly "stuck" tend to sit back and wait for the therapist's evaluation. Here the role of the therapist is threefold: (1) to provide carefully selected observations regarding dysfunctional patterns within their relationship or from across the broader intergenerational system; (2) to initiate an educational process of helping them explore how they got to this place and where these dysfunctional elements came from; (3) to challenge and push on the boundaries of their relationship to help them experience whether they both are at a place to struggle with their marriage. This session should conclude either with some verbal commitment from the couple to continue to work on the relationship but with no guarantees regarding the outcome; or perhaps by offering another structured time frame, designed to manage the continuing ambivalent spouse's caution, of working on the relationship for six to eight weeks; or with one spouse's expression that therapy is too late and they desire to end the relationship. For the latter circumstances, conjoint and individual sessions are still offered by the therapist to manage adjustment to this decision, to discuss separation issues, and to identify the children's needs and responses. (Referral for mediation will be discussed later.)

Developing Clinical Strategies

Following this assessment stage, the therapy process may proceed in one of at least three directions: (1) the distancing spouse, while still talking of leaving the marriage, remains ambivalent and agrees to work on the relationship; (2) the distancing spouse is highly ambivalent and reluctant to pursue therapy; (3) the distancing spouse is postambivalent and prepared to terminate the marriage.

From these possible clinical directions, it is apparent why the assessment is important and why the therapist must feel that he or she has developed clear working hypotheses regarding the family's dynamics. To proceed with routine marital therapy when a spouse is postambivalent and ready to leave the relationship renders the therapy process ineffective; to become trapped by the distancing spouse's talk of divorce when there is still ambivalence and potential to work on the relationship would seem irresponsible. Thus, the therapist must rely on the assessment data and focus these into a clear treatment direction.

In cases where both spouses are willing to work on the relationship, we proceed rather straightforwardly with marital therapy. This involves identifying and dealing with imbalances, complementarity, developmental shifts, parent-child issues, and intergenerational loyalties (see Nichols & Everett, 1986). However, we continue to identify the thread of ambivalence and potential threat of loss of the relationship throughout the process.

Typically we invite children for family sessions to explore the parent-child interface with the marital subsystem, as well as to evaluate their anxiety regarding their parents' conflict. We also involve family-of-origin parents, when accessible, to serve as "consultants" in the therapy and explore developmental and family separation issues for each spouse, as well as the role of intergenerational triangles and loyalties. The marital therapy will move toward either rebalancing the relationship, allowing for new growth and diminishing the ambivalence of the distancing spouse; or toward confirmation of the failure of the relationship and a resultant decision, perhaps more mutually agreed-to now, for divorce.

In polarizing couples where the ambivalence is high and there is reluctance to pursue therapy, the clinician has a difficult task. The issue is how to provide a therapeutic structure that allows the distancing spouse to participate in therapy. Often the agreed-upon time from of six to eight weeks makes this comfortable. Certainly the therapist must be clear that the intent of the therapy is not to "save" the marriage but to help each spouse explore their own feelings about the relationship and arrive at a comfortable direction.

Because of the reluctance of the distancing spouse, the therapist needs to be careful not to become trapped siding with the preambivalent spouse by trying to talk the ambivalent spouse into participating in therapy and, by implication, the marriage. The straightforward approach will often fail here. Thus, we may take a more strategic role by creating metaphors or reframing the distancing spouse's discouragement and ambivalence into a more workable clinical dynamic. This may take the form of identifying marital therapy as a potentially painful and stressful experience. We might say, for example: "Sometimes the pain of looking at the disappointments and anger that you have experienced over the years in your relationship can be more overwhelming than simply walking away from the relationship as it is. I am not encouraging you to do that, but you need to know that this process can be very painful." This takes the power of the distancing spouse's discouragement away by focusing a more immediate ambivalence with regard to the opportunity of therapy and the unexpected caution expressed by the therapist. Such an approach will often dissipate the distancing spouse's need to pull away, capture some of the other spouse's discouragement, and shift the focus to the question of the future of therapy rather than the future of the marriage.

In some instances, the continuing ambivalence of the distancing spouse may actually pull the other spouse into an ambivalent and angry stance. It may appear here that the therapy is stalled and there is simply no movement in any direction. The first attempt that we will make to diffuse this impasse might be to invite children or family-of-origin members into the therapy process. This must be done more carefully than in normative marital therapy because the same commitment to the therapy process has not been achieved here. However, by broadening access to other components of the system, the therapist can often gain new leverage or develop new strategies.

When this approach has not been successful, or appears too unsettling to pursue, we will often attempt to perturb the relationship system by refocusing abruptly on the reality of the divorce process. We ask the couple to imagine what it would be like for them to live by themselves and to care for their children as a single parent. We will often "walk through" a postdivorce scenario with a couple and blend aspects of fantasies regarding dating and new relationships with pragmatic concerns of doing laundry and handling financial matters. We introduce the adversarial legal system to them and have them decide what they would say to their attorney about the marriage and one another, and about who gets custody of their children. Most polarizing couples use the threat or fantasy of divorce without any practical awareness of its implications for them. This intervention adds a dose of reality to further help them test their attachment and ambivalence.

The next level of intervention, intended to further perturb a rigid system, utilizes ritual to introduce a new level of noncognitive drama for the couple. Here we will acknowledge the spouses' mutual pain and unhappiness and suggest that perhaps the marriage relationship as they knew it needs to be buried and let go of. The burial of the relationship will allow them either to start over and begin to build a new marriage or will help them in their decision to walk away from it.

The actual ritual must be designed for each case situation. In some situations the couple may help design the ritual and it will involve children and other family members. In other situations the ritual may be performed for the couple. For example, one of our former graduate students, who was also an active clergyman, discussed a couple's willingness to participate in a ritual that would help them let go of the old relationship. Without elaborating on the content of the ritual, he entered their next therapy session garbed in his clerical robe and carrying a Bible. The couple's response was a curious blend of laughter followed by "dead" silence. A brief nonreligious service "burying" the relationship was enacted during the session which dramatically gave the couple permission to share their grief and disappointment over what they felt they had lost in their failed marriage. This opened new emotional levels to pursue in therapy and at a later date the couple made a mutual decision to separate and end the marriage.

In another similar case where the polarizing spouses had been separated for six months and were working in therapy on the potential for getting back together, the therapist helped them plan a ritual involving their children and other family members. This took place in a park setting where they used to go early in their marriage. Here they recited new vows and intentions toward one another in the presence of their family in preparation for renewing their relationship. The use of rituals and metaphors can be an effective therapeutic intervention for polarizing couples who are either immobilized by their ambivalence or moving toward ending their relationship.

The third clinical situation involves the postambivalent spouse who has made a decision to seek a divorce. Often this is a spouse who has been dissatisfied with the marriage for many years and either has not verbalized the seriousness of the unhappiness or has not been able to get the spouse's attention or earlier involvement in therapy. This spouse has simply disengaged emotionally from the marriage, perhaps over a period of six to eight years. Often developmental issues, such as children leaving home, or external events, such as career moves or the death of a family-of-origin parent, trigger the overt move to leave the relationship. The result is a preambivalent spouse who never recognized the depth of the other's dissatisfaction, and who is now overwhelmed by the spouse's level of accumulated anger and resentment, and the fear of losing the relationship. In some systems the shock is shared equally by children and family-of-origin members, while in others it appears that everyone knows but the unsuspecting spouse.

After the initial assessment confirms the postambivalent intentions of the spouse to leave the relationship, the focus in therapy must be balanced between trying to help the preambivalent spouse recognize what is happening and "catch up" emotionally, and slowing down the process of the exiting spouse in order to deal with practical issues of separation, divorce planning, and telling the children and other family members. In many cases, a period of three or four therapy sessions can be defined as an interim stage where both spouses can express feelings and concerns of what happened and failed in their marriage. This allows for a recognition of how far apart emotionally the spouse may have grown. It also allows a relatively safe setting for the mutual expression of anger that must be recognized. It has been our experience that couples who move toward divorce too quickly, without this opportunity to say things to one another and to

achieve some understanding of what has happened, will not only
carry latent resentments and disappointments into adversarial
custody battles but also continue to act them out with their
children years after the divorce (see Everett & Volgy, 1983).

It is often useful to schedule a couple of individual sessions
at this point. These would be intended to offer support to the
preambivalent spouse and a setting where they can explore the
range of feelings from rage to loss. Individual sessions for the
exiting spouse focus on understanding the reactions of the other
spouse and anticipating separation and divorce issues for the
family. Depending on the dependency and vulnerability of the
preambivalent spouse, the individual sessions may continue pe-
riodically.

However, we believe it is crucial to return to conjoint sessions
so that the spouses can verbalize their responses to one another,
deal with letting go, and begin what we call "divorce planning."
Here we follow a model of introducing to the couple a range
of pragmatic issues that must be recognized as they enter the
divorce process. These issues serve to represent reality, to slow
the process down, and to provide a structure and sequence for
preparation for the divorce. These issues include: how to tell
the children and other family members; anticipating and managing the children's responses; separation—how, when, where;
timing of the divorce process; anticipation of postdivorce parent-
child and personal adjustment; the role of grandparents; the
recommendation for mediation. While the specifics of working
through the divorce process are beyond the scope of this chapter
(see Everett & Volgy, in press), we want to identify the role of
mediation as a resource to both the spouses and the therapist.

We introduce mediation as an alternative to adversarial divorce
proceedings and an opportunity for the spouses to work out a
self-determined agreement regarding custody and access which
they believe to be in the best interest of their children. Depending
on the mediator and the setting for mediation, most other aspects
of the divorce regarding support and the division of assets and
debts can be included in the agreement. We believe strongly in
the role of mediation (see Volgy & Everett, 1985a, 1985b) and
recommend that therapists working with divorcing couples iden-

tify experienced mediators to whom they can refer. (In certain cases, we may offer the mediation ourselves because of the continuity of working with these cases. However, we do not recommend that therapists do such unless they have had considerable training in mediation and experience working with attorneys and the courts. The professional liabilities can be great.) Where a couple will not pursue mediation, we identify family law attorneys for them who will not unnecessarily escalate the divorce into destructive litigation.

Following referral for mediation, it is certainly appropriate for the therapist to continue the clinical process for the family. After they separate, we will usually schedule several family sessions, often including young children and family-of-origin members. These sessions allow everyone to process what has happened and reflect on where they are going. Occasionally, separate sessions may be scheduled with the sibling group if we are concerned about their adjustment at this point.

It is important that the therapist define an ongoing clinical role with the family throughout and following the divorce process (see Everett & Volgy, in press). We are concerned when we learn that a therapist has discontinued working with a couple or family after the decision to divorce has been made. We find it equally disturbing when a therapist who has been working with a couple offers only individual therapy to one of the spouses after the decision to divorce has been made. Such clinical choices appear to completely disregard the couple's and the family's need to work together to get through the divorce process with some integrity.

SUMMARY

This chapter has defined the predivorce polarizing process that occurs in couples and has identified central clinical assessment dynamics of collusion, ambivalence, and developmental factors. These have been operationalized in a variety of clinical interventions and strategies. Polarizing cases represent a challenge to family therapists and demonstrate the importance of integrating ongoing assessment with systemic treatment planning.

REFERENCES

Boszormenyi-Nagy, I., & Spark, G. (1973). *Invisible Loyalties.* New York: Harper & Row. (Reprinted 1984. New York: Brunner/Mazel.)

Dicks, H. (1967). *Marital tensions.* New York: Basic Books.

Everett, C. A. (in press). *Treating family dissolution.* New York: Guilford Press.

Everett, C. A., & Volgy, S. S. (1983). Family assessment in child custody disputes. *Journal of Marital and Family Therapy, 9,* 343–353.

Everett, C. A., & Volgy, S. S. (in press). Treating divorce in family therapy practice. In A. Gurman & D. Kniskern (Eds.), *Handbook of family therapy, revised edition.* New York: Brunner/Mazel.

Nichols, W. C., & Everett, C. A. (1986). *Systemic family therapy: An integrative approach.* New York: Guilford Press.

Strange, J. (1987). The intergenerational effects of death upon marital attachment and dissolution patterns in cohesive and non-cohesive family systems. Unpublished doctoral dissertation, Florida State University, Tallahassee, FL.

Volgy, S. S., & Everett, C. A. (1985a). Systemic assessment criteria for joint custody. *Journal of Psychotherapy and the Family, 1,* 85–98.

Volgy, S. S., & Everett, C. A. (1985b). Joint custody reconsidered: Systemic criteria for mediation. *Journal of Divorce, 8,* 131–150.

Winch, R. F. (1971). *The modern family* (3rd Ed.) (pp. 487–489). New York: Holt, Rinehart and Winston.

5

What's the Rush?—
A Negotiated Slowdown

Candyce S. Russell and
Charles M. Drees

Throughout the psychotherapeutic literature, there exists the notion that marital partners participate in a mutual selection process that results in an "exquisite" match. Within this relationship each finds a safe arena in which to regress to earlier stages of development where issues unresolved in the family of origin can either be relived and thus perpetuated or reworked on the way to further individual growth (e.g., Dicks, 1967). Authors writing from several theoretical positions reference the uncanny precision involved in mate selection (Bowen, 1978; Dicks, 1967; Humphrey, 1983; Sager, 1976; Whitaker, 1982). Bowen (1978) suggests that individuals usually choose to marry a person with the same level of differentiation. Whitaker (1982) states that the "marital partners have chosen each other with great wisdom, with the wisdom of social propriety, with the wisdom of their bodies, as well as the unconscious awareness of how they compliment each other's person" (p. 186). He goes on to say that this "exquisite accuracy" of choice continues to exist even when there is evidence of pathological "sickness" present in the choosing process. However, despite this somewhat comforting notion of "exquisite choice," the fact remains that nearly one-half of all first marriages in the United States will end in divorce by the seventh year of marriage (Humphrey, 1983; Spanier & Thompson, 1984), and of those divorced persons who remarry, almost half (44%) will experience a subsequent divorce (Norton & Glick, 1979; Sager, 1986). It appears that for many people, what started as an "exquisite choice" ends in the painful process of divorce.

However, not every troubled marriage needs to end in divorce in order to reduce the pain of its partners. It is possible to assist the couple in exploring the current challenges to the "accuracy" of their original marital choice, as well as alternatives for a new type of relationship contract. The challenging of the original match may result in a new marriage to the same partner, separation, or divorce.

THEORETICAL FOUNDATIONS

We assume that marital relationships take on a "life" of their own. The marriage and the individuals in it are constrained to a certain degree by "relationship rules" (Watzlawick, Beavin, & Jackson, 1967), unspoken "contracts" (Sager, 1976), and a legacy from each partner's family of origin (Kerr, 1981). Relationship rules are unspoken, agreed-upon limits to acceptable behavior. These rules develop over time, outside the awareness of the participants and become noticeable usually as they are violated. In a similar fashion, the contractual foundations of the relationship are unspoken and unwritten and become most recognizable when one partner changes and fails to "live up" to his or her side of the relationship bargain. The strengths and vulnerabilities each brings from the family of origin can frequently be identified in the multiple clauses of a relationship contract.

Among polarized couples where "one wants out and the other wants in," distance is typically regulated by a pursue/withdraw cycle where one partner threatens divorce and the other pleads for time to figure out the unspoken expectations of the changing relationship contract. The pursue/withdraw cycle, in turn, prevents the relationship from evolving to a new level with a revised contract.

Furthermore, when "one wants out and the other wants in," we assume that each partner lives out the side of the ambivalence about the marriage that the other partner is moving too quickly to experience for him- or herself. If the pace of the pursue/withdraw cycle can be slowed, the two partners are likely to experience more of both sides of their ambivalence about themselves, the marriage, and commitments to friends, work, and family of origin.

The therapist, in thinking about the marriage as an entity with its own life and rules of operation, can assist the couple in depersonalizing their struggle. He or she can model for the couple an interested, yet detached curiosity about the development and operation of their system that reduces blame and increases the maneuverability for each spouse within the relationship. As previously unspoken rules and contracts become spoken, relationship-level constraints are loosened and the "degrees of freedom" are increased.

Drawing upon the Circumplex Model of Marital and Family Systems (Olson, Russell, & Sprenkle, 1983), each relationship must develop rules regarding *distance* (a balance between separateness and connectedness) and *change* (a balance between stability and variety). The optimal balance point on each of these dimensions will change over time. The famous "seven-year itch" and "20-year-review" (Whitaker, in Neill & Kniskern, 1982) can be thought of as crises over separateness versus connectedness and/or stability versus change. Patterns of indebtedness from past generations, unresolved losses, loyalty ties to each family of origin, and reciprocal projections (Dicks, 1967) complicate the balancing act and help us to understand some of the historical factors that may be preventing the couple from locating a new and more satisfying balance point in their relationship.

Contemporary stressors such as the addition or loss of family members, job or residence changes, and changes in health, financial status, or friendship networks may further complicate the couple's attempts to balance separateness with connectedness in their relationship and to find a comfortable mix of stability and variety. Finally, there are a host of contemporary "markers" that partners may use to measure whether they are "on time" or "off time" (Neugarten, 1979) in their personal conceptualization of how well they are doing in their development as adults. The press from these groups of stressors (contemporary and historical) operate to maintain the pursue/withdraw cycle within the marriage and to "split" the ambivalence about the relationship so that one partner overfocuses on stability and connectedness while the other overfocuses on change and separateness (see Figure 1).

If the press from contemporary and/or historical stressors can be reduced, the intensity of the pursue/withdraw cycle will lessen and partners may start to experience *both* sides of their ambivalence about relationships (including this marriage) (see Figure 2).

While one step in our therapy is to focus on the couple's relationship as an entity separate from the spouses, in later phases of therapy we hope the partners will begin to *focus on the self* (Kerr, 1981) as the appropriate target for change. A review of each partner's previous attempts to change the other typically reveals how fruitless an overfocus on the other has been. The longer each partner has been involved in attempting to change the other, the more depressed she or he is likely to become at this phase of therapy as she or he begins to take responsibility for her (his) own happiness in life. This is a turning point in therapy. The spouse who has been the pursuer, overfocused on the other, and the champion of closeness and relationship stability now backs off and focuses on self. If the new focus on self is genuine (not designed to get a response from the partner), the second partner may notice that she or he is no longer being pursued. This *may* allow the second partner to focus on him/her self with greater clarity and openness now that there is less need to defend self against pursuit from the spouse—and less need to champion the cause of separateness and change in the system.

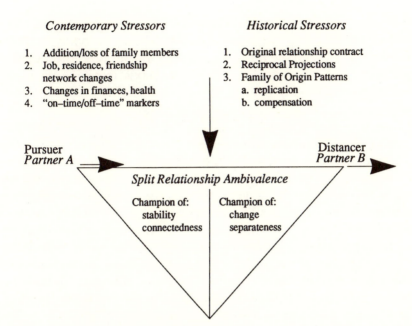

Figure 1. Pressures that perpetuate the pursuit distance pattern and split relationship ambivalence in polarized couples.

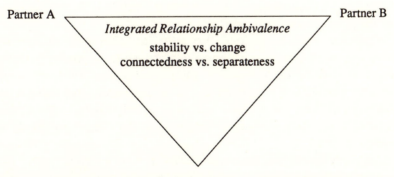

Figure 2. Consequences of moderated pattern of pursuit distance and focus on self in previously polarized couples.

Neither the therapist nor the couple knows what the outcome will be of this new focus on self within one or both partners. However, it is our belief that decisions made after the pursue/withdraw cycle has slowed will be decisions to which each will feel more personally committed.

INTERVENTIONS

In dealing with polarized couples, there are usually two implicit (sometimes explicit) beliefs underlying the presenting problem. First, there is the belief that if one spouse can only disassociate from the other, perhaps he or she can find happiness or discover who he or she is. According to Whitaker (1976), this is the issue of self-discovery by denial of the other. It is one of the delusions of divorce. As part of this pattern, one spouse believes that the "cause" of his or her unhappiness is the other person. If only the other spouse were different, had not changed, treated me better, and so forth then my life would be better, more fulfilling, or happier. It becomes a short step to believe that if I leave my partner, then I remove the major barrier to my happiness. This may work well until the person enters the next relationship and repeats the same patterns that made him or her miserable.

The second belief is that any solution is acceptable so long as it is quick and involves a minimum of pain. Comments such as "I'll do anything, I just want to save my marriage" or "I don't feel anything anymore; I just want out" are frequently heard when working with polarized couples. Inherent in this is the notion that a "quick fix" will solve the problem, as well as numb the pain of change and/or loss.

While we wish to relieve the pain underlying both of these positions, we believe it is beneficial to slow down the process before any decision is made regarding divorce. Only after the partners understand themselves, their partners, and their interactional patterns more fully will they have reliable information on which to base a decision regarding the future of their relationship.

It is our contention that until both spouses recognize and take responsibility for their part in the successes and problems that exist in their marriage, they are doomed to repeat these patterns in this or subsequent relationships. In explaining this to the couple, we suggest that both partners can benefit from therapy. The spouse who wants out can discover whom he or she is divorcing. Likewise, the spouse who wants to save the marriage can explore whether or not his or her needs are being met in this relationship or if they might be better achieved in another one or alone. Finally, both spouses can decide if it is feasible to create a new relationship together or whether they should divorce.

In working with polarized couples, we find that our therapy proceeds in stages. Although these stages are somewhat artificial and they often overlap, the following is a general outline of our therapy. In the first stage, we get to know each other. This involves sharing our beliefs about our roles as therapists, as well as our beliefs about responsibility and change. We also ask the couple to contract to work. Next, we gather information concerning the presenting problem as each spouse takes turns venting his or her feelings and concerns about these issues. The next stage involves assessment of the relationship system. The fourth stage is the heart of therapy. In this stage, we focus on the couple's relationship as an entity unto itself, as well as the process of self-differentiation (Bowen, 1978). In other words, how can each spouse exist as an individual yet remain in a relationship? As each partner struggles with these issues, we find they often come to a decision concerning the relationship and the continuation of therapy. At this point, we reevaluate the process and offer various alternatives based upon the couple's goals and choices.

Stage I: Therapist's Position

Among the most important issues when working with polarized couples is the therapist's stance concerning responsibility for change and his or her feelings concerning marriage and divorce. It is our belief that the couple, not the therapist, is responsible for changing their behavior and for deciding to remain married, to separate, or to divorce. This is congruent with our belief regarding self-responsibility and the development of a more differentiated self (Bowen, 1978). As therapists, we are responsible for the conduct of the session, not the couple's life. Part of that responsibility is to ensure, to the best of our abilities, that both partners have information to facilitate their choices. The couple is responsible for making use of or ignoring this information in making their future life choices. One way to ensure that we respect this is by remaining neutral.

Our conceptualization of neutrality concurs with that proposed by Selvini Palazzoli and her colleagues (1980). It concerns not only the therapist's dealing with each spouse, but also remaining neutral to the continuation or dissolution of the marriage. Through neutrality, the therapist attempts to balance support for each spouse, avoid coalitions, and avoid making judgments about the couple's decisions. This frees the therapist from becoming overly invested in the couple or in "solving" their problems. The responsibility for change remains with the couple. Thus, the therapist has the freedom to move in and out of the marital system, one time supporting a spouse, another time challenging, yet another time admitting his or her confusion regarding what is occurring between the spouses. At no time does the therapist assume responsibility for leading the couple's life. That is their job.

It is important to note that remaining neutral to the couple's choices does not imply that the therapist should remain valueless. We do not believe this is realistic. However, if the therapist is an "unabashed marriage-saver" (Weiner-Davis, 1987) or a believer that marriage is a relic that maintains repressive power structures, we believe these values should be shared. Withholding this type of information from the clients may hinder their ability to make informed, responsible choices. Remaining neutral to the continuation or dissolution of the marriage also provides a therapeutic benefit for the therapist. This stance frees the therapist from measuring success or failure in terms of the numbers of marriages "saved" or "split up."

Having discussed these issues with the couple, we often ask that they contract for a number of sessions to explore their options. Usually, we ask for six to eight sessions, with an opportunity to evaluate the progress/process at this time. This allows both the couple and the therapist an opportunity to assess whether or not to continue therapy with each other. It also provides the therapist with an indicator of the couple's commitment to their marriage, as well as therapy. By contracting for sessions, the therapist is indicating that he or she is willing to share with the couple information, impressions, and aspects of the therapist's self that may help in their struggle. Also, the therapist provides an arena for the couple to examine their relationship, and any decisions they make. By asking the couple to agree to a number of sessions, the therapist is also indicating that the couple will be responsible for their changes. It is a start in self-responsibility and decision making, as well as a means of demonstrating that neither spouse is all-powerful or a helpless victim (Jones, 1987).

Stage II: Venting

Having obtained an agreement with the couple to try therapy, we ask the spouses to discuss why they are here, why this is a problem/concern for them, and what steps they have taken so far to solve these issues. We ask one spouse at a time, usually starting with the spouse who did not initiate therapy, to tell his or her story. We tell them that they will both get a chance to tell their side of the story. By doing this, we indicate to both spouses that we take very seriously how each perceives the marital situation. Also, we believe that it is crucial for developing rapport that the spouses be allowed to vent whatever emotions are associated with these issues. Through this, we show the couple we are not afraid of their conflict and will provide an arena to help them with their struggle. In our experience, we find that this venting serves several useful purposes: (1) it allows each spouse to voice his or her concerns and feelings; (2) it provides each spouse with information regarding the other's viewpoint; (3) it provides an emotional release that, paradoxically, calms down the system; and (4) it creates an atmosphere for problem solving since the issues are now out in the open.

By exploring what attempts the couple has made in problem solving, we avoid duplicating, as much as possible, unsuccessful solutions. The couple does not need solutions that are "more of the same," but rather solutions that provide second-order change (Watzlawick, Weakland, & Fisch, 1974). In other words, they need solutions that alter the nature of the system such that new levels of functioning are achieved.

Finally, by asking for each spouse's perceptions, we raise the possibility that there are at least two sides to the problem, and that neither spouse's viewpoint is the only possible viewpoint. The "reality" of the situation may elude both of them. It is our job to help them discover a "common reality" on which they can base their decisions regarding their relationship.

Stage III: Assessment

Having listened to each partner's viewpoint, our next step is an assessment of the relationship system. Like Nichols and Everett (1986), we believe assessment is an ongoing process that provides an understanding of the strengths and weaknesses of each individual, as well as the couple as a system. Because it is ongoing, assessment provides a basis for working hypotheses about the couple's relationship which can be tested through the therapist's interventions. The couple's responses provide feedback which leads to a modification or confirmation of the hypotheses and, thus, provides more information for assessment.

In an effort to understand the couple's attempts to balance distance and change, we collect multigenerational information through a genogram. Also, we obtain a picture of the couple's relationship through constructing a time line of important events and issues in their history. Through these, we attempt to slow down the pursue/withdraw cycle by removing the focus from the heated issue of whether or not the couple should divorce. Instead, we demonstrate that they possess a history, both as individuals and as a couple, that brings them to this point in their relationship.

In our framework, the genogram is basically an annotated family tree that allows us to collect data about an individual's family of origin, as well as the relationships among family members. Usually, we extend it through three generations in an effort to examine various behavioral patterns or attitudes that may have been passed down through the generations. This allows us to examine behavior in the context of the developmental cycle of the individual and the family of origin. In the genogram we include names, ages, occupations, highest level of education, geographic locations, and other factual data of all family members. We also include dates of nodal events such as births, deaths, marriages, separations, divorces, retirements, and other important dates. While recording this, we encourage the individuals to comment on the various relationships within their family of origin, as well as in their spouse's family, especially regarding the management of distance/intimacy and stability/change. This provides a richer picture of both families and sheds light on how information is shared by the couple. The following is a partial listing of the types of questions we might use while doing the genogram:

How would you describe your mother/father/siblings? To whom were you closest?

Who would comfort you when you felt badly?

Describe the relationship between your mother-father-siblings.

Who was the favorite/the black sheep/the clown?

What was/is the relationship like between your parents and their parents?

Who are you closest to/most distant from in your family?

Which parent handled the discipline? Did one think the other was too harsh or too lenient?

How were decisions made in your family?

How could you tell when your parents had a fight or were mad at each other?

How could you tell when they were affectionate with each other?

What were/are their attitudes toward work/play/education/sex, etc.?

What happened when the oldest child left home?

How did your parents meet? Describe their courtship.

Did either of your parents think the other drank too much? How did you know?

What happened when someone in your family died? How did your parents react when their parents died?

Would either of your parents be surprised at your marital difficulties?

Could either of them have predicted you would have these problems?

Having removed the focus from the couple's heated relationship through the use of the genogram, we refocus on the marriage by constructing a time line of the couple's relationship history. This flows from the genogram as we move from each successive generation. However, rather than jumping into the "problems" of the relationship, we explore how the couple "chose" each other. We also examine key issues, events, and expectations that helped the relationship evolve into its current state. This exploration helps us examine the developmental issues occurring in the marriage. The following is a partial listing of the kinds of questions we employ in examining the relationship:

What attracted you to your partner/how did you get together?
Did you see any weaknesses back then?
What was going on in your family during this time?
Describe your dating. Did you date each other exclusively?
How soon after your first date did you have your first fight/ have sexual intercourse?
How were these decided? Was it what you wanted?
How soon after your first date did you get engaged/married?
What were your expectations when you got married? Who influenced these expectations?
How did you decide/decide not to have children?
What went on when you left home?
How did the two of you decide who wants in and who wants out of this marriage?
Are you free to initiate sex or does one of you typically initiate it?
How are problems solved and decisions made? Is this different now?
What seems different about your partner now versus when you started dating?
How have you tried to "change" your partner? How successful are you?
When fighting with your partner, do you bring up past issues or hurts?

How satisfied are you with the quality and quantity of physical and nonphysical affection?
What types of intimacy do you share with your partner? How has this changed/remained the same during your relationship?
What happens after you fight? How do you make up? How has this changed?

In gathering relationship history in this manner, we can obtain a richer picture of the couple's "exquisite choice." It also allows us to integrate information from the genogram with the time line. For example, we might ask, "Jill, we noticed that the year you started dating Bob, your mother started working. This left Dad without his usual support system. You mentioned he became more critical of you and your mom. Do you notice any similarity in your relationship with Bob now that you are working?"

By integrating this information, we hope to show the couple that their current relationship is a product of both their families of origin and their own interaction. Also, we can show that some of their stress is a result of developmental influences, or "stuck points" in making the transition between life-cycle stages. In other words, their relationship is bigger than both of them; it has a life of its own that evolved through the contributions of their respective families as well as their own interactions. Neither by themselves could have made the relationship what it currently is. Therefore, much of our effort in therapy is designed to help the partners change their focus from what the "other person" is doing wrong to what is going wrong in the "relationship." One way to facilitate this process is by helping each person discover his or her part in maintaining current behavioral patterns. The next stage in therapy involves helping the couple differentiate, while shifting the focus from the "other" to the "relationship."

Stage IV: Self-differentiation Within Relationship

Since most people do not exist in a vacuum, most couples can understand that their actions affect others and, in turn, are affected by others. One method for simulating this is to have the couple enact (Minuchin & Fishman, 1981) around an issue. It is not necessary to use the issue of divorce for this. Having done the genogram and time line, we find there are many sensitive issues (e.g., sex, finances, decision making, and child-rearing) that mirror the behavioral patterns that exist with regard to the issues of divorce. Because they are convinced the problem lies in the other, each spouse ignores significant aspects of his or her behavior and how this helps maintain the problem. While observing the enactment, we obtain a clearer picture of how each person contributes to the maintenance of the problem. The next step is to broaden the picture.

This is a most sensitive part of therapy. In this, we try to expand the couple's definition or view of the problem by challenging them to see that they both contribute to the problem. Often, this is most difficult to accomplish. Both spouses have an emotional investment in their positions and have resisted the other's attempts to change their minds. However, we believe this is a result of viewing the other as the "problem." Instead of trying to "change their minds," we try to change their definitions of the "facts" through reframing the behavior. In other words, we attempt to restate a situation so it can be perceived in a new or different way, thus changing the meaning for the person. One method for doing this is through positive connotation (Selvini Palazzoli et al., 1978). This involves connoting each spouse in positive terms or positively reframing behaviors as a way the couple chose to solve problems, express their caring, regulate the pace of change, or obtain intimacy. Thus, symptoms are connoted as useful and as evidence of the desire to preserve the integrity of the marriage. However, the old system "rules" and relationship contracts no longer work effectively and may need to be updated. Both reframing and positive connotation offer techniques for introducing to the couple a new way of looking at the same behavior and its functions. It is a way of introducing information into the system that may make a difference and lead to change in the relationship's patterns.

Another technique that takes the focus off the other spouse is to ask both members to use "I" statements when conveying thoughts, feelings, or intentions. We find this helps to reduce the tendency of the spouses to overfocus on the other. This procedure helps each partner "own" his or her feelings and behaviors in the relationship, as well as to take responsibility for them. Concurrently, we teach listening skills such as "shared meanings" (Miller, Nunnally, & Wackman, 1975), in an attempt to help the couple reach accurate understanding, not necessarily agreement, around a particular message. We find that through these exercises couples often discover that they have made assumptions about what their partner wants or intends to communicate. Also, it becomes easier to see what each partner's expectations are concerning the relationship or what feelings are projected onto the partner. These techniques help to uncover previously unspoken relationship "contracts" (Sager, 1976) that may need revision.

As used here, contracts refer to the set of assumptions and expectations each spouse has for the self and the other in the relationship (Sager, 1976). These include the fulfillment of personal needs and expectations of the marriage. The marital contract concerns the "shoulds" of the marital interaction which develop as the marriage evolves. In this process, the spouses, consciously or unconsciously, work out the "rules" that will govern their future relationship, as well as fulfill their own needs.

Often, both spouses are unaware of their own needs, much less those of their partner. However, both spouses proceed with the assumption that their spouse is aware of their needs and has agreed to the implicit and explicit exchanges inherent in these contracts. Frequently, the type of contract is the quid pro quo (Jackson, 1965), in which something is exchanged for something. Examples might include exchanging material goods (i.e., home, money) for emotional security ("I'll never leave you") or sexual favors; or one partner "agrees" to have an affair to "heat up" the marriage, while the other expresses outrage (Whitaker, in Neill & Kniskern, 1982). Thus, the marital contract is usually collusive in that the partners unconsciously agree to avoid certain topics, deny certain problems, or play certain games that test the system's boundaries or test its flexibility. Since much of the contract is not shared with the partner due to lack of awareness, confusion sets in, expectations are unmet, and conflict results.

There are methods for uncovering both the individual and marital contracts in the relationship. The more direct way is to ask each partner what his or her expectations were when they got married. Some questions that might be helpful include, What was your fantasy about marriage? What roles did you expect to play? Who would work/stay home? Did you both want children? How would you raise them? How would decisions be made? With whose friends would you socialize? How would you get alone time? In exploring these issues, it is important to integrate this information with that obtained through the genogram and time line to show the influence of each partner's family of origin on the relationship.

The less direct method for uncovering contracts is by asking each person to describe, in detail, what his or her ideal relationship would look like. How would decisions be made? How would the partners express desire for change? How much differentiation would be allowed? How would the partners pursue their individual goals/dreams? What kind of communication would exist? Would you or your partner work? What kind of partner would you look for, and what traits would he or she possess? How would affection be expressed? Would you have children? If so, how would they be cared for? When using this method, we look for unrealistic expectations as well as similarities to previous expectations found in the current relationship. In this way, there is a greater likelihood that we can caution the partner either that he or she is repeating the same patterns that brought him or her here, or that the expectations may need to be modified in order to be achieved. It is a way to perform a "reality check" so that the person is not setting him- or herself up to fail. However, any decision is theirs to make.

Another difficult part of therapy occurs when the couple attempts to translate insight into action. As the couple tries to change the pursue/withdraw cycle, the therapist must provide support for both spouses. For some spouses, it is difficult to maintain clear boundaries and a focus on self. During this stage, we encourage each spouse to identify and focus on a personal challenge or issue that each wants to work on irrespective of the partner's requests. For example, the wife's issue might involve how to maintain an independent identity yet remain emotionally close to a man, or how to assert her needs without scaring a partner. The dilemma for the husband might be how to become close without sacrificing his identity, or how to express his frustration or anger without distancing from a significant other. By identifying personal issues, we encourage differentiation of self for each spouse. Conceivably, at this point both spouses will have a better understanding of what they can or cannot control in the relationship, as well as what they are or are not responsible for in the marriage. Armed with this knowledge, they may modify their expectations of their mate, or realize their part in maintaining the dysfunctional aspects of their relationship. By focusing on self, they may stop trying to assign blame for common problems; instead, they can explore how to best meet their needs and goals in this, or subsequent, relationships.

Stage V: Reevaluation

At this point, we reexamine the therapeutic process. Depending upon the couple's goals and their choices, we may continue with therapy or terminate. For some who desire to explore further, conjoint or individual therapy may be recommended. For those who are learning to differentiate, we suggest family-of-origin work and caution that this is lengthy, often a lifetime project. At this point, we are often consultants and guides in a learning process, one that is as much our own as the client's. As we assist others in differentiating, we open ourselves to further exploration and growth.

CASE STUDIES

The two cases that follow illustrate our approach to working with couples when one wants in and the other wants out. The first couple divorced after deciding the costs of changing the original relationship contract would be too great; the second couple renegotiated their relationship and continued the marriage.

Case #1

Mr. and Mrs. B were a remarried couple—the first marriage for him, the second for her. They parented two children from her first marriage and two from this marriage. He was a skilled laborer and she a secretary. Mr. B (31) was a small man, of slight frame, who avoided eye contact and slouched as he walked or sat. Mr. B was also illiterate. Mrs. B (38) was a robust woman, though not overweight. She was energetic (though getting very tired), an excellent organizer, and attentive to each of her four children. Mrs. B's complaint was that her husband was very little help to her in managing the family and that, in fact, he was like "one of the kids." As the older children entered their teen years, conflict between them and their stepfather increased, and Mrs. B was convinced that she could manage the family better alone and was considering a divorce.

Mr. B accepted his wife's characterization of him with little resistance. The couple reported that not only did Mrs. B work full time, but she managed most of the household tasks alone, handled the family's finances, and was the children's primary disciplinarian. They did, however, report that Mr. B occasionally negotiated with creditors when the couple were unable to meet their monthly obligations. In general, they had arranged an overfunctioning/underfunctioning relationship, which the wife was now challenging. Their previous attempts at involving Mr. B more in the running of the family typically ended in Mrs. B criticizing Mr. B's efforts. Mr. B felt belittled by his wife and scorned by the children, especially his two stepchildren. Both partners agreed to postpone any decision about the marriage until the "bigger picture" was better understood.

Conjoint couple sessions included a focus on relationship history and family-of-origin material. During their courtship, Mrs. B had been attracted to Mr. B's gentle manner and his sense of humor. Mr. B had been attracted to Mrs. B's caregiving qualities—her supportiveness and thoughtfulness. As an oldest child, Mrs. B had become very skilled in that role, just as Mr. B was comfortable in the role of a charming but somewhat irresponsible youngest child. Their challenge as a couple was to "become closer in age" and to move beyond their original mother/son arrangement. On an individual level, her challenge was to learn to leave room for the competent effort of a partner. His challenge was not to be "run over" by the women in his life (e.g., his mother, teachers, and wife).

Mrs. B's intense focus on "getting her husband to grow up" shifted to a curiosity about women in her family of origin. She was able to recognize a family pattern in which the men were noticeably absent and the women were "bigger than life." She was able to recount many more stories about the women in her family than about the men. The therapist wondered what role the women may have had in "erasing" the men from the family's memory. In her own history, Mrs. B recognized that she had chosen men who were exceedingly quiet and who spent more time with either alcohol or "buddies" than with their families. More important, she was able to recognize how her efforts to "protect her children" from her first husband's influence replicated her family's pattern of "erasing" men. The therapist challenged Mrs. B to identify a goal for herself. The goal she chose was finding a way to "back off" so that her children could know their father better.

As Mrs. B decreased her focus on changing her husband, he became more involved with the two younger children. However, he continued to underfunction in other areas of the marriage and had not really identified a goal for himself in therapy. Mrs. B made it clear that although she appreciated her husband's increasing involvement with their children, she was discouraged about his distance from her. They seldom spent time together or talked together, and even in therapy Mr. B said very little.

Mr. B had a series of failed relationships with women whom he saw as competent but angry with him. These women were usually older than he and offered assistance by providing a place to live, financial assistance, or help in finding work. Each relationship ended with the woman complaining of Mr. B's irresponsibility. Mr. B knew little about his family of origin. His father abandoned the family when he was an infant, and his mother had a series of nonmarital relationships. Each of the children left home before completing high school, and Mr. B knew little about their lives. The therapist noted that Mr. B was becoming a "pioneer" in his family by virtue of his continued involvement with his children, and asked if he was also interested in finding a new way to relate to the woman in his life. Mr. B was not sure he wanted to do this, and therapy shifted to a discussion of what the couple might lose if Mr. B were to spend more time with his wife. One of those costs for Mr. B was the risk of disappointing his wife—of "boring" her and therefore humiliating himself. He had chosen a woman who was seven years older than himself, considerably more verbal and very involved with her children. He wondered if he might not be more comfortable with a woman closer to his own age.

Mrs. B eventually made the decision to leave the marriage. She organized the children to be more helpful at home and reserved time for herself to do something special, either alone or with friends. As the noncustodial parent, Mr. B continued a playful and friendly involvement with the two children who were biologically his own. Mrs. B did not block these attempts. However, she consciously refrained from inviting Mr. B back into the home or in other ways offering to make his life easier. At follow-up, Mr. B was living alone, visiting his children frequently, and dating a young woman. Mrs. B was living with her four children and had not established a new romantic relationship. They were functioning competently as co-parents although they had chosen not to continue the marriage.

Case #2

Mr. and Mrs. C, a young couple with two preschool children, came for therapy. Their presenting problem focused on their frequent arguments. Because of these, the wife was extremely unhappy and disclosed that she was unsure if she wanted to continue the marriage. During the initial session, the therapist indicated that the couple, not the therapist, would be responsible for any decision regarding their marriage. Accepting this, the couple contracted to pursue therapy.

During the remainder of this session, both spouses vented their feelings and concerns. Mrs. C was a full-time wife and mother who felt her abilities were inferior to her husband's, but also resented her greater burden in caring for the couple's children. Her life consisted of raising the children with little adult stimulation until her husband came home. Mr. C was an engineering student who studied long hours to achieve and maintain high grades. He spent his evenings studying at home or the library. Generally, much of their marital conflict centered around the issue of time—his time spent away from Mrs. C and the family, and her time spent with little adult stimulation. In addition, a number of current stressors further complicated the situation. First of all, there existed the heavy financial burden of raising two children while attending school. Also, Mr. C was competing in a highly demanding curriculum. For her part, Mrs. C had few friends because of the demands of child care. Finally, both spouses were physically cut off from their families of origin by more than 1,500 miles. Mrs. C commented that she missed the "free babysitting."

In the next several sessions, while exploring each spouse's family of origin and gathering relationship history, the therapist discovered a very strong traditional sex-role bias. In both families, women were expected to marry, stay home, and raise the children, while the men were to be breadwinners and decision-makers. Both spouses stated that neither of their parents had "close" relationships. In addition, Mr. C came from a family where men were either "leeches" or overly responsible "workaholics." His father, as patriarch of a family business, was a workaholic, while his uncle, who was an employee of his father, was seen as a leech. During exploration of the couple's relationship history, Mr. C indicated that he had gone through a period of irresponsibility, at which time he and Mrs. C had conceived their oldest child. However, since making the decision to marry Mrs. C, he had followed the pattern of his father, feeling a heavy burden to support others and to achieve great success in his chosen vocation.

Mrs. C's family was less educated than Mr. C's family and it was considered unnecessary or indulgent for women to pursue a college degree. Mrs. C's was also a family where women married young, were pregnant at marriage, and, consequently, were not easily assured of their value to their husbands. Women in this family "redeemed" themselves by sacrificing their needs for their children and family, and asking little from their husbands.

The therapist pointed out that the couple brought these patterns and expectations with them into their marriage. There appeared to be two major unspoken contracts: "I'll make few demands for emotional involvement from you if you will protect me from testing my competence"; and "I'll work hard to achieve in the outside world as long as you are content to remain at home and not outshine me." Both spouses colluded by keeping their part of the bargain.

During the examination of the relationship, it became apparent that the wife craved personal fulfillment and adult stimulation, neither of which she believed she was receiving. For his part, Mr. C encouraged Mrs. C to go to college and do something on her own. However, in doing so, he also indicated that she might be less adequate than he and in need of his "guidance." Although Mrs. C complained about her confining, unstimulating life, she remained ambivalent about her choices and resented her husband's "pushing" her into school—an arena where he was successful.

Having obtained a working assessment of the relationship system, the therapist reframed the couple's marital conflict as an effort to remain loyal to their families of origin. It was suggested that this loyalty kept them stuck in their current situation and protected them from having a more intimate relationship than either of their parents' marriages. During the sessions, when the husband spoke for his wife or analyzed her situation, the therapist pointed to the similarity between Mr. C and his father, and suggested that Mr. C might consider taking a less burdensome role in his family. Likewise, when Mrs. C acted helpless and/or confused, the therapist asked how Mrs. C's mother might feel if Mrs. C were to achieve a more equal and intimate relationship with Mr. C than Mrs. C's mother had achieved with her husband. In doing this, the therapist indicated that both current and historical stressors impacted upon the couple's relationship.

At this stage in therapy, the therapist encouraged each spouse to be responsible for his or her own career and to avoid attempts at manipulating or controlling the other spouse. Each spouse focused on a personal issue. Mrs. C's challenge was how to be a wife and still define "self." For Mr. C, the challenge was how to be a man and avoid being either a "leech" or a "workaholic." At the same time, each spouse was encouraged to view the other as a resource in areas in which they were unskilled or unfamiliar. In slowing down the process, the couple had time to understand their original "contract" and the ways in which they had limited their individual growth. Mrs. C decided to remain in the marriage, and the couple reported greater intimacy and fewer fights. Mr. C chose a job in another state rather than working in the family business. Mrs. C chose to remain home with the children until they became settled in their new location. However, she planned to become involved in the community and entertained the possibility of completing her college degree. At termination, the couple reported feeling confident in their ability to continue working on issues related to their new marital contract without continued therapy. The couple was seen for a total of nine sessions spanning three months.

SUMMARY

In both of the cases described above, the therapists maintained a neutral position with respect to the decision of whether or not to divorce. However, they did assist the couples in slowing down the decision-making process long enough to clarify the history of the relationship and each partner's investment in the original relationship contract. This allows for increased commitment to the eventual decision as well as a direction for future individual growth.

REFERENCES

Bowen, M. (1978). *Family therapy in clinical practice.* New York: Jason Aronson.

Dicks, D. V. (1967). *Marital tensions.* New York: Basic Books.

Humphrey, F. G. (1983). *Marital therapy.* Englewood Cliffs, NJ: Prentice-Hall.

Jackson, D. D. (1965). Family rules: Marital *quid pro quo. Archives of General Psychiatry, 12,* 589–594.

Jones, B. W. (1987). The ambivalent spouse syndrome. *Journal of Divorce, 10*(1/2), 57–67.

Kerr, M. E. (1981). Family systems theory and therapy. In A. S. Gurman & D. P. Kniskern (Eds.), *Handbook of family therapy* (pp. 226–264). New York: Brunner/Mazel.

Miller, S., Nunnally, E. W., & Wackman, D. B. (1975). *Alive and aware: Improving communication in relationships.* Minneapolis, MN: Interpersonal Communication Programs, Inc.

Minuchin, S., & Fishman, H. C. (1981). *Family therapy techniques.* Cambridge, MA: Harvard University Press.

Neill, J. R., & Kniskern, D. P. (Eds.). (1982). *From psyche to system: The evolving therapy of Carl Whitaker.* New York: Guilford Press.

Neugarten, B. L. (1979). Time, age, and the life-cycle. *American Journal of Psychiatry, 136*(7), 887–894.

Nichols, W. C., & Everett, C. A. (1986). *Systemic family therapy: An integrative approach.* New York: Guilford Press.

Norton, A. J., & Glick, P. C. (1979). Marital instability in America: Past, present, and future. In G. Levinger & O. C. Moles (Eds.), *Divorce and separation: Context, causes, and consequences* (pp. 6–19). New York: Basic Books.

Olson, D. H., Russell, C., & Sprenkle, D. (1983). Circumplex model of marital and family systems: Theoretical update. *Family Process, 22,* 69–83.

Papp, P. (1984). *The process of change.* New York: Guilford Press.

Sager, C. J. (1976). *Marital contracts and couple therapy: Hidden forces in intimate relationships.* New York: Brunner/Mazel.

Sager, C. J. (1986). Therapy with remarried couples. In N. S. Jacobson & A. S. Gurman (Eds.), *Clinical handbook of marital therapy* (pp. 321–344). New York: Guilford Press.

Selvini Palazzoli, M., Boscolo, L., Cecchin, G., & Prata, G. (1978). *Paradox—counter-paradox: A new model in the therapy of the family in schizophrenic transaction.* New York: Jason Aronson.

Selvini Palazzoli, M., Boscolo, L., Cecchin, G., & Prata, G. (1980). Hypothesizing—circularity—neutrality: Three guidelines for the conductor of the session. *Family Process, 19,* 3–12.

Spanier, G. B., & Thompson, L. (1984). *Parting: The aftermath of separation and divorce.* Beverly Hills, CA: Sage.

Stuart, R. B. (1980). *Helping couples change: A social learning approach to marital therapy.* New York: Guilford Press.

Watzlawick, P., Beavin, J. H., & Jackson, D. D. (1967). *Pragmatics of human communication.* New York: W. W. Norton.

Watzlawick, P., Weakland, J., & Fisch, R. (1974). *Change: Principles of problem formation and problem resolution.* New York: Norton.

Weiner-Davis, M. (1987). Confessions of an unabashed marriage saver. *Family Therapy Networker, 11*(1), 53–56.

Whitaker, C. A. (1976). The hindrance of theory in clinical work. In P. J. Guerin (Ed.), *Family therapy: Theory and practice* (pp. 154–164). New York: Guilford Press.

Whitaker, C. A. (1982). Psychotherapy of marital couples. In J. R. Neill & D. P. Kniskern (Eds.), *From psyche to system: The evolving therapy of Carl Whitaker* (pp. 182–195). New York: Guilford Press.

6

Early Fit and Faulty Fit: Object Relations in Marital Therapy

Laura J. Singer-Magdoff

Anguish and anxiety accompany couples who seek marital therapy because one of the pair expresses a wish to leave the marriage. Ambivalences and ambiguities are expressed by the mate who does not want the marriage to end. In my experience these marriages rarely terminate in divorce.

Marital pairs in which one wants out fall into one of the following categories: (1) those few couples who do ultimately divorce; (2) those who divorce, then date each other, and after a while, remarry; (3) those who separate, inhabit separate domiciles, sign financial agreements, then reconcile, sometimes renewing formal marital vows; (4) those who separate, sign legal financial documents, inhabit different domiciles, and get together for birthdays, holidays, but otherwise live separate lives; (5) those who remain on the fence.

A number of useful constructs helpful to the marital therapist in understanding and interpreting some of the underlying causes for the marital disharmony come out of object relations theory, which focuses upon the interactive relationship between the mother and the child during the first years of life. The marital therapist is able to observe how the early child-caregiver inter-actions are recapitulated between the spouses, and between each spouse and the therapist. Since marital therapy engages dyadic interaction, a dynamic opportunity is provided for each spouse to be understood and empathically responded to in the presence of the other. It is also an opportunity for the enlightenment of each concerning the mate's early history, often barely known or acknowledged by the other.

OBJECT RELATIONS

The following object relations concepts have been found to be especially useful in marital therapy. Balint's (1968) formulation of the possible lack of "fit" between a mother and her infant which he calls a "basic fault" is a failure of "fit" and leads to insecurity in future object relations. This "basic fault" may manifest in a marital dyad in one spouse's clinging desperately for support out of an underlying fear of abandonment, while the mate feels engulfed and smothered and anxiously wishes to flee.

Mahler, Pine, and Bergman's (1975) subphases of separation-individuation can also be helpful in lending understanding to aspects of the spousal relationship. If the infant has suffered from a "poor fit," a failure in empathy on the part of the caregiver, as an adult in a marital relationship he or she may experience an unending desire for a symbiotic attachment to a mate who is seamlessly and totally and perfectly empathic, while selecting a mate who has difficulty in providing the desired fit. One problem is that it is never enough. Paradoxically, the reality can never measure up to the imagined fantasy of a love that can anticipate one's every wish, that is completely in tune with one's desires and needs and that is the "perfect fit." Unwilling to give up the fantasy, the individual feels the only solution is to leave the marriage and continue the endless quest for the perfect, empathic mate.

When a pair come into therapy and it becomes apparent that each has suffered early deficits in the caregiver-infant relationship, that the "fit" has left large gaps, it is also evident that the need and hunger for each other has created an illusion which has turned into disillusion. The spouse who once was idealized is now experienced as critical and rejecting, and the mate as demanding and engulfing. One begins to look for an out, for liberation, or for a new love.

Object relations theory, with its emphasis upon projections, splitting, and projective identification, offers interpretative modes to the marital therapist. These modes, when employed with empathic delicacy, can generate insights which can correct distortions in perceptions and slowly serve a reparative function in marital disharmonies. Application of techniques culled from object relations theory will be described in the case studies that follow.

The formulation of early deficits, of empathic failure in the mother-infant dyad, has been developed by the self psychologists (Kohut & Wolf, 1978). When the experience of the early empathic failure of the caregiver is repeated in a spousal empathic failure, the result is acutely distressing. Most painful is a failure in the idealizing functions or the admiring function of one spouse for the other. What becomes of great significance is that there is no failure of empathy on the part of the marital therapist; or, if it does occur, that there be a nondefensive acknowledgment by the marital therapist. Applying this formulation to couples in distress has proven to be effective in helping each spouse to feel understood by the therapist, and it certainly facilitates the development of a therapeutic alliance in a nonjudgmental atmosphere.

THE STRUCTURE OF THE INITIAL INTERVIEW

When couples come in for an initial interview, my immediate goal is to determine the degree of narcissistic vulnerability in each of the spouses, to attempt to assess problems around rage, dependency and self-esteem. I do this by gathering the following information:

1. I ask the couple to talk to each other about their concerns, and let me listen in. I ask them to face each other directly to try to get a sense of their involvement and commitment through eye avoidance or contact and a variety of nonverbal gestures and motions, as well as their communications modes. Talking about their concerns also helps to make them more aware of their responsibility for any changes they may wish to engender.

2. Sometime during the course of the interview, I ask: "Why did you marry him (or her)?" In this way, the initial idealizations, the hopes, the fantasies, and the expectations may be elicited and whether or not they have been met and fulfilled in any way may be determined. In this manner it is possible to get a quick overview of the fantasy aspects of the relationship, the covert as well as the overt wishes, and to begin to get a glimmer of what may be unconscious and not verbalized; some beginning glimpses into splitting, projection, and projective identifications may emerge.

3. If the complaints are multiple, I use the complaints and the designations articulated to introduce a paradoxical question: "Why did you choose such a lazy, unattractive, stupid, messy person to be your spouse?" By the nature of the response, (that is, coming to the rescue of the spouse by saying, "But I loved her/him"; or the reverse, agreeing with the designation of lazy, and so on), it is possible to begin to get a sense of the degree of caring and commitment, or the opposite.

The foregoing interactions give the marital therapist an opportunity to formulate a tentative sense of the nature of the holding environment, the degree of permeability of ego boundaries, and a peep into the split-off, repressed, denied, unacceptable parts of the internal self, as well as a chance to look for manifestations of ambivalence and projections of inadequacy or hyperadequacy, in couples who are polarized.

4. I try to get some estimate of the following: How early in the relationship did the problems start? Was there ever a time when the marriage was happy and stable, or was it stormy from the outset? Did the problems emerge at a particular time in the marital life cycle? During the first year? After the birth of the first child? When the wife started to work? When the husband didn't receive his promotion? When a parent or a sibling got sick, or died? Any of the significant crisis points may determine the nature of the contextual holding patterns as well as the central support core. It is here that one may also be able to arrive at some beginning notions of the prognosis. Frequently, but certainly not always, the earlier the onset, the poorer the prognosis. Data can be very helpful if the goal is to have either a well-functioning marriage or a separation and divorce.

5. When the couple report feeling bad, I ask: "Who else in your past made you feel this way? Were there any people in your family of origin who also made you feel this way? Were there any people in your family of origin who also made you feel humiliated, demeaned, like a fool, as if you could never do anything right?" Again we begin an awareness of possible early internalizations and identifications with early object representations. We often see projections on to the spouse and the marital therapist of some painful, unacceptable aspects of the self, difficult and dangerous to "own." Empathic awareness of earlier hurts takes the heat off each spouse and gives them new insights to share. The sharing constitutes a moment of core relating (Scharff & Scharff, 1987).

6. As marital therapists, we need to be emotionally equidistant from each spouse. If we find that we are on the side of one of the partners, it is a countertransference signal that we are reacting to our own internal impulses, momentarily sidetracked from our task of providing an empathic milieu for each spouse. It is essential to be alert to the transferential signals that we receive from each spouse so that we may use our empathic understanding in the interpretations we may tentatively offer. When couples come into a session and continue during the session to complain, to fight, and to be abusive to each other, an empathic acknowledgment of the underlying hurt and longing may help lodge a tiny wedge of

insight and compassion into the monstrous projections and accusations.

I shall now recapitulate some of the preceding formulations that are applicable to the treatment of those couples who articulate the polarized stance of one spouse pressing for a divorce and the other frantically holding on to the marriage. It is helpful for the marital therapist to provide an atmosphere in which the couples discover that their anger or criticism will neither destroy the therapist nor each other. Since ambivalence emerges in all polarized couples, it is crucial that the therapist process the projective identifications and provide a modeling experience for the couple. Transferential similarities, projections, and anxieties are carefully noted, understood, and appropriately and empathically addressed. The anxieties that occur quite regularly during the course of treatment of these polarized couples cluster around fears of abandonment and engulfment, loss of autonomy and identity. These reflect the lack of attunement in the early caregiving interaction experiences. This causes them to be convinced that their needs will not be met and that the only recourse is to leave the marriage, even though in my experience very few of them, in fact, do.

CASE #1

Mike and Mary had been married for four years and lived together for five years prior to the marriage. There were no children. Mary was a 28-year-old research scientist, and Mike was a 30-year-old doctor. Mary, competent and hardworking, expressed her discontent:

> I feel at my wits' end in the marriage. I can't stand the ups and downs. We're always fighting, constant hassling. But I think it's all him. He's very sensitive. I get very disgusted every time I open my mouth. I can't win.

They came to see me after having read an article about me and wanted to check it out to make sure I wasn't committed to keeping spouses together no matter what. They, especially Mary, wanted to be certain that if they couldn't make it, I would help them separate. But, said Mike, "I really want this marriage." Mary described the marriage and her childhood in this fashion:

> I married Mike because he was so kind and sympathetic and understanding. He is very expressive, no matter what the cost. When he is nice, it's very unhassled. I remember the first time I had sex with Mike. He was so inept, so strange, like I wasn't even there. Over before we started. I could teach him, I thought. He was very masculine looking, but I had the stronger role. I was earning the money, I had the checkbook. While Mike was going to medical school, I was supporting us and running the marriage. Mike would never be able to control me. I don't trust him. He's sloppy. I feel if he took over, he wouldn't give me an inch.

Early "Fit"

Mike married Mary in order to hold his impulses and grandiosity in check. He was content to be a passive participant, delighted that Mary was there to take care of him. She was the good maternal introject, the nurturer, undemanding, enabling him to keep his ego boundaries intact. Mary was a strong, competent, cold, and aloof woman who was very hardworking and organized but very frightened of closeness and of dependency, as well as of her rage. Mike's impulsivity was intriguing to her, as long as she felt that she could be in control. Mary continued:

> I was always blamed for things. I remember being accused of stealing cookies or crackers. When I was nine, I used to steal nice little things to give to my mother—jewelry or perfume. She really got angry and annoyed. There never was much money. I was afraid to ask. I was always trying to win my father's love. My father favored my older sister. I had to be the tomboy, very independent, very quiet. My father was always leaving. An ob-

stinate man, he could never be wrong. When he got angry, he walked out. My father dreamed of being a millionaire. He was a travelling salesman who couldn't stay put in a job. My sister was really a shit-ass older sister, nasty. She said that if my parents got divorced, I would have to go with Mommy and she would go with Daddy. She would tease me to the point of tears and my parents would threaten to send me away if I didn't stop crying. My father put my mother down for being a nagging wife. She was always a simple-minded dummy who started doing clerical work when I was 11 and my father went into bankruptcy. When I started dating and would come home late, my father would scream at any boy I was dating: "You animal, taking out your animal instincts on my daughter." Sex was taboo. With Mike we've had trouble with our sex life from the start. I've been afraid of him. I've cut myself off. I'm afraid to initiate because he turns me down or he starts demanding more and more and more. He wants me to respond instantly or he'll have to make other plans to have sex. I can't be conned, forced, or physically pushed into it. One night he climbed on top of me and attacked me and I felt horrified and vile and disgusted. He just needs a receptacle. I was frightened. He beat me. I did leave a few weeks ago in the heat of anger. I've broken a chair, bashed in a door. I don't take it out on him. One Sunday he started out being brazen and bold and aggressive. I started screaming and crying and I left the house in the afternoon and came back in the evening. I couldn't stay there but I was too insecure to leave. I feel that when I leave, that's it. I don't think I'll ever want to go back to that. Mike is an indulged, spoiled child. I've been the one to run our marriage, and it's very hard to let him do it.

Faulty "Fit"

When Mike got his degree and began to earn money, his grandiosity broke through and he threatened to take over all of the money, make all of the decisions. With Mike's new status came his omnipotent fantasies. He felt free to express his contempt for Mary, and in fact became physically abusive when he felt thwarted or rejected. This was his way of warding off his need for and fear of closeness, which to him meant symbiosis, merging, loss of self.

To Mary, Mike became the authority figure, the harsh, judgmental, internalized father image who blamed her for all the difficulties of their marriage. Through splitting and projective identification he began to see Mary as all bad; she was the recipient of all the shameful, contemptible, scary parts of his negative, hostile, rageful, repressed inner world. When Mike expressed anger, Mary withdrew into hurt silence which frightened Mike, who then felt as though he had destroyed her with his rage. Overcome with guilt, he would attempt a reconciliation. The moment he came close and disclosed his vulnerability, her rage would surface and she would direct it against him. Her anger then evoked a barrage from Mike and so it went.

Discussion

The couple's constant quarreling, plus their early histories, made it apparent that although they each desired closeness, because of the early empathic failures in their relationships to caregivers they were very frightened to risk the deep pain that another empathic failure would entail.

Each had a combination of individual therapy, couples group therapy, and conjoint therapy. Therapy for Mary meant working through her fears of closeness and learning how to separate and individuate until she was finally able to divorce Mike. Mike's therapy was devoted to working on his "basic fault," the serious deficits in his early caregiver relationship which left him feeling empty, hungry, enraged, full of impotent anger at being frustrated, and fearful of that hateful world outside and inside. Mike suffered a depletion which required slow, careful, endlessly empathic understanding and the ability to process projective identifications. The therapy provided a model for Mike that he was able to emulate and internalize.

CASE #2

Joe (aged 40), a freelance photographer, and Judy (aged 35), an executive in Joe's father's manufacturing business, were referred by Joe's therapist for marital therapy because Joe was having a hard time reaching a decision about whether or not to remain in the marriage. They had been married for four years and had lived together for two years prior to the marriage. Joe described their experience:

> There has been a 180-degree shift in what she wants. I married her because she was fun, loved me like no one else. She was smart and funny and she continued to be someone special and different. We were a fabulous love match. Then sex was nil. All she did was wrap herself in a blanket and refused sex. She wouldn't let me get near her at all. I felt like a eunuch. Then she began to nonstop want things. So I gave her whatever she wanted! Think she was satisfied? No, then she wanted something else! And then something else! She generally gets what she wants, but she's changed. She was never like that before. I wanted her to sign a prenuptial agreement but she wouldn't. She is so materialistic I don't think she sees me at all. She doesn't know who I am. I want to be loved and appreciated for what I am, not for what she would like me to be.

Early "Fit"

Joe was the first-born child of an affluent, entrepreneurial father and a controlling, overprotective mother. His sister was two years younger than he. His father was distant, preoccupied with making money. Joe was struggling to be a successful photographer—a task made more difficult because of his father's denigration of his attempts and easier because of a substantial trust fund endowed upon him by his parents which enabled him to work or not work at his own discretion.

Judy had suffered grave deficits because of her controlling, dictatorial mother who rejected her in favor of her sister, who was two and a half years older than she, and a much-indulged and loved younger brother. She had a gentle father whom she adored, but saw as weak and at the mercy of her domineering mother.

Judy and Joe each idealized the other and both were able to join forces in reinforcing separation from the parents to whom they had been symbiotically attached. They were 1960s people who seemed to share the same values. Judy felt loved, protected, and adored by Joe who delighted in her intelligence, which had been demeaned by her mother's overvaluing the other siblings. Joe was supportive and not critical. Judy was warm and loving and fun and they played well together.

The difficulties started when Judy began to work for Joe's father. She described her ambivalent reactions to the work and to the marriage:

> I thought we'd have a more traditional marriage, home, family, doing things together. I work for Joe's father, travelling and buying for the company. I can't stand his father, but it's a good job. Joe doesn't have to work. I leave him in bed. When I come home, he's watching television or reading. I'm torn between being a wife and a homemaker. I'm frightened about my age, worried about postponing a baby. My sister is pregnant with her second child. I cried myself to sleep every night last week and took tranquilizers every day. I want to move to a more comfortable apartment; he wants to stay where we are because it's cheap and he doesn't want to spend more money. I love Joe and want to spend the rest of my life with him. He says it's not easy for us to make a decision about anything, the least little thing.

Faulty "Fit"

Both were highly ambivalent, obstinate, and desperately trying to hold on to their own fragile ego boundaries. Joe viewed Judy as his powerful, invasive, constantly demanding, insatiable, and controlling mother. He didn't trust any of the changes they had both reported (i.e., the atmosphere had changed from very tense and cruel and they had made real efforts to be nicer to each other). He labeled these changes as "cosmetic" and not real. He was afraid to trust, to become vulnerable, and to expose himself to another empathic failure. Judy was very envious of Joe's ability to stay home, to make the money decisions about where to live. She saw him as a tyrant, withholding, rigid, controlling, and critical like her mother. Just as Joe withheld money, Judy withheld what she thought was the only thing she had that made a difference to Joe—sex.

Discussion

Judy and Joe were locked into a collusive power struggle from which they were just beginning to emerge. Joe was still questioning his decision about whether to remain in the marriage, which certainly echoed Judy's ambivalence. They continued to declare their love for each other and Joe clung to his old narcissistic wounds and was afraid to trust that Judy's demands would not deplete him, would not intrude and take over his territory. He kept projecting his invasive, demanding, controlling mother onto her, and therapy had in part focused upon bringing these to his conscious awareness. Judy saw Joe as her critical withholding mother (the tyrant). This projection was altered when she got sick and felt miserable and he was able to be very comforting and loving to her. She then saw him as her loving caring father, less powerful and withholding. Neither had achieved a differentiated sense of self and both remained emotionally attached to their families. Joe had developed his own isolated activities which were a resource he cherished in his reaction to his intrusive mother. Being a freelance photographer had helped him to maintain his boundaries. When Judy wanted to change apartments, he felt as though she was invading his boundaries.

Judy had deficiencies in her empathic capacity because of her early experiences with a mother who was seriously lacking in empathy. In conjoint therapy, during role reversal, Judy was unable to empathize with Joe's feelings. Joe was able to take her role with a good deal of accuracy, so that his caregiver appears to have been somewhat in attunement with him during that crucial first year.

One of the treatment goals was to aid each of them toward achieving a more consolidated sense of self, identity, and adequacy, since conflicts around inadequacy are rooted in ambivalence. It was to this resolution of the ambivalence that had led them to designate each other as "tyrant" and/or "capitulator." It was hoped that in a more benign, nonjudgmental, empathic environment, both would be able to accept and internalize the small increments that they already acknowledged and to grow in the ability to become more attuned to each other.

CASE #3

At 66 and 67 years of age, respectively, Barbara and Ben were an attractive, energetic, stubborn, and ambivalent couple. Each needed to be "right," each needed to be seen as rational. Ben's greatest anxieties concerned his intellectual superiority and his sexual competence. He demanded that Barbara be a dutiful wife, totally task-oriented.

At the mercy of a punitive superego, Barbara tended to be indecisive, albeit very rebellious and desirous of breaking free. Married 45 years, the couple had four adult children and three grandchildren.

Twenty-five years ago Ben wanted out. He said that outside of college, he had never had an opportunity to be on his own. He took his three sons with him, and Barbara took responsibility for their daughter. The separation lasted two months. Ben felt that he could not cope with adolescent children. He called Barbara and returned home.

Now it was Barbara's turn to want out. Ben disclosed that he had been having an affair with a secretary in his firm and described his desire to be able to have scheduled time with his lover. Barbara flew into a rage and asked him to move out. After a few months of procrastination, Ben found an apartment. After two months of being on his own and free to spend the time in any way he wished, he asked Barbara for a reconciliation. Although she was ambivalent, she wanted out of the marriage. She had been unhappy about their endless quarrels, his unavailability, and his constant demands.

Early "Fit"

Ben and Barbara were friends in a small midwestern high school. He went east to a prominent college for his engineering degree and she stayed behind to get a degree in teaching. They married right after graduation. On the surface, Ben was enchanted by Barbara's robust good looks, her competence as a sportswoman, and her zest for life. Ben's deeply unconscious wish to be a playboy, together with his unacceptable needs and wishes, were projected onto Barbara. Ben played the role of rescuer.

To Barbara, Ben was a real prize. She had been deposed and displaced by a younger brother at age three. Her mother's hitherto somewhat detached attention was shifted to a frail, sickly, but very appealing and cuddly infant who became the acknowledged favorite of both parents. Years later, when Ben came along she was delighted to be rescued by him. He was her friend. She trusted him and felt he would take care of her always.

Ben was the only son of a rigid, demanding, and overbearing mother and a warm but ineffectual father. They viewed Ben as the able, conscientious, rigorous performer who would get their approval only to the degree that he would continue to perform. No performing, no approval.

Having dutifully cared for her younger brother, Barbara became the nurturer whom Ben felt he could depend on. In the early years of their marriage, that is indeed how it was.

To Barbara, Ben was the idealized provider, dependable and very hardworking. Although she was the primary caregiver to her four children, Barbara experienced the early years as the happiest and most fulfilling time of her life. The unconscious resentments she may have felt at Ben's lack of participation in this process were deeply buried and offset by the unquestionable centrality of her position and her feelings that she was in control. Ben felt protected and nurtured. His unconscious resentments at always having to be the performer and the provider only emerged at a much later time.

Faulty "Fit"

Barbara was in a rage at once again having been displaced, this time by a younger woman rather than a younger brother. The self-hatred that she felt for not having been born a boy she now externalized and projected upon Ben for evoking those

early, painful feelings of impotent rage. To Barbara, Ben became
the withholding, demanding, hysterical mother who wanted her
to be a "good" girl, living a life of duty and work with no
thoughts of fun or sex. His need to control, to make Barbara
perform (as he was made to perform) is illustrated by his poking
Barbara on a Saturday morning and saying: "You're late. Get
up. Didn't you see the list I left you? You've got a load of work
that has to be done. Get out of bed, now." To Barbara, this
felt like an attack, and it made her furious. What she used to
think of as reliability she now saw as rigidity and betrayal. He
became the bad, punitive part of her internalized mother image.
Through "splitting," she retained her "good" self as victim and
saw Ben as all mean and critical.

She consciously saw herself as a playful little dog, wagging
her tail, wanting to have fun and to be petted and loved. She
was not able to accept her hostile and aggressive aspects, which
she then projected upon Ben, seeing him as mean and hostile.
Ben, through projective identification, saw her as a witch or a
lioness, roaring and raging. They were in collusion, seeing each
other as the repository of all the "bad," unacceptable aspects of
the self which they projected onto the other. Barbara needed
to see herself as good, dutiful, pure, and right. Ben needed to
see himself as good, rational, logical, misunderstood, and right.

Discussion

In this polarized couple, Barbara wanted "out" and Ben wanted
"in." Each had the need to disavow the roaring, angry "lion"
and "lioness" within. Ben remained rational, logical, reasonable,
divorced from his aggressive, unacceptable, internal aspects. The
more he disavowed this aspect of himself, the more he provoked
and induced Barbara to express unacceptable feelings for him.
Then, what Ben formerly admired as spontaneity, he now saw
as being out of control. She was expressive and explosive for
him; he was restrictive and disciplined for her. Then Barbara
rebelled and became passive or silent and refused to carry out
the demands of Ben's endless "lists." Instead of her protector,
she saw him as a punitive, restrictive mother, actively against

pleasure, telling her what a bad girl she was and how unacceptable she was for not attending to all of her duties. In addition, she was unlovable, or else why would he have sought the favors of a younger woman? She could not be a boy for her parents, nor a younger woman for her husband. She was helpless to change the situation when she was a child, but now she could do something about it. She could leave.

Barbara mostly wanted out. She wanted to "try her wings" but was afraid that if she went, she would have to give up all of her wishes to be taken care of, all of her dependency strivings. Her self-doubts concerning her attractiveness and desirability as an older woman kept her ambivalent and indecisive. She also struggled with her fears that her rage toward Ben would destroy him.

To Ben, when Barbara wanted out, he repeated what he did as a child to win his parents' approval. He performed. He strove compulsively to sustain an image of great productivity and imagination. At the same time, he combatted regressive manifestations of passivity and dependence. Ben, with his having left for two months and having come back, was in the rapprochement subphase of separation-individuation. He expected and hoped that Mommy would be there to greet him and welcome him back. He wished for the all-loving mother of his fantasies who would nurture and sustain him, as indeed Barbara had during the early years.

In marital therapy, work was directed toward helping Ben and Barbara accept those aspects of the internal self that they had disowned and projected onto each other. Understanding the early origins of the "splits" and how they were being acted out in the current relationship began to give them a sense of what had been distorted and disruptive in their relationship. Within the benign therapeutic atmosphere these painful aspects of the self became less frightening and gradually became more acceptable. Through role modeling they learned to process their projective identifications. Through the therapist's empathic sharing of her mistakes they were able to be less harsh and more accepting of their own. Currently, resolution of the ambivalences is still a long way off, but they have begun to reap small benefits.

CONCLUSION

This chapter has described some useful constructs drawn from object relations theory and self psychology in the treatment of couples who seek help because one of the pair has expressed a desire to leave the marriage.

Object relations theorists, influenced by the more sophisticated data accumulated during the last decade by the "baby watchers" (Stern, 1985), now see the neonate as born with a capacity for a highly organized social interaction. Lachmann (1988) sees the neonate as having a capacity to regulate his or her own self-esteem, and notes that the self-regulatory capacity is affected by the mutual regulatory system between the mother and the infant. The significant point is that what takes place between the infant and the primary caregiver gets replayed in the spousal relationship. Since object relations theorists postulate the universality of internalized mental representations of those people who have been most significant in the earliest years, it is those internalized objects that predispose our view of our closest and most intimate relationships. Confusion occurs when the inner representations from the past are projected upon the present objects and we fail to make the distinctions or to see the differences between early love objects and current ones.

Balint's formulation of "basic fault" and "fit" have been applied to the couples described and the nature of the early "fit" and the faulty "fit" were delineated in detail.

The theoretical constructs of projection, collusion, splitting, and projective identification were applied and shown to be of help in enabling the marital therapist to reach beneath the manifest projections of rage and power and to reveal the longing and anguish.

From the self psychologists come the useful formulations of early deficits in the empathic attunement in the mother-child dyad. These formulations open up some ways of relieving the bitterness manifest in these polarized couples through the sharing of moments of deep pain in an empathic, nonjudgmental setting.

An initial interview was described in detail with recommendations specifically for the engagement of polarized couples. The three case studies presented in this chapter are at different places on the continuum of couples who are polarized. One ended in divorce, while the other two studies describe couples who are at different stages in the life cycle and are working diligently toward the resolution of conflicts that are ambivalence-rooted. Whether they remain in the marriage is still uncertain, although the object relations approach seems to be a most promising one. All three cases called for empathy, warmth, and acceptance on the part of the therapist.

REFERENCES

Balint, M. (1968). *The basic fault: Therapeutic aspects of regression.* London: Tavistock Press.

Kohut, H., & Wolf, E.S. (1978). The disorders of the self and their treatment: An outline. *International Journal of Psychoanalysis, 59,* 413–425.

Kohut, H., & Wolf, E. S. (1982). The disorders of the self and their treatment. In S. Slipp (Ed.), *Curative factors in dynamic psychotherapy* (pp. 44–59). New York: McGraw-Hill.

Lachmann, F. M. (1988). Unpublished presentation, annual conference of the American Association for the Advancement of Psychoanalysis, New York (April).

Mahler, M., Pine, F., & Bergman, A. (1975). *The psychological birth of the human infant.* New York: Basic Books.

Scharff, E. D., & Scharff, J. S. (1987). *Object relations family therapy.* Northvale, NJ: Jason Aronson.

Stern, D. N. (1985). *The interpersonal world of the infant: A view from psychoanalysis and developmental psychology.* New York: Basic Books.

7

Power and Presence: When Complementarity Becomes Polarity

Luciano L'Abate and
Doris W. Hewitt

THREE DIMENSIONS OF POLARIZATION

Most couples who marry on the basis of a negative complementarity, that is, on the basis of deficits in the self-structure that supposedly will be fulfilled and satisfied by the partner, eventually become polarized along three major dimensions. These dimensions are: (1) the experience and expression of emotions and feelings, where typically, but not always, women express their feelings of sadness, dissatisfaction and unhappiness by blaming their husbands, while the men avoid dealing with both their own feelings (except for anger) and consequently their wives' feelings altogether by emphasizing a rational ("reasonable") approach to the marriage and marital differences; (2) self-definition, where the selflessness of one partner, usually but not always a woman ("You are important, I am not"), is complemented by the selfishness of the other, usually but not always a man ("I am important, you are not"); and (3) admission (usually in women) versus denial (usually in men) of vulnerability, fallibility, and neediness.

These three dimensions deal with what we think is the major polarization in marriage: power versus presence. In functional marriages both aspects are clearly defined and fairly well differentiated. They are used additively to increase marital growth in a multiplicative fashion. In dysfunctional marriages both aspects are ill-defined and poorly marked, fused, confused, and diffused to the point of a subtractive division in the marriage. By power we mean the ability to negotiate *doing* (information and services, i.e., performance) and *having* (money and possessions, i.e., production). Presence means *being*, that is, loving oneself and the partner unconditionally as important human beings, regardless of what one does and has, mainly on the basis of one's existence ("I am important because I am; you are important because you are"), that is, selfullness or selfhood (L'Abate & Bryson, in press).

THE THEORY

These polarizations are derived from a theory of developmental competence (L'Abate, 1986; L'Abate & Bryson, in press; L'Abate & Hewitt, in preparation) that assumes two basic orthogonal dimensions of (a) movement in space, or distance, defined by extremes in approach-avoidance, and of (b) control in time, defined by extremes in discharge-delay. The dimension of *space* is basic to the development of emotional attachments and love, while the dimension of *time* is basic to the development of problem-solving and negotiation skills, with their inevitable victories and defeats ("I win, you win, we both win," I win, you lose," "You win, I lose," "I lose, you lose, we both lose").

The Dimension of Space

Each set of abilities is made up by different resources. The *ability to Be* loving is made up by love itself and status. The ability to love is made up by at least four different skills: (a) caring and commitment, or the everyday, routine, physical, and practical demonstration of love, such as holding a job, making a living, and carrying the bedpan if necessary; (b) seeing the good, or the cognitive choice to emphasize the positive aspects of self and other (loved one) and disregard negative aspects; (c) forgiveness, or the decision to accept, tolerate, and forget one's demands for perfection, performance, problem solving, or production in self and other; and (d) intimacy or the ability to share one's self and a loved one's hurts and fears of being hurt, which, in turn, requires the ability to be available emotionally to self and other.

Status, on the other hand, consists of attribution of importance to self and to other. This definition allows derivation of a fourpartite classification according to: (a) attribution of importance to self and other, of *Selfullness,* as seen in victorious interpersonal outcomes ("I win, you win"); (b) attribution of importance to self and denial of importance of other, or *Selfishness,* which brings about a defeat ("I win, you lose"); (c) attribution of importance to other and denial of importance to self, or *Selflessness,* which also brings about a defeat ("You win, I lose"); and (d) denial of importance of self and of other, or *No Self,* which brings about a double interpersonal defeat ("I lose, you lose") (L'Abate & Hewitt, in preparation).

From this framework, L'Abate and Bryson (in press) have derived a classification of personality types and of psychopathologies. For instance, selfhood represents healthy functioning. This is a position where equality, positive reciprocity, and intimacy are possible. Both selfishness and selflessness are at the extremes of a continuum of reactive (negative reciprocity) intimate relationships, characterized by manipulation, immediacy, rebuttals, and revenge. Most women, at least 40% of them, are socialized for selflessness (self-defeating personalities, depression, affective manic depressive disorders) and, more often than not, choose for partners males who have been socialized for selfishness, who also comprise 40% of the entire male population (Type A driven personalities, addictions, and criminalities). These reactive relationships furnish the bulk and context from which some individuals raise themselves toward selfullness (25%), while some others fall down into destructive pathologies (borderline conditions, psychoses, and schizophrenia) with No-Self (25%).

The Dimension of Time

When two resource classes of information and services are combined, one obtains the modality of doing or *performance*. The two classes of goods and money are combined into having or *production*. Both performance and production are the basis for power, which, depending on the relationship, "should" be negotiable, as in democratic relationships, where equality of importance is assumed. In autocratic relationships, power is held tightly and becomes nonnegotiable. Whoever has the power does not want any change that may decrease it. By the same token, presence is not negotiable but is sharable. If and when power and presence are confused, conflicts ensue.

THE COUPLE

The following case study will serve to illustrate some of the points made above, that is, power versus presence, selfullness versus selfishness, admission versus denial, and emotionality versus rationality. (The primary therapist for the case was Doris Hewitt with occasional supervision by Luciano L'Abate.)

The couple we are discussing illustrate how all of the three polarized dimensions we have presented are relevant to their interaction. Adrian Jarrett grew up in an environment in which doing and having were heavily emphasized. The only child in the family, he was more spoiled than overtly abused. He was lonely as a child and received essentially everything he ever wanted, while few restrictions were placed on him. He never felt that he truly had his father's approval, and he worked hard to achieve and be successful, which seemed to be the most effective way of getting his dad's attention and support. As a young man, Adrian was rather promiscuous and developed no close, lasting relationships. At age 26 he met Evalyn, who was 22, and they began dating and were married a few months later. It was the first marriage for both of them.

As the years passed, Evalyn tried to get pregnant and was unable to, and after eight years of marriage they adopted a son, Robert. Robert's development was somewhat slow, and by the time he was school age, it became clear that he had some learning disabilities and would need special education and a lot of help and encouragement from his parents in order to get a reasonable education and function normally. Adrian tended to look upon Robert as just being lazy, and he left all responsibility for Robert's education and school work to Evalyn, who resented her husband's lack of empathy for his son and tended to overcompensate by being overly protective of the child. Conflicts gradually mounted over parenting, finances, and social issues. At about the same time that Robert started school, Evalyn became ill, and when her doctors could find no physical problem she was eventually hospitalized in a psychiatric ward. However, two weeks later it was discovered that she had breast cancer, and she was transferred to a regular hospital.

At the time the Jarretts came for therapy, Evalyn was still regaining her health after surviving the cancer several years earlier. At one point during the illness her doctors had estimated she would live only several months or a maximum of two years. She said that Adrian, upon being told by doctors that she would not live, "wrote me off." He had little patience with her, she said, and seemed resentful: "He begrudged the money paid on my medical treatment, and he essentially waited for me to die. He seemed angry that I eventually recovered," she said. Evalyn lacked the physical stamina to look for a job and go to work. Also, she lacked any specific job skills, not having worked outside the home in years. She continued to have a great many medical bills and feared how she would manage financially if her husband were to divorce her.

Adrian was a successful businessman with a very high income, and money should have been no issue in the marriage. He spent freely for himself but allowed his wife to have very little knowledge of their financial matters. He gave her a personal and household allowance and expected her to account for every dollar she spent; he became very angry whenever she contended that the food or clothing money he gave her was insufficient. Partly because of her great insecurity about whether she could support herself and her son financially, and partly because of her strong commitment to marriage, Evalyn clung to the hope of making the marriage work.

However, after 21 years of marriage Adrian left Evalyn and Robert and filed for a divorce after intense conflict over his long hours away from home and whether or not he was seeing another woman. Despite many indications of an affair, Adrian strongly denied any extramarital interests and declared that he was deeply insulted that his wife would even think of such. However, upon her attorney's recommendation Evalyn hired an investigator, who within several hours had secured undebatable evidence that Adrian was involved in at least one ongoing affair. After learning that Evalyn's attorney had evidence of his unfaithfulness, and sensing that odds were stacked against him in financial settlement, Adrian "had a change of heart." He asked his wife to go with him for counseling, which she welcomed, having suggested counseling herself earlier. Thus, they began therapy.

Evalyn was the more vulnerable and needy as shown by her persistent dependence on her husband, with this dependence being proliferated by her illness. Adrian had the power of money and saw himself as important according to what he Did and what he Had. He was, and probably still is, unable to deal with his feelings, which he denied and avoided. While Evalyn would be defined as initially selfless in regard to the marriage, he could be defined as being selfish, as shown by his lack of concern for the material and emotional welfare of his wife and of their child.

He was obsessed with sex as performance and was unable to be available to her with his presence. He kept the power of the purse strings and did not allow her to have any such power at all. Her emotionality and dependence were completely threatening to him as he coped with her physical condition allegedly in strictly rational ways, denying the importance of feelings and emotions in himself and, ultimately, in her. Her illness and depression and the attendant feelings were conceived as intolerable burdens and demands on him which he was not ready for nor able to deal with.

Whereas at the beginning of therapy she was unable to give up the marriage because of her needs and love for her husband, eventually, as therapy and the relationship progressed, she was able to see how costly her position was for herself and for her child from an emotional viewpoint. Once she realized this, she was able to give up the relationship without injuries to her self-esteem and self-worth and, in fact, was able to develop better self-esteem and self-worth in the process of an unusually stormy divorce due to her husband's increasing irrationality. Whereas at the beginning she could not conceive of life by herself and without the marriage, by the end of the relationship she considered herself as being better off without it.

At first, the man wanted out while the woman did not. She felt she could not make it by herself. She had given everything of herself to the marriage (i.e., selflessness). The man, by the same token, operated from a self-centered, "selfish" position that made it very difficult, if not impossible, to relate to him. In spite of the fact that he was visibly and blatantly depressed, he continued to deny any possible depression because he was gainfully and successfully employed and managing to function satisfactorily on the job. When the cost of being married to this man became too expensive for the wife, she switched her position and eventually decided that she was better off without him.

THE THERAPY

In the first therapy session with me (DH), Adrian repeatedly insisted that they ought to get back together, meaning that he wanted to move back home: "Evalyn says I can't right now, but if I don't, there's no way things can get better between us!"

"Oh, I definitely recommend that you two *not* get back together yet," I responded. "Your chances of really making this marriage work will be much better if you wait."

"I agree!" Evalyn chimed in.

Angry and frustrated, Adrian confronted me: "How on earth do you expect us to get our differences worked out if we're not together to do it?"

"You can certainly spend time together and in fact ought to do so, and yet not be living together. If you get back together prematurely, one or both of you may feel trapped. Right now, nothing is different in your situation than before. It will be best if there are some real changes before you attempt to *live* together again."

"How do you expect things to change or us to ever become a *team*?" Adrian demanded of me.

"Oh, there are a lot of ways you can make things change," I replied, continuing slowly and using as much of their own wording as I could. "I'm concerned that when you get back together, Adrian, both of you will be on the same team pulling together rather than being so polarized as you are now; that you work *together* on planning for Robert's education and assisting him; that you discover some ways to make sex more mutually satisfying; that you, Adrian, learn how to express more soft, tender emotions so that Evalyn can become less sensitive; that you, Evalyn, become tougher and less fragile. I'll serve as your coach and help you both to develop better communication and negotiation skills so you can get along better. And if you really want, I can help you become closer emotionally."

It was also in that first session that Adrian focused on what an inadequate wife Evalyn had always been and how he left her "because she must be crazy, because she's always talking crazy talk."

Confused, I asked, "Crazy talk? What do you mean by that?"

"You heard her do it just now! That's her crazy talk!" After further discussion I realized he was referring to her persistent, hysterical sort of nagging when he distanced most from her. At those times her speech got faster and faster, and the pitch of her voice rose as she continued. The more he distanced emotionally, the more frantic she seemed to become; and the more hysterical she became, the angrier and colder he became. This was particularly true as we discussed Adrian's affair. Adrian contended, "I can't see that I did anything wrong in having the affair. After all, she's been sick, and even when she could, she didn't always meet my needs for sex. And a man's sexual needs have got to be met somewhere!"

As he justified his affair, Evalyn's voice got shrill: "See! He not only won't apologize, but he expects me to believe that he didn't mistreat me or do anything wrong!"

"That's a perfect example for you," Adrian said, as he pointed his finger at Evalyn, "of her crazy talk!"

"Adrian, I see what you mean. But I am uncomfortable with your term 'crazy talk.' I'd rather call it hysteria. And I hope you are willing to learn to be comfortable with a degree of hysteria, and to even appreciate it, because it's a marvelous way your wife has of letting you know exactly how high her frustration level is. Perhaps you can learn to listen to the hysteria, and perhaps she can learn to listen to the message that you sent her (via an affair) about your own frustration level. When each of you learns to recognize and control what you do to agitate the other to the extent that such messages from the other are subdued, you will have learned to live together! And when you have learned to share your innermost thoughts, feelings, and vulnerabilities with each other, you will have learned how to be truly close, or intimate, with each other."

In the second session I repeatedly reminded Evalyn to relax at those times when her voice became shrill and her speech fast, and soon she began noticing when this happened and would relax at those times without being reminded. She seemed to be open to help and seemed to learn easily. There was further discussion of Adrian's affair, and again he was very defensive. I wondered if he really saw no harm or wrong in an affair and, thus, if his value system was very different from Evalyn's, or if it was just exceedingly difficult for him to admit he'd made a mistake. If Adrian saw nothing wrong with extramarital affairs, then perhaps he'd had numerous others and Evalyn just didn't know about the others and hadn't been suspicious. I increasingly noticed Adrian's attitude that money speaks and is extremely important. Whereas in typical marriages one spouse tends to control money and the other sex, in the Jarretts' marriage the husband seemed to control both. Meanwhile, Evalyn exercised control over Robert's upbringing and education, and after Adrian decided he wanted to return home she gained additional control by refusing to allow him to move in. Adrian continually pushed harder and harder to move back in.

At the end of the session, I said: "Adrian, I'm glad you're eager to return home and know that would be more convenient for you. Both of you have made some progress thus far. But these new behaviors need to become internalized, automatic. If they aren't internalized before the two of you get back together, you'll both be less motivated to continue them once you're together. You may start taking each other for granted again."

The third session dealt with negotiating practical matters related to child's irritations, Robert's school difficulties, and Evalyn's need for additional money. In the fourth session we focused on what love is and how one can show it. Adrian's response was typical: "I work hard and provide for the family well, so of course I love them! They know it!" I kept looking diligently for evidence of Adrian's capacity for emotional intimacy and found little reason for hopefulness, while Evalyn seemed to yearn for intimacy but found it very difficult to get emotionally close to Adrian. I encouraged her to find some close female friends, and she responded by spending more time with her two best friends and by getting to know the ladies in her church better by joining a study group there.

Near the end of the fourth session I said, "I'd like you to do a simple exercise today that will be helpful to me in assessing just where each of you is with intimacy. It may also help you in evaluating your relationship and progress in therapy, as well as helping with developing better intimacy skills. Will both of you please stand in the middle of the room, join hands, and face each other?" They complied. "First, Evalyn, will you please look Adrian in the eyes and take a minute or two to tell him *why* you love him? Now please talk to *him*, not me! Just try to forget that I'm even around if that makes it easier." Adrian seemed uneasy and kept rubbing his nose and looking at the floor.

"Adrian," Evalyn began, "I love you. I love you because when we first met, you seemed to notice me, and I noticed you. That made me feel special, and we had a good time together. I love you because I think you're good-looking, and you're smart, and you know how to do a lot of things. I love you because we've shared a lot of happy times together, and because you like children and helped me adopt Robert and raise him. I appreciate the way you work hard and have been a good provider, and especially how you've paid so many big medical bills of mine. I love you, even though we've had a lot of problems, because when things are good between us, they are *very good*—sex, talking. That's why I hope and pray we can get things straightened out," she finished.

"Good!" I said. "Now Adrian, will you please tell Evalyn why you love her."

"Oh, she knows I love her and why!"

"I do *not*," Evalyn retorted.

"Well, let's see," he said as he scratched his head. "You're right, that when things between us are good, they're *really good*!" By now he had shifted and was talking to me, and he had not looked into her eyes.

"Adrian, remember to talk to *Evalyn*. Forget I'm here."

He turned back to her but never did look into her eyes: "You're good at sex. You could meet all my sex needs as well as any woman could, if you just would!" he continued. There was a pause. "And if I didn't love you, I wouldn't want to move back home like I do." He turned to me to indicate he was through. He look satisfied, and Evalyn looked very frustrated.

I stood up and said: "Adrian, that's a beginning, and I appreciate it. I think you realize, though, that you have difficulty expressing tender emotions." He nodded agreement. "If you don't mind, I'd like to pretend that *I* am *you*, and I'd like to express to Evalyn what I *think* you may feel toward her." Taking Evalyn's hand I added flippantly, "Of course, I'm not nearly as handsome as Adrian," and they both laughed and the tension was eased. "I may be wrong about some things you feel, so listen carefully."

I paused before starting, just for the effect, and looked straight into Evalyn's eyes. "Evalyn, there are a lot of reasons why I love you. When we first met I noticed you in particular amid the group of girls because I thought you were pretty and very striking. You still are, and that's one reason I love you. Your appearance, as well as the way you act and get along with others, makes me very proud to be seen with you. When I'm out around other people, I feel more comfortable when you're along. I love you for the tenderness and gentleness I see in you, like when Robert was a baby and you helped take care of him, and how you do that now sometimes. I love the way you 'baby' me when I'm sick or feel hurt about something, and the way you console me. I love you for the way you try to see the good in almost all situations, and the way you encourage people. I love the zest you have for life, and how you had that zest even when you were so ill. I love you for your smile and laughter and sense of humor. You're great to be with when we're not fighting; things are *really good* then. Even when we're fighting, you will talk with me about how you feel. Even though you get very upset, I know it means you care. I guess that's why I love you most of all, because I know you care about me, and that helps me to love myself and respect myself better."

Evalyn was moved to tears, and Adrian seemed touched. "Yeah," he said enthusiastically, "that's what I feel! How did you know? I feel all of that! But I'm no good with words."

"Adrian, you're fine with words!" I responded. "You just aren't comfortable with 'feeling' kinds of words at this point, but you can develop that with practice. I'll help you practice during our sessions, and you can practice when the two of you are together. There are ways you can practice even with other people, such as at work." He seemed encouraged.

Things began going very well. Adrian seemed more accepting of Evalyn's emotionalism and began talking more about his own feelings and showing hints of empathy about her hurts. Things were going so well, in fact, that Evalyn believed the marital problems were largely resolved. Privately, her attorney had warned her that Adrian may have suddenly become interested in the marriage only because he knew he would have to share all property and monies with her if he divorced her, once he knew there was evidence of his affair. The attorney told her that the improvements might not be genuine and might not last. On occasion, I saw both Adrian and Evalyn alone, and I shared this concern with Evalyn, feeling she was somewhat naive and too willing to trust others. In discussing this in session with both of them, I explained to her that even though Adrian seemed genuinely thrilled with the new-found level of closeness and being that they had achieved, the changes were not yet nearly internalized, and most of his underlying attitudes appeared to be unchanged. Adrian protested. Evalyn felt vulnerable and greatly feared divorce. She was still unable physically to work, and she was very aware that it would probably be difficult for her to find a suitable job with reasonable compensation. Thus, after only several weeks of therapy, the Jarretts arrived for a session happily announcing that Adrian had moved back home.

"What a surprise!" I exclaimed, tongue in cheek. "I thought you weren't ready for that, Evalyn."

"Well, Adrian has been so good to me lately! We've learned how to really open up and share and enjoy being together. We've made so much progress, I felt we were ready."

I responded: "I wish you both had allowed me more input before making that decision, because I still have the same concerns that I shared earlier. However, it's your marriage and your decision, and certainly you have a right to choose. I do hope you'll both continue your hard work and not become lax just because you're back together." I suspected that this move back home would blow whatever chances existed for saving the marriage, but I was well aware that I'd been wrong about such matters before.

THE OUTCOME

Evalyn's exuberance faded within a month. It bothered her increasingly that Adrian still had never once said "I love you" nor apologized in any way for his infidelity or for deserting her emotionally during her illness. Evalyn consoled herself with thoughts that perhaps this admission would come later on, but it didn't. There were times of closeness and sharing, and she valued those times, but she was unable to discover any way to bring about such times. They seemed to happen strictly as a result of Adrian's mood. Adrian's demeanor was one of great depression which did not lift, so I shared my concern about his depression and the belief that he should see a psychiatrist and be evaluated for possible medication. He not only refused to discuss medication with *any* physician, but also strongly denied his depression. Meanwhile, his sex drive was unusually high, to an obsessive level. Early in the marriage, sex had usually occurred one to two times daily, but now in their forties when Adrian was home and they were not fighting, he expected sex at least twice every morning and sometimes as many as three or four times. It became clear that as long as Evalyn was sexually available whenever Adrian wanted it, and in the ways he wanted it, they got along relatively well, but that the pace was exhausting for Evalyn physically and she felt very controlled and used.

After Adrian returned home there were many intimate moments, but these by no means constituted an intimate relationship. Once when the Jarretts were feeling especially close on a beach vacation, Adrian had been drinking and was very relaxed and sharing more of his feelings than usual. He confided in Evalyn that he was in contact with five or six "girls" in various cities, implying ongoing affairs with them. He apparently thought at that time that Evalyn would accept this information complacently, but she could not. He later tried to altogether change the meaning of what he had told her about the women. This experience led Evalyn to take more seriously Adrian's failure to assure her of his love and also his contention that extramarital sexual activities were not so bad and that she ought to be more accepting of them. She became more aware that his position about extramarital sex was in conflict with her own religious belief system and emotional needs, and she concluded that being able to trust in her husband and living according to her own value system were far more important to her sense of security and well-being than was being married to Adrian. Even though she felt that at times the sexual relationship had been meaningful, she was unable to tolerate sex with Adrian any longer. She was increasingly able to acknowledge that in certain ways he was irresponsible and that this quality was not likely to change. Adrian began finding excuses to avoid therapy sessions and then quit therapy altogether.

After about three months Evalyn asked Adrian to leave. He protested but left, saying, "Everything is okay in the marriage except that she's started thinking and talking 'crazy' again." The divorce was long and drawn out and very expensive, due to Adrian's stance of feeling he should accept no financial responsibility for Evalyn or Robert since *he* didn't want the divorce. Adrian's behavior during the divorce proceedings, which lasted over a year, also revealed a distorted sense of responsibility. He gave his retired parents a gift of $10,000 to build a fish pond on their property but refused to pay $10, per week for a tutor for his child who was of borderline intelligence. When Evalyn would not give in to Adrian's financial expectations, he decided to pursue custody of Robert, and a jury trial was held eventually after numerous postponements. Adrian preferred to pay attorneys about $30,000 per month for endless months rather than to assume responsibility for Evalyn's medical bills if he could find a way to avoid it.

Evalyn can see in retrospect that this lack of responsibility prevailed throughout the marriage and prevented the development of real respect and intimacy. She has continued individual therapy and gradually developed a better sense of self-importance. She has increasing confidence that she can succeed as a single adult and single parent. She is learning to involve herself more heavily in several close friendships and to rely on spiritual resources rather than to feel isolated and lonely and to remain in a continual struggle with Adrian. She is gradually moderating her actions and reactions as she becomes more aware of Adrian's ways of controlling her. In other words, she is gradually "depolarizing."

CONCLUSION

The partner who wants out feels pushed out by blame and by feelings that are left unexplored and unexpressed. When doing and having are the only two models of problem-solution, there is a serious deficit in being. Power (doing + having) is negotiable if both partners know how to negotiate. More often than not power is confused with presence ("If you loved me you would do . . . ," "If you loved me you would buy me . . ."). Presence in and by itself is extremely difficult to achieve because emotional availability (listening and sharing) implies a degree of selfhood or selfullness that most of us did not receive from our parents and were not prepared to achieve in a culture where doing and having are the two predominant modes of exchange. When power is negotiated without presence we may obtain a pseudo or functional relationship. When presence is shared, we may achieve a certain degree of closeness, but if we do not negotiate, closeness may be short-lived. We need *both* power and presence to reach a level of contentment and security in marriage that will withstand the inevitable stresses and strains that are part of living.

The partner who wants out is usually the one who cannot express feelings in a positive or full fashion. This inability is usually the outcome of emphasis on doing and having issues without attention paid to issues of being. Wanting a divorce may be tantamount to a selfish action that is designed to find legal separation if and when an emotional separation seems impossible. Usually the partner who stays is the one who has selflessly dedicated herself or himself to the home, the family, and the children. He or she may be angry, dependent, blaming, and just as inarticulate in dealing with his or her feelings as the partner who wants out. Neither selfishness nor selflessness are positions designed to bring about a positive reconciliation or outcome, since one's victory can be achieved only with the other's defeat in an either-or fashion.

The partner who wants out needs to deny any personal inadequacies or problems in order to "monsterize" and to distantiate from the partner who stays. The partner who stays is usually the one who is more depressed, angry, and dependent and is willing to admit to it. However, admission may be just as much an obstacle to change as denial: "As long as I do admit to a problem I do not have to change it!" Consequently, both partners are stuck in a quagmire of their own making from which they can only extricate themselves through the magic of divorce for the one who denies and keeping the status quo for the one who stays. The status quo can be seen as dangerous and as threatening as a breakup. The one who leaves sees staying in the marriage as more of the same, while the one who stays sees divorce as the end of his or her existence! Neither can win in the long run because both are operating from ultimately destructive positions. Neither can change the self to include the other in a positive fashion. Negative complementarity eventually spirals into destructive polarity!

REFERENCES

L'Abate, L. (1986). *Systematic family therapy.* New York: Brunner/Mazel.

L'Abate, L., & Bryson, C. (in press). *A theory of personality development.* New York: Brunner/Mazel.

L'Abate, L., & Hewitt, D. W. (in preparation). *Doormats and muddy boots: Selfless women and selfish men.*

8

Therapeutic Deadlock in Impending Divorce Situations

Wayne E. Oates

When one marital partner expresses a strong resolve to divorce and the other expresses an *equally* strong resolve to remain married, they are deadlocked in a test of the strength of each other's resolve. Both pour the major portion of their energy into maintaining the impasse. Each wistfully desires "to get on with his or her life" but there seems to be no way to do so. As Shakespeare has Hamlet say: "And thus the native hue of resolution is sicklied o'er with the pale cast of thought, and enterprises of great pith and moment with this regard their currents turn awry and lose the name of action" (*Hamlet* III,1). Parenting responsibilities, job efficiency, effective management of money, home maintenance, and goal choosing for the future grind to a halt in the clutch of the deadlock.

For the marital therapist, couples who present with such deadlocks are a therapeutic challenge. In my own care of couples over the years, this kind of situation not only challenges me, but also causes many otherwise useful theoretical orientations to collapse when held to slavishly. The therapist, therefore, has the responsibility of formulating his or her own unique hypothesis and therapeutic approaches to the spouses as individuals and as a couple. The wide range of theoretical orientations are informative, but the therapist brings his or her own uniqueness to the task. This uniqueness is his or her main forte in caring for a couple in an impasse over whether or not to divorce.

In this chapter I address the following hypotheses which have become my working assumptions in marital situations where one spouse is resolved to divorce and the other is eager to maintain the marriage. First, the therapist may have major difficulty and only occasional success in involving both partners in conjoint therapy. Second, more often than not the spouse who is eager to get a divorce leaves the abandoned spouse for the therapist to care for and sustain through the divorce and its sequelae. He or she leaves the spouse on the therapist's doorstep. Third, the therapeutic deadlock seems to occur most often in sudden demands of one partner for a divorce, throwing the other spouse into the shock of acute grief. Fourth, not all therapeutic deadlocks over divorce are sudden. Some follow a definable, cumulative course which I have charted. This course, when carefully diagnosed by the therapist, provides him or her a pattern for defining his or her own therapeutic approach, that is, the extent of deterioration of the relationship gives perspectives on whether the relationship can be reconstituted or whether it will continue on toward dissolution. In essence, by identifying the stage of dissolution, the therapist can determine whether he or she is doing marital therapy or divorce therapy. This decision will determine the therapist's procedures.

THE INITIAL INTERVIEW AND
THE THERAPEUTIC ALLIANCE

How the problem comes to the therapist's attention varies from couple to couple. In some instances, both partners come for therapy together. They can express their feelings which are already known to each other. They cannot express secrets they are withholding one from the other. The therapist can ask to talk privately with each spouse, after having heard them out as a couple. At this time private agendas can be explored. Then the therapist can bring them back together to make plans for continued therapy. The formation of the therapeutic contract is a major concern at this point. If the therapeutic goal is to attempt to rebuild the marriage and if it is apparent that the couple's decision about divorce revolves around an extramarital affair, alcoholism, homosexuality, and so on, then there is a need for a moratorium on these behaviors while therapy is in progress. Is the partner who is involved in the behavior willing to agree to that? If not, the couple is separated psychologically, even if not separated from bed and house. Possibly another therapist for one or the other is indicated. Or, the therapy now being considered is aimed not at marital therapy but at divorce therapy.

Another issue is important in the therapeutic contract. The couple may not be at the stage of separation, but in the legal stage of marital dissolution. They may simply have consulted a lawyer, or they may have already filed for divorce. What is their need for therapy? Have they come for the purpose of rebuilding the marriage? If so, the legal process must be frozen in place pending the outcome of therapy. Even if they have not come for the purpose of working on the marriage, the therapist may be in the position of helping them rethink their decision to file for a divorce. Have they missed some very important factors in making that decision? My own practice is to ask for a moratorium both on the behaviors described above and on legal action while therapy is in progress.

However, the problem is not usually brought to the therapist by the couple, but by one or the other of them individually. One of the real advantages of seeing the first spouse who calls for help individually is that hidden agendas or secrets can be discussed openly. One of the most common of these secrets is either accusations of infidelity or confessions of infidelity. Other secret and nonsecret issues which may need to be discussed with only one partner are alcoholism, drug addiction, homosexuality, severe financial stress, and chronic depression of one or the other.

However, it is important to note the following hazards to this approach:

The hazard of "belonging" to the spouse who is seen individually. The rivalry between the spouses can turn against the therapist. The spouse who has seen the therapist for a few interviews may resent the intrusion of the other spouse becoming a part of a conjoint therapy endeavor. The left-out spouse may feel that his or her spouse and the therapist will have formed a coalition. These two situations can be offset by shifting to individual sessions and providing "equal time" for the other spouse. Or, the other spouse may already be in individual therapy with a therapist colleague. If both partners grant the right to the two therapists to collaborate, then later, when both sides of the impasse have been softened and each is amenable, reconstruction of the marital covenant in cotherapy by both therapists can be done.

The hazard of forfeiting the opportunity to involve the other spouse. This is the hazard of miscalculation inherent in not knowing the other spouse. In some instances, the other spouse is known to the therapist, especially if the couple is a part of the same social, occupational, political, or religious organization as is the therapist. This happens more often than is usually theorized inasmuch as these common affiliations have much to do with the choice of a given therapist in the first place.

The hazard of not being able to involve the other spouse, however, may be caused by the naivete and ignorance of the spouse who does come to the counselor. The spouse who does *not* want the divorce is the most likely one to be first to seek therapy for their marriage. The one least likely to do so is the one who has a strong resolve to divorce. While the former is seeking therapy for the marriage, the latter may take unilateral actions such as "moving out" of the house when the other is not there, of instituting divorce procedures, of withdrawing all the family money from a joint account and putting it in his or her own account in a separate bank, of going on a journey with a paramour, and so on.

These actions further deteriorate the marriage while the counselor is trying to be of help to the individual spouse who came to the therapist first. If the therapist assesses the story of this spouse and has even an inkling or a hunch that the marriage is in far worse repair than the denial mechanisms of the spouse at hand permit him or her to admit, then the individual therapy approach must be forfeited in behalf of crisis intervention approaches to the absent spouse. Efforts to involve the other spouse may bring his or her unilateral decision making under the influence of the therapist and forestall impulsive unilateral actions such as have been mentioned.

STRATEGIES FOR INVOLVING THE OTHER SPOUSE

When one spouse has sought therapeutic intervention and the other has not, and when the therapist's decision is to involve the other spouse, no one way of doing so works in all instances. All efforts may fail in some instances. A repertoire of approaches is necessary, and bases for choosing one or the other are finitely constant. I use an "If . . . , then . . ." method for decision making.

If the spouse whom the therapist is treating shows real evidence of being a *reliable* messenger, *then* he or she can be asked and urged to advise the spouse that he or she had sought therapy and to extend the invitation to the spouse that they come together to the next appointment or to call and ask to be seen separately. *If* the spouse who first comes seems too depressed, distraught, suspicious, or punitive to be a reliable messenger, *then* the therapist can offer to write such an invitation or call the spouse by telephone. Permission will be needed to do this wisely. I have been astounded to see how often such permission will not be granted. In some instances, the spouse says that it is useless and predicts that the spouse will not want to do this. I am inclined to insist and not to take this fatalism as a fact. On asking the other mate to participate, I would say that in about three out of five cases the other spouse was cooperative. In two out of five, the prediction of the initial spouse was right.

In writing a letter of invitation to nonpresent spouses, I learned from veteran marital therapists to explain to the absent spouses that their wives or husbands have confided personal problems of their own in me and that I need *their* help in being of service to their spouses. I prefer to use a letter as a first means of communication because it does not demand an immediate answer. The person can think about it for a while. A telephone invitation must be answered "on the spot." That can be used later if there is no response to the letter.

Ordinarily, the first line of communication with the other spouse is to place the responsibility for persuading him or her in the hands of the first spouse to come to the therapist. Thus the therapist can learn much about how the couple communicate or fail to communicate with each other.

A MARITAL GAME: "THE THERAPIST'S DOORSTEP"

In the last 10 years, I have paid close attention to how one or both spouses come to my attention as a therapist. Occasionally both partners come for the first interview even though only one partner continues in therapy. The scenario is somewhat like this: The couple come for therapy together. They usually arrange for the first interview in a stressful appeal for emergency, immediate attention. The impasse of one wanting out of the marriage and the other wanting to sustain the marriage is not expressed. They are having severe conflicts with each other and want to enter marital therapy. Both of them agree on a process of working on their marriage together. The therapist uses the rest of the first session to identify with them areas of tension and conflict that beset them.

Certain phrases appear in their dialogue: "He has been unhappy for some time and has little to say"; "I care a lot for her, but I'm not happy with her"; "Things are just not what they used to be." Notice how vague and nonspecific these statements are. The therapist senses that there is a big hidden agenda and can easily be seduced into asking a lot of "detective questions" such as, "How do you folks spend your spare time?" Rather than do this, inasmuch as the therapeutic alliance has not yet been clarified, it is much better to concentrate on what sort of contract or understanding we should have with each other. Or, would they like to defer conjoint therapy for a while and each of them be seen separately with the goal of exploring private misunderstandings each has of the other and anything that each would be reluctant to discuss in the presence of the other until they had discussed it with the therapist? Or, do the couple have suggestions of ways of approaching their dilemmas other than these suggestions? They have come for therapy, what do they expect of the therapist?

Briefly stated, the spouse who is eager to get a divorce "cares" for the other spouse, does not want "to hurt" him or her, and yet does not "love" him or her. He or she may continue in therapy for a few interviews but then drops out, leaving their spouse on the therapist's doorstep to see to it that he or she is cared for, does not hurt or get hurt any more, and so on. I have found that therapeutic deadlocks tend to end this way more often than not. The person committed to divorcing finally does so.

IDENTIFYING THE PROCESS OF
DISINTEGRATION OF THE FAMILY SYSTEM

The discussion thus far has focused heavily on the crucial quality of the initial interview. It points up that *two* interacting covenants exist alongside each other: the covenant of the couple with each other and the covenant they are forming with the therapist. In my earliest work as a marriage and family counselor, I developed the concept of the marriage relationship as a teaching-and-learning covenant. A covenant is characterized by the confidence, trust, respect, and a degree of intimacy the couple have that prompted them to get married in the first place. A synonym for "covenant" is "understanding" or "contract." Upon entering marriage, the couple "know" each other to a certain extent. This "knowing" consists of their verbal agreements with each other. Yet a considerable amount of "not knowing" (i.e., mystery, unspoken assumptions, unconscious assumptions, ignorance of each other) exists. The marriage covenant that lasts includes both the "knowing" and the "not knowing," coupled with commitment to learn from each other and to teach each other concerning the mystery or unknown each has in relation to the other. Stubbornness, unwillingness to learn from each other, and unteachableness are the stuff of which divorce is made. Therefore, the covenant of marriage may be so devoid of knowledge and even be full of conscious deception that not enough real understanding exists to sustain the life of the marriage. Just as a conceptus of a baby may be so lacking in gene material that it will not sustain life through gestation and naturally aborts, a man-woman covenant may be so devoid of genuine knowledge of each other as a couple that it breaks up before marriage can take place.

A statistically high proportion of divorces occur in the first three or four years of marriage. This is not by chance. At best, two people getting married are strangers to each other. Chronic marital unhappiness is characterized by couples willfully remaining strangers to each other and refusing to learn from one another. Marital happiness is characterized by courageously carrying out a commitment to learn from each other and to grow and change by incorporating each other's differences in completing each other's selfhood. Divorce is the end-result aborting of a marriage relationship through the settled resolve of one or both partners' refusal to increase their knowledge of and empathy for one another. Marital deadlocks emerge in one of two ways, suddenly or cumulatively. My theoretical formulation calls for a differential diagnosis as to which type of deadlock the couple presents.

SUDDEN DIVORCE

Twenty-five years ago, I would have routinely assumed that there is no such thing as sudden, traumatic divorce. Today clinical observation yields plenty of evidence that sudden, cataclysmic divorce does happen far more often than we have any statistics to show.

Here is an example of sudden divorce. I saw a 25-year-old graduate student whose wife had decided to divorce him and had moved all her belongings from their home. He said: "I have no idea why she did this to me. I thought everything was fine between us. I didn't know anything was wrong. I told her I was coming to you for counseling. I begged her to come back home. Home with her is the only home I have."

Detailed inquiry revealed that he was financially dependent upon his wife who was a nurse. He was also dependent on student loans. He spent practically all his time studying. They had little or no time for each other because of his studying and her working. Things were less complicated in that they had no children.

His wife called for an interview. She was an attractive 26-year-old nurse. She said: "It's all give and no get. I pay all the bills, care for the apartment, prepare meals, and wash our clothes. He studies. He rarely approaches me sexually and when I approach him, he can't get an erection. It is not a marriage. It never has been."

I asked her if she were willing to undergo marital therapy along with him to see if some of these problems could be faced together and changed. She said: "I appreciate your offer, but I see no future for us and am not interested." She communicated this to him and told him she was filing for divorce. The marriage ended quickly in divorce.

However, my therapy with him continued. He became acutely depressed. I arranged overnight hospitalization for him. He attended classes in the morning and attended therapy in the afternoons. This was a bridge for him in his severe grief. He faced his dependency, impotence, and compulsive study habits. He sustained his work as a student and graduated two years later. At that time he had not remarried. Therapy consisted of moving with him through the grief process. This included working with the struggle between the fantasy that his former wife would come back and facing the reality that she would not. It also included working with the shock of his being abandoned and working through his grief, enabling him to mourn his loss and restore his self-esteem.

The sudden divorce is a unique form of the deadlock situation of one partner expressing a strong desire to divorce and the other partner expressing an equally strong resolve to remain married. The phenomenon seems to happen in the following manner.

Couples living in large urban areas and pursuing two careers in two widely separate work situations can easily develop different routines, different social groups, different sets of values about man-woman relationships, and fewer and fewer rituals that they share together. Even the rituals of eating together and sleeping together can become sporadic. They develop parallel lives, much as children below the age of three tend to have parallel play rather than cooperative, collaborative, intimate friendships with each other.

In fact, it is possible for persons in large urban areas (where anonymity is the order of the day rather than face-to-face communication) to have ongoing relationships with more than one sexual partner. Some people seem to be able to do this with little or no pangs of conscience. In fact, it is no recent thing that some spouses, more often wives than husbands but not uniformly so, tacitly assume that their spouse has other partners. They will say, "I don't worry about it as long as I don't know about it." Their spouse justifies his or her extramarital affair by saying that what their spouse does not know won't hurt him or her.

Sooner or later, though, the paramour of the spouse who is living a double life begins to pressure for marriage. He or she agrees to do this and is faced with the task of *telling*, not asking, his or her spouse that he or she is going to divorce him or her. It is a fait accompli in his or her mind. Then, with no prior conversation, notice, or preparation he or she announces to the wife or husband, "I am going to get a divorce!" The spouse is thrown into shock. The unknowing partner protests that he or she did not know that anything was wrong. In paroxysms of emotion the unknowing partner asks, "What on earth has gotten into you? Who ever heard of such a thing?'' Surprisingly, these persons are often strong in their resolve to remain married. One of the first things they think of is for the two of them to seek marriage therapy.

This interview consists of a time of catharsis for the spouse who has just learned of the divorce crisis. He or she is in shock. The partner contending for the divorce then needs consideration. He or she may not have the wisdom to appreciate the fact that he or she has known about this possibility for a long time and the other partner has just learned it. Can he or she delay divorce action in exchange for therapeutic time to enable the partner to "catch up" in the process of grief, which divorce surely is? Then, too, the exiting partner, with all the time spent in thinking about divorce, has been doing so in a vacuum of fantasy and imagining what it would be like. Now the exiting partner is dealing with the real thing; getting a divorce is not as easy as he or she may have imagined. The spouse being divorced does not vanish, disappear, or even "go away." Especially if there are children of whatever age, divorce does not *break* the relationship with the spouse; it simply changes it from a collaborative one to an adversarial one. In spite of all the bonny optimism of self-help books on divorce telling the couple to "remain friends" and be "civilized" toward each other, the exiting spouse needs to be aware of the amount of rage and the punitive forms it can take in a rejected spouse. In brief, the exiting spouse does not dissolve a marriage with the snap of a finger or a simple announcement.

Therefore, both of the spouses will need a nonadversarial third person to facilitate their moving out of the realm of shock and denial in the case of the spouse who wants to sustain the marriage, and unrealism and fantasy in the case of the person who is strongly resolved to get a divorce. They can be told that their relatives and friends will appoint themselves to the task of being their advisers. They will be more than likely to "choose up sides," thereby becoming a part of the problem. In most instances involving consultation with lawyers, the attorney becomes the advocate of one and the adversary of the other. Exceptions to this are both rare and refreshing. Therefore, the therapeutic relationship offers the couple the opportunity to get acquainted with each other in depth. The situation they have presented is evidence that they are in a real sense strangers to each other. Even if after the passage of time they both agree to divorce, it is important to *know* each other and not to divorce as strangers!

A covenant of communication is necessary if the spouses are to gain the most from the therapy. They should be assured that the therapist will not convey their situation to anyone else without first discussing it with them and getting their permission to do so. In turn, they need to agree that they will not discuss their problems with anyone else without first conferring with the therapists. The commonsense reason for this is to localize the conflict and to keep it from spreading to their whole daily environment. Furthermore, this keeps them from triangulating friends, co-workers, and family.

Inherent in this therapeutic alliance is the need to delay precipitous decisions for divorce. Panic decisions impaired by shock and denial, and unrealistic decisions impaired by fantasy and a lack of foresight can be avoided. The Episcopal Book of Common Prayer says that marriage is "not to be entered into unadvisedly or lightly, but reverently, discreetly, soberly, and in the fear of God." This is doubly true of divorce.

CUMULATIVE DIVORCE

Far more frequent than sudden divorce is what I have chosen to call *cumulative divorce*. This is where one partner's resolve to divorce arises out of a long series of cumulative stresses in the marriage relationship. The following is an example of cumulative divorce.

Both partners were 46 years old. Only the wife came for counseling. The husband was under treatment by a psychiatrist. They were at the stage of separation at the time of the wife's seeking therapy. Over the last four years there had been several separations. Both of them were Catholic. For this reason and the fact that they had three children, ages 3, 11, and 14, the wife was deeply opposed to the divorce. The husband had moved out of the home into an apartment. I did not have therapeutic contact with him. Upon offering collaboration assistance to his psychiatrist, I was rebuffed because he considered the husband as his patient and the relationship confidential. Hence, no interdisciplinary or cooperative work was possible.

The wife formed a clearly defined therapeutic relationship with me that extended over three years on a once-a-week basis. The therapeutic goals were to enable her to process her resistance to the divorce, to gain control over her rage, to readjust to the new parental situation of joint custody, and to deal with her own personal issues in continuously developing new relationships with men. Interlocked in all of this work were her convictions as a Catholic and her periodic encounter with the Church and its pastors. She repeatedly said that her husband had set out with her in a faithful Catholic marriage, but that he had changed the rules without telling her.

The therapy went through several phases: (1) absorbing the shock and social humiliation of being abandoned; (2) debriefing the events of the week among the children, the ex-husband, and herself (she was often overwhelmed by repeated catharses of rage and recrimination toward her husband); (3) dealing with the nitty-gritty issues surrounding her job (she fortunately had a Ph.D. degree and commanded a moderately good salary as a teacher; also, the divorce settlement provided her with the house and a somewhat adequate sum of monthly child support); (4) assessing her loneliness and conversing with her about her involvements with new male partners. She terminated after three years of therapy and occasionally makes another appointment when an event occurs that cues in or reenacts her old hurts in the divorce.

The longer-term or cumulative dissolution of a marriage goes through a somewhat predictable pattern of stages. The therapist's tactical approach to the couple varies from stage to stage. It is vitally important to understand that the process of dissolution may be reversed at any point or in any stage. As the couple progresses through the stages, reversal becomes increasingly difficult. The identifiable stages of marital dissolution ending in divorce are as follows:

Stage One: Conflict in Adjustment

This kind of conflict arises in the earliest years of the marriage. It centers around several issues:

- Establishing and agreeing upon a mutually understood routine for work, meals, sleeping, making love, social interaction with people outside the home, the performance of household chores, and so on.
- A mutual understanding of the balancing of roles in decision making, management of money, initiative in sexual activity, and the expression of such emotions as tenderness, anger, and fear.
- Dealing creatively with their joint interaction with the rituals and needs for attention and control of their families of origin.
- Learning each other's elaborate system of nonverbal cues and communications so that much understanding takes a minimum of verbal communication. This is often described as becoming sensitive to each other's feelings as well as listening to each other's words.
- Arriving at a clear understanding with each other about the possibility of having children.

Each of these areas is a potential source of conflict that can prompt threats of separation, threats of divorce, or divorce itself. Even at this stage one partner may want out of the marriage while the other partner is strongly committed to working on the relationship.

The covenant of trust, respect, and commitment to the marriage is, however, still intact at this first stage. One of the best therapeutic tactics at this stage of dissolution is to involve the couple in marriage enrichment groups. Couples can challenge, sustain, and inform each other of ways and means of dealing with adjustment conflicts. They become a part of each other's life support system.

Another approach proved to be highly successful in a case where the partners were each enmeshed in their respective family of origin and the partners were being driven apart by conflicting styles of family living. The couple, who were at first in conjoint therapy during which little progress was made, were then involved in a weekend series of sessions, with both parents of both spouses participating with them. The intergenerational stresses were faced directly, in which both pairs of parents "set them free" and "put them on their own." After that, threats of divorce by one partner and plaintive appeals by the other were resolved, and negotiated decision making replaced the deadlock. The couple did not divorce. The tactic of bringing in both sets of parents appeared to be crucial in helping the couple free themselves from parental enmeshment.

Stage Two: The Collapse of the Covenant of Trust and Withdrawal of Selves

In this stage, the covenant of trust, respect, and intimacy collapses because of any one of a large range of events. For example, one spouse learns that the other has a criminal record; the truth comes out when they try to negotiate a loan to buy a house. Or, a spouse reveals that he or she is gay or lesbian in an active way. Or, a spouse learns that his wife has a child by a previous marriage about which he has not been told. Or, a previous wife of a husband continues to call him for help and he spends inordinate amounts of time talking on the phone with her, attending to her business affairs and having evening meals with her. More often the breach of trust occurs when one spouse discovers the other spouse is having an affair. In such shattering of the covenant of trust, threats of divorce are purely nonverbal but the erosion of the marriage has begun to accumulate exponentially.

The couple withdraw into themselves and begin to live parallel lives. Any one such event is enough to strain the best of relationships. The degree of deception involved is a measure of the prognosis at this stage. The decision of the offended partner to divorce is highly probable. The offending partner may strenuously object and resolve to sustain the marriage.

If these couples bring this impasse to the therapist, arresting the process of dissolution depends upon dealing with the fear and distrust of the offended partner that other secrets are being withheld. Underneath this is the lurking question, "Can I believe anything my spouse says?" These barriers have to be surmounted before dealing with the difficult task of the offended partner being able to forgive the offending partner. I have seen in at least two instances that the offended spouse, the wife, did not forgive her husband. Nor did she divorce him. In one case, the alternative of overriding loneliness in living alone as a divorced person caused the wife to "put up with his ornery behavior." In the other case, the couple were involved in a family business that was very lucrative, and the wife "was not about to turn any part of the assets over to him to do with as he pleased." From that point forward the "offense" was used as a tool for controlling the husbands in both instances. Although these two wives had been resolved to get a divorce, their own self-interests deterred them, not genuine reconciliation with their spouses.

Stage Three: The Stage of Private Foreboding

At this stage, the deadlock is at its most acute intensity. Both have despaired of each other and of the future of their marriage. One may have resolved to get out of the marriage, but feels hopeless about how to do it. The other may cringingly live in fear of the time when what he or she has sensed from the nonverbal messages of the other will finally be voiced. The spouses hold these ruminations privately from each other. They have not told anyone else about what they are thinking. Thus it is a *private*, nonverbal response. Each is isolated from the other and suffers in silence apart from all other people.

The marriage and family therapist is no exception to the exclusion. If he or she is related to the couple or one member of the couple in a teaching situation, as fellow members of a religious or some other organization, or if he or she is a friend of the extended family of both spouses or one spouse, then the therapist may observe and "sense" the depression that is a hallmark of this stage. If, in addition to being a therapist, he or she is the family physician of the couple, the person may confide in him or her during a routine examination. If the therapist is the family pastor and senses the sadness of one or the other spouse, a pastoral home visit may enable them to "open up" their despair (Oates, 1974). Or, one or the other partner may "have stood it as long as I can" and decide to break out of the isolation and share his or her plight with someone. This ushers in the fourth phase.

Stage Four: The Stage of Social Involvement (Going Public)

This happens when one or the other (or both) decides to blurt out his or her story to someone else. Until this time it has been to them at least a "personal" or "family secret." This is the most critical stage in the process. Whom they reach out to and share this with is of the greatest importance. Who are the most commonly chosen confidants?

Members of their extended family or personal friends are most often chosen. These persons can be creative guides and a part of the solution rather than the problem. It is not my experience that in-laws are *routinely* harmful complicators of the couple's marital distress. Especially in cases where there are children, I am always aware that I am not just dealing with in-laws. These are grandparents! They have a vested interest in the resolution of marital discord between the parents of their grandchildren. If the marriage fails, they may well be called upon to care for the children. Yet even this is a tender trap. The grandparents, reliving their own parenthood, may feel that they will be more competent than the parents of the children to care for them. On balance, I have found that in-laws are more often helpful to, than sabotaging of, their son's or daughter's marriage.

Close personal friends become the confidants of persons in marital desperation. However, the possibility that one of these personal friends is of the opposite sex is very high. A woman listens in an understanding and empathic way to a man's marital troubles, and vice versa. They already have a warm friendship. It is very easy for this gradually to slide into a clandestine liaison with sexual involvement.

Clergypersons and physicians are among those who rank exceptionally high in the confidence of those who are choosing a professional person in whom to confide personal problems and are productive sources of referrals for longer-term marital therapy. Their forte is crisis intervention and short-term therapy. Their other responsibilities must be balanced with the amount of time they give to any one individual or family. The optimal time to be a therapist for a deadlocked couple is at the earliest moment as they break out of their marital involvement and begin to share their woes with others.

Therefore, in the initial inquiry with a couple when one wants out and the other doesn't, the imperative question to ask is: "To whom else have you been able to talk about this?" I ask this routinely of everyone whom I counsel, but it is especially important with these couples. In exploring answers to this question in detail, I get an overview of the family system of which they are a part. Occasionally I unearth a plexus of other "counselors" and many of the dynamics of the marital discord between the couple. Exploring the answers to this question often reveals to the couple insights that help relax and inform the deadlock they are in together. One excellent way to do this is by constructing a family genogram with the couple.

Stage Five: Threats of Separation and Divorce

Ordinarily a couple are in this fifth and advanced stage of marital dissolution when they present an impasse to the "to-divorce-or-not-to-divorce" dilemma. Much water has already gone over the dam. Arresting and reversing the process of marital disintegration is an Augean task! The question of whom else they have talked to about their plight leads both the therapist and them back to the stage of social involvement.

I use two questions to "change the subject" away from divorce. The first has two parts: "How did you two people meet in the first place and what did you see in each other at that time that caused you to decide to get married?" This question leads them back to a time when things were much better. It elicits the positive strengths of the union.

The second question is: "What kind of understanding about your life together did you have when you got married?" This question puts them back at the time when whatever covenant or contract they originally had was in effect. I tend to let their attention focus on that covenant and how they got from that point to this point in their life together. Very gradually, the deadlock becomes less the focus of their attention. They begin to experience the "other side of their ambivalence" toward each other. The one that is resolved to get a divorce begins to see what he or she is eager to leave. The one who is resolved to stay married begins to catch a few glimpses of what brought him or her to this state of desperation. My underlying assumption in these situations is that such a line of questioning will reopen the teaching and learning dimension of the husband-wife relationship, a responsibility they have both neglected too long. The softening of their hardened stances toward each other may or may not occur.

If this mellowing does not occur, the partner who is set on getting divorced pushes and shoves the process along. The other partner, however, has had little time for reflection; impatience flares into anger. When this happens, until I have data to the contrary, I hypothesize one of several possibilities. The person seeking the divorce has an intense extramarital relationship with someone else that he or she is compelled to turn into a marriage. This is one possibility. Another is that one person has decided to be openly homosexual. A third possibility is that one or the other is in an acute depression and no longer wants to be a burden on their family. The possibilities, of course, are limitless. Frequently, the first hypothesis proves to be correct. In order to pursue the matter further, I ask for individual time with the contender for the divorce and frankly discuss my hypothesis with him or her.

If the person confides in me that this is the case, then I point out that it is hazardous for his or her later happiness with the paramour in marriage for him or her to dash out of this marriage and into that one. That person will have a lurking doubt whether he will treat her as the present spouse has been treated. Will his haste come back to haunt them? I also suggest to the person that the paramour has a right to be chosen for himself or herself alone and not as an escape from this marriage. These are efforts, admittedly often futile, to slow down the decision to divorce and give time and reason an opportunity to mature such a decision.

Stage Six: The Legal Phase

In the sixth phase of marital dissolution, the couple may herald its beginning by asking legal questions of the therapist, such as: "What about the custody of the children?" or "Will she get the house or will I?" In other words, I feel that I am being consulted *as if* I were a lawyer. However, many couples in this deadlock have already been to a lawyer about their legal rights before they seek therapy. A considerable number of lawyers and judges will insist that some couples seek therapy for their differences before they proceed to finalize a divorce. Occasionally, one will suggest a time of separation as a "cooling-off" period before instituting divorce. Hopefully this approach will gradually replace the legal practice of becoming adversaries in behalf of one or the other spouse. Divorce mediation and conciliation are a fledgling but discernible positive trend in the practice of law.

If the person who is resolved to get a divorce has already engaged the services of an adversarial lawyer, it is my practice to advise the spouse who does not want a divorce nevertheless to consult a lawyer about his or her legal rights. Regardless of how badly one member of a marriage wants to keep the marriage intact and does not want a divorce, when this last ditch has been reached, I feel obligated to urge that person to be adequately defended legally when the spouse sues for divorce. The grief I feel at standing at this juncture with a couple is increased by seeing the waste of the few financial resources they have in an adversarial legal hassle.

POSTDIVORCE BEREAVEMENT

When one spouse forces a divorce upon the other in spite of the latter's protests, the abandoned partner is left in a profound state of bereavement. Often this is a complicated grief amounting to a clinical depression. If this is true, suicidal risk is present. In such cases I do four things:

1. I encourage the person to seek medical assistance from his or her internist. If he or she does not have a physician, I recommend a physician with whom I am accustomed to working. In either event, I ask permission to confer with the physician to see what extent a psychiatric referral is or is not indicated.
2. I involve the person in a divorce recovery group of recently divorced persons. This group must have skilled and competent leadership.
3. I continue to see the person in therapy. In most cases fees need to be scaled down because of the economic disaster many divorces entail.
4. Finally, I interpret and facilitate the grief resolution process over the next full year. Shock, numbness, a struggle between fantasy about reestablishing the marriage and the reality of this possibility, the catharsis of despair and rage, the passing through of the "first" wedding anniversary, Thanksgiving, Christmas or other holy days, birthday celebrations, and the anniversary of the divorce itself are all stages of grief.

The financial and emotional cost of divorce to both spouses is difficult to overestimate, especially if there are children to be nurtured.

SUMMARY

In this chapter, I have considered several sequelae of a marital deadlock in which one person wants a divorce and his or her mate does not. The difficulties and hazards of getting a workable therapeutic relationship started and sustaining it have been considered. Getting both spouses equally involved therapeutically calls for specific strategies which are discussed. I described and labeled the marital game of leaving the abandoned spouse for the therapist to care for as "The Therapist's Doorstep." I explained my own therapeutic orientation by showing how to assess or diagnose the degree of suddenness or cumulativeness a given marriage deadlock presents. Two case studies illustrating sudden and cumulative divorce were considered. The discussion of cumulative divorce included six stages. Reversibility is possible, yet increasingly difficult as one progresses through these stages. A final section on postdivorce bereavement concluded the chapter.

REFERENCE

Oates, W. (1974). *Pastoral counseling* (p. 124). Philadelphia: Westminster Press.

9

The Divorce Dance: Doing Therapy with Polarized Couples

Marcia Lasswell

INTRODUCTION: THE ONE-SIDED DECISION

In the course of nearly 30 years of working with couples whose marriages are in turmoil, I have experienced far more one-sided decisions to divorce than mutually agreed-upon ones. This is not to say that there have not been some couples over the years who have exhibited surprisingly little conflict over the decision to end their marriages. On occasion, both partners have agreed that their relationship was too troubled or too devoid of positive feelings to continue and with surprisingly calm and rational discussion they have brought their married years to a close. This pattern is not a frequent one, however. As I think back over my own practice, there may have been fewer than a dozen such "mutual" couples among the much larger number

175

of divorce-bound marriages where only one partner initially wanted out.

Several studies on divorce have suggested that my experience is not unusual—divorce is not very often an equally agreed-upon decision (Dixon & Weitzman, 1982; Kitson, 1982; Levinger, 1966). More likely than not, one partner has realized that he or she is dissatisfied enough to think of separating and begins one or another of several patterns to bring things to a head. The other partner may ignore these actions, protest them, attempt to work things through, or some combination of these or other reactions. This "divorce dance" between the partners may continue for months or even for years. Usually, the initiator gets his or her message across eventually and the partner who does not want the divorce must deal with the reality that there is serious trouble. I have known several couples, however, where one spouse's request for a divorce comes as a complete shock to the other. Immediately, four couples come to mind where the husbands returned home one evening to find that a moving van had carried away the bulk of the household goods and a note explained that divorce papers would be forthcoming.

Marriage therapists are called upon at a variety of points in the "divorce dance" sequence. Intervention necessarily depends upon several factors, such as how long the dissatisfaction has lasted, the depth of the dissatisfaction and whether or not there is hope for the marriage, the degree of awareness of the reluctant spouse, and whether the initiator is motivated to participate in counseling. As a therapist, I must know the agendas of both partners. Usually they are not the same, although the spouses are often unaware of this.

DIVORCE DANCE PATTERNS

Typical patterns are the following:

Pattern I: Immediate Solution Demanded

> Mrs. L. called to make an appointment for herself and Mr. L. On the day of their scheduled visit, only Mrs. L. arrived. She

told me that her husband had been having an affair and the evening before told her that he wanted a divorce. He saw no point to "marriage counseling" since he did not want to be married any longer. She was miserable, shocked, and felt powerless to change his mind.

The above scenario is a frequent pattern. It is not always the wife who is in this situation, of course, because as women's lives more closely approximate those of men outside the home, wives often are the ones who want a divorce to be with another man. The client who is sitting before me, male or female, obviously needs support. One of the most frustrating and painful human experiences is to have one's life turned upside down by another person and to have little or no choice in the matter. The feeling of powerlessness to gain some sort of control over the situation is at the root of much depression and even suicidal ideation.

One of the best kinds of support seems to be to explain that there may be more to the story than we know. Without giving false hope that things might work out, I feel strongly that I must encourage the client to get his or her spouse in for at least one session. I explain that there is not only "marriage therapy" but also "divorce therapy" and before I can be of help, I must be certain which is called for. Almost always, if I have explained myself well, the client can persuade his or her spouse to come for one visit (alone, if that is less threatening). In that visit, I must determine the next step; usually, it is to ask for a joint session and then to reassess where we go from there. If this is refused, then most often the follow-up is supportive therapy for the first spouse. It is not uncommon to get an initial refusal from the spouse who wants out, only to have him or her agree to come in at a later date.

Pattern II: Long-Term Dissonance

Mr. G. made the appointment and he and his wife arrived together. In the course of our initial session, it became clear that Mrs. G. was unhappy to the point of leaving. She said that she loved Mr. G. but was not "in love with him the way a wife should love a man." She said there was no one else, although Mr. G. said that she was "having an affair with her career." Mrs. G. was a buyer for a major department store chain; Mr. G. was an electrician for the city.

This couple is typical of many who have had long-term conflict over their differences in personality, values, interests, and desired lifestyle. Mrs. G. had been dissatisfied with her husband and had attempted to get him to change to her specifications for several years. Repeated but unsuccessful attempts to change a partner's behavior is one of the most frequent reasons for divorce. It is common for feelings of intimacy and love to decline with the disappointment of not seeing desired changes. Mr. G. alternated between open anger and passive resistance as reactions to his wife's criticisms. His reason for making the appointment at the specific time that he did was because there had been an argument which came close to violence and Mrs. G. left the house overnight. As a result, they both agreed to see a counselor.

Even though one spouse says he or she wants a divorce while the other states that the marriage is salvageable, I do not take these statements as necessarily true, especially when both are willing to seek therapy. It is especially important to reframe their troubled relationship into a two-way interaction rather than to allow one partner to be blamed. So often, when the blaming cycle has existed for a long period of time, resentment is high on both sides. I often suggest one or two individual sessions so that each can air complaints to me without the other having to suffer through them once more. In these individual sessions, possible solutions to their differences are elicited from those spouses, as well as what, if anything, each is willing to do to enable the other to make changes. This is especially helpful to me to diagnose personality traits, flexibility, motivation to work on the marriage, and level of trust each partner feels for the other.

Studies of conflict in marriage have shown that the level of trust each partner has for the other is a strong predictor of how the couple will work together to solve their problems and determine if the marriage can be maintained (Haun & Stinnett,

1974; Indvik & Fitzpatrick, 1982). If the couple agrees to try counseling to work toward reconciliation, enhancing trust becomes a first order of business along with new problem-solving behaviors.

Pattern III: The Provokers

> Mrs. S. called for an individual appointment concerning one of her preschool children who was exhibiting some behavior problems. After a few minutes of the session, it became quite clear that while her son was indeed having some problems, Mrs. S. really wanted to talk about her marriage; more specifically, her husband was rarely at home and saw little of her or the three children. The couple seldom had sex or went places together, and they seemed unable to talk about the emotional distance between them. Mrs. S. had spoken to her mother, sister, in-laws, and friends who had suggested drugs, alcohol, another woman, or a midlife crisis (Mr. S. was 39 years old) as possible reasons for this behavior.

As adults, most of us have learned our lesson well that if something seems to be wrong, we should try to fix it. Being unable to make things right, or at least to salvage something out of chaos, not only is a helpless feeling but also gets right to the heart of one's self-esteem. Such powerlessness often makes a client feel insignificant and childlike. Feeling helpless can cause one to feel devalued. Mrs. S. had all of these feelings and was searching for what she was doing wrong. She blamed herself for her husband's absences and indifference, and with her childlike feelings she had talked to nearly everyone she knew about the problem. This had given Mrs. S. justification for even more distance. Her five-year-old son was reacting to the strain in the household and Mrs. S. decided to seek professional help for him although she said she had not considered marriage counseling. All therapists who work with families and children frequently see this "back-door" cry for help. If a child has been the identified patient, I often use this path to involve both parents. A reluctant spouse often is not a reluctant parent.

It is essential in cases such as this one to see both partners to determine what the problem really is. Obviously, it could be any one, or all, of the reasons that were suggested, but in this instance, the husband's motivation was divorce, only he did not want to be the one to make the decision. Mr. S. is typical of many spouses who choose to behave in such a fashion that they provoke the reluctant spouse into the position of making the decision to divorce.

It may seem strange in this era, which is relatively free of the social stigma of divorce, that there still are countless men and women who do not want to be the instigators of divorce proceedings. They often give lip service to wanting to maintain the marriage while, in fact, they continue behavior that is calculated to provoke the partner into leaving. Their reasons may be to protect themselves from what they believe will be negative feelings from children, relatives, and friends. On the other hand, just as often, it appears to be the result of fear about making such a complex decision or a childlike absence of taking responsibility for the consequences of their behavior.

Intervention with couples of this sort is twofold. First, the provoker needs to face up to his or her actions and to understand the pattern that has developed. If there is true ambivalence about the divorce, exploring the issues often can change that person's behavior into a more honest approach, after which a decision, one way or the other, can be made responsibly.

The second part of the therapy is to help the spouse who is being provoked to assess the situation as objectively as possible. This must include an understanding of his or her part in letting this happen. It is frequently the case that the provoked spouse feels the most responsible for the relationship and often is in a dependent role. Sometimes he or she has lower self-esteem than the partner and has come to expect little in the way of attention or affection. He or she is a perfect victim for neglect and lack of consideration. The provoked spouse continues to hope his or her partner will change, while usually the behavior escalates until it is unbearable. Should a divorce occur, postdivorce therapy is often needed for the spouse who actually sought the divorce that he or she had never wanted in the first place.

Pattern IV: The Compliant-Resistant Couple

Mr. and Mrs. K. explained in their first session that they wanted marriage counseling. Mrs. K. had been in individual therapy, and through this process, she had come to recognize many traits that had acted as negatives in their relationship. She was working to improve her relationship with her husband and Mrs. K.'s therapist had advised conjoint marriage counseling. The K.s had agreed not to see Mrs. K.'s past therapist so that Mr. K. could obtain a "neutral ear." Mrs. K. had several major complaints about her husband. Each time he raised some objection to her behavior, Mrs. K. was quick to acknowledge the problem and to say she was already working on it. In addition to therapy, Mrs. K. was a prolific reader of self-help books which she urged Mr. K. to read. He said he had little time to read but he had read one or two books at her request.

On the surface, this couple reminded me of other couples who come for help with their floundering marriages. The problems seemed routine enough, nothing that could not be resolved fairly easily. On the other hand, I am always somewhat uneasy about such sensible, cooperative couples with run-of-the-mill problems who pay a hefty fee to come to marital therapy. There have been a number of such couples I have seen over the years and usually I have not found these cases to be all that simple. Most of the time there is a hidden agenda on the part of one or both of them.

One scenario that has emerged several times with the compliant-resistant couple is that one of them wants out of the relationship. More often than not, it is not the passive partner but the active one, such as Mrs. K. The partner who seems to be making every effort to save the marriage (while the other one is simply going along with the program) may have as a hidden agenda one or more of the following: (1) if the divorce-bound spouse expects trouble over the divorce, he or she may be enlisting the therapist to smooth the way and to support the reluctant spouse to adjust; (2) the active partner may want to give the impression of having tried everything, even therapy, before throwing in the towel with the added hope that the therapist will also decide that their marriage is hopeless; and (3) I have many times discovered that the active spouse had made up his or her mind 90% of the way but has remaining questions or doubts that need to be addressed. Frequently, one of the doubts is about how to tell the reluctant spouse and how to work out a divorce settlement and custody. Often this latter, one-sided agenda has another agenda that "marriage counseling" will actually turn out to be "divorce counseling."

STAGES AND THE TIMING OF SEEKING COUNSELING

There is an almost infinite number of variations of the Divorce Dance patterns. In addition, couples may seek professional help at any one of a number of times during the development of their particular pattern. Much has been written about the stages of divorce and the sequential time periods commonly observed. For example, one stage which is not unusual is for one spouse to seek counsel when he or she first becomes cognizant that divorce may be a solution to existing problems, but long before the other spouse suspects such thoughts exist. Usually, the one seeking professional advice is wrestling internally with the need to make a decision and may not have involved others, including his or her spouse in the deliberations.

Another more frequent stage, however, happens once "divorce talk" has started. Interspersed with attempts to work things out or put up with their discontent, one or both parties may seek help. When either spouse threatens divorce as a solution rather than working on the problem, it usually gets the other's attention rather quickly and can precipitate a call for professional intervention. Emotions run high at this stage and there usually is a strong need to blame. Very often other parties have entered the picture as support for the beleaguered spouses. There may be a lover, close friends, or family members who offer advice and support. Frequently outsiders confuse the issue and, more often than not, may actually escalate the problems.

At this point I usually tell couples that whether they ultimately divorce or decide to stay together, working through some of their conflict will be beneficial. I usually also volunteer at this point that I do not believe every marriage should continue but that I do strongly believe that they both will feel better, should they decide to divorce, if they have left no stone unturned to see if they can salvage their relationship.

A third variation occurs when a decision has been made by the initiating spouse who has begun to make preparations for the divorce. He or she may have seen an attorney, made plans to move, changed financial arrangements, and have told significant others of these plans. This is an especially difficult period for the reluctant spouse which can be met with anger, illness, denial, resignation, or whatever coping mechanisms come to the surface. Objectively, there appears to be no hope of reconciliation and yet, the reluctant spouse does not want to let go. Sometimes the initiating spouse seems cold and calculating at this stage but, more often, he or she has some ambivalence about what is happening, along with sadness and sometimes guilt. These feelings often result in actions that are misread by the reluctant spouse as offering hope that his or her partner will have a change of heart.

ISSUES INFLUENCING TYPE
AND TIMING OF INTERVENTION

Is the Marriage Really Over?

The therapist's intervention must be carefully weighed according to the stage in the divorce process in which help is sought. Even though the couple is talking about divorce, many marriages are still very much alive and careful assessment to determine marriage viability may result in marriage therapy rather than movement toward divorce. Involving the other spouse and discouraging involvement of outsiders is usually the most beneficial path to follow.

In our initial interview, a couple married for seven years who are the parents of three young children said that they had made the appointment to discuss how to tell their children they were divorcing.

Rather than immediately exploring how and why they had come to this point, I told them how impressive it is to see parents who have such concern for their children under the trying circumstances of splitting up. We explored their concerns and what they had already told them until nearly half of the session was over. All three of us grew silent as the sadness of their plight hung in the air.

The husband broke the spell by telling me how he admired his wife's way with the children and her love and caring for them. This was my opening to ask if he had once felt that he received the same. "Not since the children were born," he replied. I asked if that was a factor in their decision to divorce and he said that indirectly it was. The real problem was that he had been having an affair and felt he no longer loved his wife even though she wanted to continue the marriage. His lover was encouraging him to move along with his divorce.

Two sessions later, an agreement had been made to explore the possibility of staying married after all. The husband's affair seemed directly related to his uncertainty about whether his wife loved him and he was able to see how he had felt displaced by the children. His wife recognized that in her desire to be a good mother she had pulled her warmth away from her husband. Together we decided against divorce counseling just yet. Instead we would analyze what had gone wrong in the marriage. If that exploration proved useful, we could then decide between marital therapy or divorce therapy. The difficult task would be for the husband to take a "vacation" from his lover for three months so that we could do our work. He thought about it for a week and agreed that he wanted to explore the viability of his marriage and could not do so effectively with a lover to turn to every time he felt discouraged.

For couples who may not be able to identify any hope for reconciliation in their first visit, some attempt at problem-intervention sprinkled with a heavy measure of the "realities of divorce" (custody and financial arrangements, child and spousal support, and other painful decisions) are needed to be sure that practical as well as emotional issues are being faced. While practical issues may not be sufficient reasons to maintain a marriage, a clear picture of what lies ahead sometimes makes the alternative to divorce look more appealing and stimulates the desire to work on the marriage.

After the third visit, both partners to a 15-year marriage had nearly convinced me that they were no longer in love and that a divorce was best. A small voice kept warning me not to move too quickly, nonetheless.

I decided to go for the "as if" approach, that is, acting as if the divorce would be a certainty, by posing the problems that we must solve to prepare for the separation. We discussed what to tell their children and other interested kin and friends. They had a reasonably easy time with this assignment. Next I asked who would be moving out or if the house would be sold and both would move. The house was already on the market, they said, and both had in mind new places to live. We discussed visitation and custody and they had already discussed and agreed how they would work out these issues.

Next I brought up the area of finances since it is my experience that money is a symbol of much that disturbs troubled couples. This proved to be a fruitful area since it uncovered some problems that were very basic to what was involved in the divorce.

The husband was frequently unemployed and had changed jobs just as frequently. His wife had a good job with a salary on which the family depended. He was very anxious about making it on his own financially and said he could not contribute much, if anything, to child support. I suggested he might wish to ask for spousal support since his income was so low or perhaps since he earned so little, he might consider having physical custody of the children so his wife could pay child support to him.

I had clearly rattled the gender-roles cage and the discussion that ensued really dug into the issues of partnership equality, disappointments, responsibility, and respect that were bothering both partners. From this came an agreement to work on the relationship before deciding whether to proceed with the divorce.

In the final analysis, there are those couples who have actually reached "the point of no return," when a decision has been made. The therapist's role then is that of divorce counselor and support to both parties and their children as they come to grips with the inevitable.

The Advantage Held by the Initiator

Although there are exceptions, the most disturbed partner usually is the one who does not want the divorce. Studies have indicated that the initiating spouse usually recovers sooner from all aspects of the divorce process than does the one who feels forced to accept what was unwanted (Ahrons & Rodgers, 1987; Vaughan, 1986). Some part of this is, of course, because the initiator usually has had longer to think about divorce and to adjust to the idea than the one who fights it to the end. The initiator may be one or two stages ahead of his or her spouse. The therapist, therefore, must be able to operate at more than one stage at the same time. This may well necessitate some individual sessions with each spouse.

> The realization that her husband really had no interest in reconciliation was a painful fact to accept for the woman who had asked for an individual session. "He seems so oblivious to how I hurt. I can't believe that he can throw away all of our years together or that he doesn't have any feeling left for me," she said.
> My role as a therapist seemed to call for support but also for words indicating that she would need time to adjust just as her husband had taken time to come to his decision. His behavior seemed sudden to her, even impulsive, rather than the result of gradual pulling away. In a subsequent session with both present, we explored the husband's lengthy decision process and he was able to express understanding that his wife needed time to adjust.

Getting the reluctant spouse to accept that holding on against his or her partner's will is not the basis for a good relationship is often a very difficult task. In this day of no-fault divorce, it is a Herculean task to explain that one kind of "irreconcilable difference" is when one partner believes the marriage is over and the other refuses to accept it.

The initiating spouse may not just be leaving the marriage but may also feel that he or she is "going to something or someone." Those who choose to end their marriage sometimes have high hopes for new-found freedom or a new partner. They may actually be experiencing parts of this new life at the same time that they are disengaging from the old. The other spouse, however, may feel that his or her life is in shambles and that it will be impossible ever to love again. It is not easy to believe that life holds much hope when one feels rejected, hurt, confused, and often still in love with a partner who wants out. This person may need far more time with a therapist to recover than the one who sees hope for a better life after divorce.

Involving Children in Divorce Therapy

When there are children, the therapist may need to involve them in family sessions, especially in difficult, disputed divorces. There is a strong tendency on the part of the reluctant spouse to use children for support. Most children naturally feel divided loyalty to their parents, but if one parent is made out to be responsible for all of the pain by wanting the divorce while the other wants the family to stay intact, the stage is set for trouble. The therapist can often intervene with the children to help them to construct their own reality of their parents' divorce, rather than simply accepting the version of one of their parents or else being totally confused about what to believe.

> The struggle over custody had turned bitter between the parents of the two girls, ages 11 and 7, who were brought in by their mother. She had fallen in love with another man and had moved in with him. Their father was hurt and angry and had refused to allow the girls to visit their mother regularly. He had told them their mother did not love them and was a bad person. He had told the girls in great detail about their mother's affair.
> Each child confided her confusion and concern since neither knew whether to believe one parent or the other. As gently as possible, I began to reframe the parents' battle over them as

showing their concern and love for their children. Their parents each had reasons for what they did to each other, I explained. "However, they both are good people and they both love you and want your love," I told them. I explained that their father was not asking for my help so I could not tell him that he was confusing them. However, knowing that he was speaking from pain might help them to see that what he said came only from his point of view. Their mother had another point of view which also came from pain. Since the two views were so different, they needed to make up their own minds. We agreed that I might serve as their sounding board until their parents resolved their struggle.

After the Physical Separation

Postseparation and postdivorce work is a major part of most disputed divorces. Even though the legal work is in process and the couple are no longer living together, the emotional divorce may be far from complete, especially for the noninitiator. The length of the marriage has a great deal to do with refusal to accept that a divorce is occurring. For a rejected spouse in a marriage where marital bonds were once well established, the reaction may be akin to losing a part of his or her body. Depression, illness, dependency, failure to engage in single-life activities, and many other signs of resistance to unwanted change are common. At this point, the therapist may need to change to a resource consultant and to be more directive in the healing process. Postdivorce group work seems especially helpful at this time.

Life out of marriage is not always what the initiator has been hoping it to be. Many find the world of singles depressing and lonely. Some may seek to return to a married state because the alternatives seem worse. Of those who had a relationship waiting to be explored, a large percentage find that finally being free to pursue the possibilities of the new romance has somehow changed the dynamics. I am especially attuned to those who cannot end one relationship without having another waiting in the wings. In many such cases, the marriage may not have been beyond saving but the initiator believed that he or she could find a chance at romance, new sexual fulfillment, and excitement. It is not easy for mortgages, backed-up garbage disposals, and children with chicken pox to provide a competing scenario. Many who separate find that the new romance cools just as the marriage had and feel regret that they had not stayed married.

While it is often futile on my part, I feel compelled to offer the advice that divorce should occur when the marriage is really a disaster, but not because one is trading in one partner for another. Admittedly, this is my bias and I state it as such. I have not found that the new relationships are ultimately any better than the old ones (and frequently, they are worse), because they were generally based on less than realistic foundations.

If the initiator is determined to divorce, my words usually fall on deaf ears, although months later I may get a phone call affirming my point of view. Where my advice has made a difference, however, is when the "other man" or the "other woman" is bringing pressure to bear on his or her lover to get on with the divorce. If I sense any reluctance on the part of the initiator to plunge into the other relationship, I may suggest to the divorcing couple that they separate for three or four months and postpone filing for a divorce. A favorite phrase of mine is, "You can always get a divorce. What's the rush?" Slowing down the divorce process and giving the initiator time to assess the other relationship has more than once reversed the decision to divorce.

CONCLUSION

Above all, I want to be as sure as is humanly possible that the couple understand what they are deciding and why. Divorce is an emotional decision to make and often feelings take precedence over common sense and practical issues as the process unrolls. This is particularly the case for the reluctant spouse, although the initiator often operates almost solely on emotions, too. Without losing my ability to be empathic and supportive, I want to be the voice of reason bringing the couple back time after time to the question of what is the best course of action to provide the least negative consequences for each member of the family.

The best of all possible resolutions to this complex problem of nonmutual divorce is, of course, that one of the partners will change his or her mind. Either both will agree to save the marriage or both will agree that a divorce is the only solution. I suppose, to be perfectly honest, this is my agenda, one I use to measure how successful my efforts have been in these very difficult and painful hours spent with couples in conflict over a divorce decision.

There have been many times, however, when the best the couple can do is to work through the hurt, pain, guilt, and anger. I believe it is important for all parties to know that I will be available to anyone who wants to continue the healing process through postdivorce therapy. As every therapist knows, obtaining the final papers is but one step in the overall process of ending a marriage. The emotional divorce may go on for decades. Doesn't tradition have it that Carl Whitaker once said, "You can never really get divorced"? Perhaps for those who never come to a mutual agreement to do so this is the truth.

REFERENCES

Ahrons, C. R., & Rodgers, R. H. (1987). *Divorced families: A multidisciplinary developmental view.* New York: Norton.

Dixon, R. B., & Weitzman, L. J. (1982). When husbands file for divorce. *Journal of Marriage and the Family, 44*(1), 103–115.

Haun, D. L., & Stinnett, N. (1974). Does psychological comfortableness between engaged couples affect their probability of successful marriage adjustment? *Family Perspectives, 9,* 11–18.

Indvik, J., & Fitzpatrick, M. A. (1982). "If you could read my mind, love . . . ," understanding and misunderstanding in the marital dyad. *Family Relations, 31*(1), 43–51.

Kitson, G. (1982). Attachment to the spouse in divorce: A scale and its application. *Journal of Marriage and the Family, 44*(2), 379–393.

Levinger, G. (1966). Sources of marital dissatisfaction among applicants for divorce. *American Journal of Orthopsychiatry, 36*(5), 803–807.

Vaughan, D. (1986). *Uncoupling: Turning points in intimate relationships.* New York: Oxford University Press.

10

Marital Therapy with Polarized Couples

Barbara E. James

When polarized couples (i.e., couples where one wishes to break up the marriage and the other wishes to keep the marriage intact) present themselves to a therapist, the therapist has the challenge of working with a system that is divided into two opposites.

Throughout any marital relationship, there are often issues on which the spouses have opposing views. In any close interpersonal relationship, the behavior of the participants is mutually reactive and interactive. This principle imposes a homeostatic equilibrium in a marriage (i.e., system). Causality of behavior is not a linear process but is circular. Behavior of spouse A may be reactive to certain behavior of spouse B which also may have been reactive to another previous behavior of spouse A, and so forth.

All marriages are subject to stress, disequilibrium, and crises, and most couples develop techniques to deal more or less successfully with these situations. As long as spouses A and B perceive that a minimum of their needs are being satisfied within the marital relationship, both usually wish to maintain the relationship. When the relationship becomes so dysfunctional that at least one spouse feels that the minimum of their needs is not being met within the relationship, that spouse may begin to want to terminate the relationship. Dramatic events such as "falling in love with someone else" or waking up one morning and "knowing that I do not wish to be married to my spouse" may lead to this conclusion. However, it is much more common that no specific event can be identified as the one trigger that leads to the decision. A slow process of negative reciprocity—that is, spouse A gives more negative than positive reinforcement to spouse B, and spouse B then gives spouse A negative reinforcement in return—has usually developed within the relationship.

If one spouse has decided to terminate the relationship, in order to maintain some sense of the equilibrium in the relationship the other spouse may immediately become convinced that he or she wants to keep the marriage intact no matter what. Thus the polarized couple has developed.

The most striking element present in the interactions of polarized couples is the rigidity of the drearily repetitive attack (hurt) and counterattack (hurt), with no change in the behavior of the partners and/or the system. On closer examination of the marriage, the antecedents for polarization often lie in the arena of the issues of boundaries, power/control, and intimacy.

BOUNDARIES

Boundaries, which are the subjective borders between one partner's symbolic self and the other partner's symbolic self, are important in marriages. A person's psychological boundary is much like that of the living cell. The living cell has integrity: it is easy to see what is inside the boundary and what is outside the boundary. Yet the living cell's boundary is permeable and can allow matter to move both in and out of the cell.

To have adequate psychological boundaries, a person must have developed adequate separation, individuation, and autonomy. The individual must know, Who am I? and What do I want? and must have the ability to tell the differences between his or her own feelings and wishes and those of another. Clear boundaries allow the individual

1. to use the past as a guide and not as a directive;
2. to accept the responsibility for his or her own life;
3. to deal with his or her own internal conflicts and desires and not to project them onto significant others;
4. to be able to make clear, appropriate choices free from the hurts, frustration, wishes, or dreams of the past;
5. to be able to negotiate for the satisfaction of his or her needs.

When individual boundaries are intact, a couple can respect each other for what they are and therefore begin to cooperate. Projection and speaking for the other (mind reading) are *not* frequently used techniques in the communication process of a couple where each has adequate boundaries.

Projection is defined as ascribing to one's spouse the attributes, feelings, and thought of one's self that are denied. In a polarized couple, projection serves the purpose of keeping each spouse from having to deal with internal conflict and shifts the battle to the spouse and away from one's self. Projection gives hope of a false solution to the problem, that is, if the spouse will shape up things will be fine.

Mind reading occurs after a projection has been made. The projecting spouse can tell the other spouse what the latter is feeling, thinking, and so on, and can translate that thought or feeling into behavior that would solve their problem.

POWER

Within marriage, power means possession of, control over, or influence upon others. This requires that one spouse has control over the other, that is, there is a winner and a loser. To win means total power and to lose means total helplessness. But one characteristic of a system is event A, which may swing in one direction and cause event B, the purpose of which is to temper event A and move it toward the opposite direction. When this happens within marriage there are no winners and losers, just losers. Power is relative and comes through competency and not absolute control or helplessness.

Within the larger issue of power/control there are three subissues: (1) money; (2) sex; and (3) "who's boss?" These are important threads in the fabric of modern marriage. The use of the term "modern marriage" is in no way meant to preclude that sex, money, and "who's boss?" have not been issues in marriage over the centuries. However, with the traditional sex roles moving toward an equal plane, the three issues have taken on special significance.

American society has begun to value both men and women for how much money they earn. This leads to marital couples valuing each other for their earning power and/or their style of money management.

Sex is a common battleground in marriages. One partner typically states, "My spouse wants sex more frequently than I do." The spouse's complaint is that he or she must feel loved, appreciated, and not taken for granted before he or she feels sexual attraction to the mate.

The battle of sexual frequency (not enough from one's viewpoint) versus quality (not enough from the other's standpoint) rages on while neither mate openly or honestly expresses latent feelings of hurt and disappointment about their nonsexual interaction. Instead of dealing with the sources of their anger and tension, they argue over sexual matters and focus on the symptoms, while the problems remain and the resentment soars. Naturally, with such treatment, sex cannot possibly be pleasurable and fulfilling, and the cycle of continued misery ensues.

Many marital struggles are waged over "Who's boss?" This represents a contest for control of the relationship and involves a complex set of individual and interpersonal needs that spouses rarely, if ever, deal with openly. Instead of questioning themselves about why each aggressively challenges the other, they take an accusatory approach and hold each other accountable.

INTIMACY

Intimacy is defined as being known and accepted by another who is loved. Each person's definition of behaviors that promote human intimacy is a product of his or her early learnings. Therefore, each spouse has a different set of behaviors that express and/or seek intimacy for him or her. In many couples these sets of behaviors, while different, are enough alike that each can understand parts of their spouse's "language of intimacy." Other couples find it very hard to do elementary translations of the "intimacy languages," much less become fluent in both their own and their spouse's "language."

To be truly intimate, marital partners must face their hopes and fears. Again, hopes and fears have roots in early interactions. Given this, we may not all have the same fears or the same degree of fears. However, one fear seems to be almost universal with humans. This is the fear of abandonment.

Partners experience hurts, disappointments, resentment, and rejection as a result of feeling unimportant to their mate. But the fear of abandonment often forces them to repress these feelings, which become masked by countless disguises that allow spouses to argue and bicker incessantly about the wrong issues. They successfully avoid the real issues. This avoidance is stimulated by the fear that arguing about real issues will worsen their problems and the marriage might disintegrate. They argue about more superficial issues and guarantee their continued misery.

The fear of abandonment is activated when one spouse says he or she wants the marriage to end. The anxiety created by this activation of the fear of abandonment causes the other partner to become helpless and clinging. In response to this behavior, the other spouse feels smothered and again states his or her wish to terminate the marriage. The one who wishes to leave the marriage may begin to relentlessly criticize and disintegrate the spouse, who in turn feels more helpless.

In other words, the behavior of the couple influences each other. The helplessness and rigidity are in direct response to the interaction. Preexisting personality predispositions appear to become more exaggerated with distressful interaction.

In this hostile, angry, "I want to break up this marriage immediately" and "no, I want to preserve this marriage at all costs for if you leave me I will collapse" position, couples present to the therapist.

TREATMENT MODEL

What follows is an outline of treatment based on psychoan-
alytic, behavior, and general systems theories. Over the years I
have developed a practice wherein primarily one member of the
couple is a physician or a physician-in-training. Therefore my
treatment model is based on the role and position of a person
who assumes authority. This treatment model can be used successfully with many different types of couples. The model is
particularly well suited to physicians who are trained in a milieu
that is populated with authority figures. These authority figures
are skilled at diagnosis, treatment planning, and prescribing
therapy. Therefore, this is what physicians respect and what they
expect when they come to a marital therapist, that he or she
will give an explanation for the problem(s), issue a general plan
and assign tasks, and expect compliance.

Assumptions

In my treatment model the following assumptions are made:

1. The therapist must be active in order to disrupt the recurring
   behavioral sequences the couple are presently provoking in
   a circular way. This must be done for two reasons:
   a. a realistic appraisal of the situation cannot be made until
      these sequences are stopped;
   b. the hurt, frustration, rejection, sadness, and other feelings
      the spouse is feeling cannot be heard until these sequences
      cease.
2. Both spouses have used ineffectual methods to try to decrease
   their hurts.
3. Both spouses are projecting their own ambivalence about
   the relationship onto the other.
4. It is highly likely that neither spouse has totally personal
   psychological boundaries.
5. Both partners need to be heard on both the cognitive and
   affective levels.
6. Both partners need support but do not know how to get it.
   In fact, they are both "experts" in making sure they neither
   get nor give support.

7. The therapist must constantly assist the couple in the translation of global, usually condemning statements into active, behavioral statements.
8. The couple is deficient in self-awareness, communication, and negotiation skills.
9. Reality lies somewhere between the two perceptions of the couple.
10. The couple is stuck in this painful place in their relationship because of shared, stereotyped, unrewarding behavior patterns.
11. Even though there is enough guilt and blame in the world, each partner feels compelled to blame the other and to try to make the other feel guilty, and furthermore wants the therapist to decide who is "worst" and to order the "worst" one to shape up. The therapist must constantly avoid speaking in terms of blame and degrees of blame and instead reframe behavior into positive, uplifting terms.
12. The therapist is viewed as the expert and therefore there is hope for the couple.
13. The therapist will attempt to:
    a. nurture that hope and transfer that hope, grounded in hard therapeutic work, into the couple's conjoint hands;
    b. assist both partners to clearly establish personal boundaries that will allow them conscious choices (1) to replace their unconscious merciless drives and (2) to separate needs from expectations;
    c. assist the couple in seeking relative conjoint power through competency rather than absolute power where they are only losers;
    d. aid the couple in developing respect for each other as they are, not how they think they should be;
    e. serve as a model for the couple;
    f. assist the couple in development of negotiation skills and strategies

The Initial Contact

The first contact the couple makes is with a secretary who does not make appointments, but takes the name and telephone number of the person who is calling and assures them the therapist will return the call at a convenient time specified by the caller. The therapist returns the call and asks the initial caller the following questions:

1. What is the nature of the marital difficulty?
2. What are the feelings of the caller concerning the marriage at this time?
3. What does the caller want to have done about the problem?

The therapist then makes a two-hour conjoint appointment for the couple (these two-hour sessions usually have at least one break).

The First Session

At the beginning of the first appointment, the therapist thanks the couple for coming to the appointment. Then the therapist says, "All I know about you is that spouse A called and asked for an appointment, and I asked him/her these questions . . ." (and repeats what was said to the therapist on the phone). The therapist then turns to spouse A and asks if that is what he or she said on the phone. If spouse A begins to add to what the therapist has said, the therapist is careful not to allow spouse A to talk for more than about two minutes.

Then the therapist says to spouse B, who is the non-calling spouse, "I have some idea why your spouse is here and how he (or she) feels about the marriage. Now could you please tell me why you are here and how you feel about the marriage?" The therapist goes on to ask this spouse all the questions that spouse A was asked on the phone. The therapist allows spouse B to talk for about five to seven minutes, then interrupts by saying, "This is very helpful, but I wonder if you could save more information until later in the interview." The rationale for this is that one spouse must never be allowed to feel that he or she is helpless in the session nor should one spouse dominate the session. This interruption also prevents the appearance of the therapist-spouse dyad.

As mentioned earlier, power/control has been an issue with this kind of couple and the leaving spouse behaves in the manner in which he or she thinks gives him or her the most power. The therapist takes the issue of power/control as defined—by who talks most frequently and longest—out of the hands of the couple and prevents it from becoming an issue in the sessions. The therapist must quickly establish clear boundaries as to who is therapist and to the fact that the marital relationship is the patient.

The therapist then says, "Thank you, this has given me some idea of the pain you are both feeling and where each of you is in your thinking. I now need more specific information. Could one of you please tell me how you met?"—and thus begins the marital history, with the therapist asking each spouse the same questions. Most couples are prepared to point out the problems at each stage of the relationship. The therapist asks specifically and repeatedly about the positive aspects of the relationship. At the end of the marital history, an individual history of each is obtained. Emphasis is placed on significant others in the early development of each spouse. The therapist expresses empathy concerning painful events. During the history taking, the therapist often checks with each spouse as to what he or she said and what the therapist has heard, thus modeling good communication.

Before the end of the first session the therapist explains the concept of marriage as a system and defines the specific characteristics of the marital system. Special emphasis is placed upon marital equilibrium and how the couple have arrived at their polarized positions. Empathic understanding is conveyed to the couple about both of their painful positions in the relationship. The therapist then says, "It is my desire that both of you grow and develop more fully in order that you can make an active, conscious decision about this relationship rather than an unconscious, reactive one. Therefore, I would suggest we formulate two contracts."

The therapist contracts with the couple for at least six sessions. The purpose of these six sessions is to look at both individuals— who they are and, to some extent, how and why they came to be the way they are. The therapist explains how this can be helpful to both spouses, no matter what they decide to do about this relationship. Then the therapist makes a second contract with the couple about the living arrangements during those six weeks. There are three options: the couple will live separately with the husband moving out or the wife moving out; the couple will live in the same house as husband and wife; or the couple will live in the same house as roommates with separate spaces and with no sexual relationship.

The purpose of the second contract is explained to the couple—that their psychic energy is to be used for each becoming more self-aware and not for struggling with each other. The therapist may have to be highly directive in establishing this contract. These two contracts are signed by all three parties. Then a second two-hour appointment is made within five days.

Between sessions one and two, the therapist forms a genogram for the couple and places each person in his or her individual growth and development life cycle.

The Second Session

The second conjoint appointment starts with the therapist asking both spouses if they have any questions about the first session or if they have anything to add to the histories that were given in that session. The therapist gives a quick review of the first session, concentrating on the contracts. The remainder of the session is round table, in which the therapist gives feedback with the aid of charts and drawings concerning normal stresses that are occurring because of where the couple is in the various life cycles. This is done very slowly, allowing ample time for questions and comments from both spouses. When this is finished, the therapist says, "You two are coping well with all these psychological events and stages." Humor such as "What makes you think you are any different from most other couples in these stages?" is often used.

The therapist then has a copy of the genogram for each partner. The therapist begins to "read" the genogram in terms of how both partners either "modeled after" or "reacted to" significant persons in their genogram. These persons are labeled "Ghosts of Christmas Past." The therapist gives an example. For instance, Melvin (the father of the male spouse) expressed love for his wife and children by giving his wife his weekly paycheck; now the son-spouse tries to show his love for his wife and children by giving them material things. Melvin would be a "Ghost of Christmas Past" who is directing the son-spouse's behavior in the present relationship.

The therapist discusses how to recognize "Ghosts of Christmas Past" and label them as such—for example, "There goes Melvin giving money to show love again." The therapist then introduces the concept that Melvin's son now has a choice of how he can express love to his wife and children and does not have to automatically repeat the pattern of his father. The therapist explains that for love to be effectively expressed, the behavior has to have some meaning of love to the person to whom it is being directed.

The therapist stresses that conscious choices concerning the relationship can only be made after each partner knows him/ herself (i.e., feelings, thoughts, dreams, expectations). The therapist says, "Each of you must sort out who you are, what you feel, what you think, what your needs are, and how you expect those needs to be fulfilled."

At the end of this session, the therapist asks each spouse to begin keeping a journal in which they write down what they have learned about themselves and their spouse in this session. This is homework assignment one.

The Third Session

The third session and all succeeding sessions last for one and a half hours and are begun with the therapist asking if either has feedback concerning the previous session or anything to add to the histories. Then the therapist asks each spouse what he or she learned about him/herself from the round table. After this, the therapist directly focuses the discussion on what each learned about his or her spouse. The same rule (as in the first session) of no one giving a long diatribe holds.

The therapist is attempting an emotional bridging by pointing out the spouses' similar feelings. The therapist emphasizes the sadness and deemphasizes the shame and anger. The sadness may help to foster further reaching out. This intervention is an attempt to get the spouses to perceive both themselves and each other differently. The therapist interjects humor at any time it seems appropriate. For example: "Why don't you turn your anger toward Melvin for teaching your spouse to express love via the giving of money, or toward God for allowing Melvin to be that way?"

The therapist leads into a discussion of how the entire range of human emotions is evoked by two people being together. Permission is being given by the therapist for each partner to feel his or her emotions. Particular emphasis is placed on anger. The therapist tells the couple that it is okay to be mad at the dead, sick, or perhaps at a higher force. Then the therapist talks about appropriate anger that arises in day-to-day living with someone and "gunny sack anger," which is actually felt toward others but gets dumped on the spouse.

The therapist assists each in discovering "who am I" in the here and now and what are past or future projections based on childhood memories, old hurts, and frustrations or dreams. The couple are shown how they each have interpreted the present in light of the past from their personal experience.

The therapist then focuses on the positive emotion of love. The homework given to the couple is that they each make a list of "What does love mean to me?", that is, "What can someone say or do that makes me feel loved?" The therapist may give an example, being careful to speak in simple behavior terms with a translation of how that behavior has taken on its emotional meaning. Thus the therapist is a model who analyzes an event in both behavioral and feeling terms. The therapist can pick one of many behaviors that he or she has "seen" in the genograms.

Only after both of the spouses have become aware of their needs and have effectively communicated them to their spouse can true negotiation begin in which each can give and take and arrive at a set of mutually reinforcing (meaning *loving*) behaviors.

The reader can easily see how the therapist is beginning to address intimacy issues.

The Fourth Session

The above work may run over into the fourth session. However, for the remaining sessions the treatment sequence is the same no matter how many sessions are held. Each session starts with the therapist inquiring about the couple's reaction to the previous session, any questions, and "How are things going with you?" If a long answer occurs, which gets back into old behavior, the therapist says, "How about your homework?" The therapist asks both to share their lists of "What does love mean to me?" The therapist gives feedback and checks out what each says and hears. No attempt is made to get the couple to agree on anything at this point. The therapist only teaches them how to listen to each other. The therapist begins to interpret by saying, "Do I hear you saying that you need x behavior from someone you are close to in order to feel loved?"

The therapist asks each to list five times or five events in the marriage when they have been very happy and felt very loved. This again is an attempt to switch the focus from what is wrong with the relationship to what has been and is good about it. Most couples have good feelings when they think of good times in the relationship when joy, happiness, warmth, and so on were felt.

Later Sessions

During the next session, the "good times lists" are processed. At this point the therapist begins to back out of the active role and encourages the couple to talk to each other.

At the end of the sixth session, the therapist says, "You can see we still have some unfinished business, so can we contract for more sessions?" Couples usually do make another contract.

If one or both spouses state that they feel the therapy is not helping them in deciding what to do about the present relationship, the therapist points out what they are learning and how future sessions will assist them in awareness of themselves as individuals and will aid in whatever relationship they have. Again, the reminder is made that conscious choices are much clearer and freer than unconscious ones.

The homework assignment for the sixth session is their "expectations" list—"What do I want in my marriage?" and "How do I want my spouse to behave in this marriage?"

During the sessions following the communication between the couple concerning their "expectations" lists, the therapist begins to introduce the concept of the "fit" between the expectations list and what they have learned about themselves and their spouse. By now most couples realize that there is some "fit" between the two, but that there are a lot of areas in which one spouse's expectations are not congruent with what the other spouse wants, needs, and/or can give. Then the therapist begins to discuss "intimacy language" and healthy selfishness. In healthy selfishness, a person constructively tends to his or her personal needs without ignoring or hurting others. This type of appropriate self-interest is in keeping with a wholesome sense-of-self and an indicator of satisfaction and happiness that allows for giving fully to others without a feeling of sacrifice or expecting something in return. This differs markedly from unhealthy selfishness, which involves a preoccupation with personal gratification, in a relentless search for pleasure with little regard for the feelings of others.

Homework for the seventh session is to ask the one who wishes to leave the relationship to imagine what it would be like to stay in the marriage for five more years and to ask the other spouse to imagine what it would be like if this marriage broke up.

In the eighth session, the therapist focuses on opposite perceptions, emphasizing what is not being seen, in order to challenge the fixated perceptions and to address the ambivalence of each spouse about his or her perceptions. The therapist comments on the ambivalence of each, thus facilitating the generation of disequilibrium within the behavior-cognitive system. This disequilibrium is necessary for the couple to evolve more satisfactory ways of relating. The therapist makes a conscious effort to gently begin disagreeing with the spouses' fixated misperceptions of one another. Once the ambivalence is exposed and acknowledged, the couple are free to work on a solution. They can discuss their mutual dissatisfaction with the boredom and monotony of their sex life, issues of control/power, and the levels of intimacy each seeks and can tolerate. These feelings can be owned and expressed by each spouse and will not be projected onto the other spouse.

Realizing that one's inescapable ambivalence is normal then leads to the capacity to resolve it and to make appropriate choices. Choice making is the height of human expression of our unique selfhood. To make appropriate choices gives us a feeling of success which leads to self-esteem.

Polarized positions can also be broken by the relabeling of events. For example, spouse A may repeatedly discuss her desire to leave the marriage. The therapist notes that she had stated this desire for five years without acting on it; therefore, she does not feel strongly enough to actually get out of the marriage. Paradoxical prescriptions can also be given at this time. For example, when the couple are raising their voices at each other, the therapist says, "I think you should yell a lot louder." Or when one spouse is portraying himself as helpless, weak, and powerless, the therapist may say, "Yes, you are as helpless as a speeding Mack truck."

Problem Solving and Negotiation

The focus of the marital therapy then becomes problem solving or negotiation training. The therapist asks the couple to bring a problem to the session which they have defined in behavioral terms.

1. The couple have jointly limited the problem to a mutually defined issue.
2. Each has become aware of his/her respective thoughts and feelings about the issue.
3. Each has searched for the roots of his/her own feelings in his/her family origin, life cycle phases, and intimacy language.

4. Each has checked for boundary and power/control issues in these feelings.
5. Each has listed realistic expectations for him/herself and his/her spouse concerning the problem.
6. Each has listed needs-of-satisfaction behaviors that each desires.
7. Each has listed what need satisfactions each is willing to give to the spouse.

During the session the therapist goes over the above and if necessary assists the couple in successfully accomplishing these seven steps. After this is completed, the therapist introduces the art of compromise, the use of which will allow partners to learn to modify their positions to the extent that they accommodate the needs of their spouses as well as themselves.

After the alternatives have been considered and a solution has been chosen, mutually agreed to by both parties, and written down, the homework assignment is given to enact it. Each is asked to record the enactment in clear, concise behavioral terms.

In the next session the therapist asks each to evaluate the outcome by answering such questions as:

1. Were the results satisfactory to you?
2. If not, can you propose changes in the enactment?
3. Can we now agree to use this solution when this problem arises in the future?

The therapist then points out to the couple that the skills learned in the homework assignment and in this session can be applied to any problem. If the therapist feels the couple needs more practice in this problem solving, the exercise can be repeated with another problem.

The next homework assignment is that the couple is to problem solve the original polarizing issue that brought them to therapy: Do we maintain or terminate this marriage? The previously mentioned seven steps are to be followed in this exercise.

The homework is processed in the last session. The therapist accepts whatever solution the couple negotiates, and states the solution in positive terms. The therapist then points out that he or she, as the therapist, has simply been a map reader of the family patterns of each spouse and of the marriage; an educator about normal stresses of marriage and family life; a coach who has given some examples of strategies that tend to get people what they want in relationships, and who, once the couple got the "play," only yelled encouragement and a suggestion or two from the sideline. Now the couple know all that the coach knows and can negotiate the relationship without a coach, but if they ever need the coach again, he or she is there at the other end of the phone.

CONCLUSION

There may be couples for whom the emotional pain and turmoil have been so severe that all efforts fail to achieve the hoped-for recapture of a satisfying and rewarding relationship. This usually occurs when each spouse is so angry and locked into his or her own beliefs that neither one can accept any new information from the other. In such cases, one or both partners experience continued emotional impairment serious enough to be unable to function. These spouses typically hold each other solely responsible for the ruptured ties and have stopped considering their own contribution to the conflict. They have come to regard the marriage as terminal and therefore no longer attempt to mend broken bonds. Such couples may require support and counseling with a view to ending their mutually destructive relationship.

At the end of the therapy work the therapist always thanks the couple for allowing her or him to share in their lives. The therapist explains that they all have become a permanent part of each other's life journey.

11

When One Wants Out and the Other Doesn't: Assessment and Treatment

Michael J. Sporakowski

When Dr. Crosby and I first discussed this therapy topic, I had a flashback to one of my earliest marital counseling cases as a graduate student at Florida State University. I vividly recalled the case for two reasons. One reason was that the male partner was afflicted with a very disfiguring disease. And second, the case was one in which both my supervisor and I experienced a great deal of frustration because it seemed to be going nowhere at all for about six weeks, even though both partners expressed a sincere interest in having the marriage "get better." The breakthrough in this case, and its relevance for this chapter, came in an individual session with the wife in which she revealed her hidden agenda. She could not face living with her husband's illness anymore and was coming to therapy to help build a divorce case in which she could claim that she had tried therapy but even that could not save the marriage. Several weeks later I received a subpoena to appear in court. She was doubtless counting on my testimony in her behalf.

In one sense there seems to me to be at least some element of the "one wanting out while one doesn't" syndrome in most, if not all, marital cases. Sometimes it is more blatant than others. Often this is exhibited when one partner either refuses to be part of therapy or is very resistant to being seen on more than a one-time or perhaps occasional basis. At another level both partners show up for the sessions, but often the participation of one or both reflects a covert, subtle, or unconscious acknowledgment that the relationship is dying, if not already dead. Bohannon (1970) referred to this aspect of the divorcing process as the emotional divorce, one of six "stations" in the passion play leading to the dissolution of the marital bond.

SOME "ONE WANTS OUT . . ." TYPES

Let's take a look for a moment at some of the kinds of "one wants out . . ." relationships you are likely to see in treatment, then move into some issues of assessment and diagnosis, and finally examine some possible strategies for dealing with this challenge in therapy. First, the varieties.

For me, one of the more typical cases, in both my personal experience and in the treatment I have supervised, is one in which one partner is threatening to leave—via moving out, finding a lover, or actually initiating the legal divorce process. Perhaps the label *The Attention Getters* best typifies this situation. Often there have been years of attempts at communication of wants and needs, but at least one of the individuals feels very unfulfilled. There have probably been "couple's nights out," weekly "marital conferences" at home, fighting, nagging, withdrawal of attention, and maybe even "Why don't you read this book?" or "Let's go to the 'Making Your Marriage Better' lecture" suggestion. Sometimes these efforts work—at least for a while. But usually such efforts end in even greater frustration and significant additions to the couple's marital problems gunny sack.

When things get out of hand and are no longer tolerable, one partner resorts to the "final," drastic measure of leaving, finding someone else, and/or filing for divorce. This marriage has progressed from what Lederer and Jackson (1968) labeled the Stable-Unsatisfactory Marriage to one that has now become Unstable and Unsatisfactory. Not only has the exchange of relationship information become less and less, but also the members of the couple have progressed (or is it regressed?) down the marital lane from "The Spare Time Battlers" to "The Weary Wranglers" to "The Gruesome Twosome," all gems you have read or can read about in the *Mirages of Marriage* (Lederer & Jackson, 1968).

A second type of "one wants out . . ." marriage that is frequently seen in marital therapy is one that parallels Cuber and Harroff's (1966) "The Devitalized." I prefer to refer to this one as The Lazys. This couple, often middle-aged, has lost the enthusiasm and vitality of earlier years—if such really did exist before—and might best be described as complacent. One, or possibly both, may want out of the marriage, but the current situation is more comfortable and secure than uncomfortable. It certainly does not warrant the effort and risk a divorce might require. Often the "wants out" partner achieves some sort of personal, intrapsychic martyrdom, perhaps not shared with others at all. The process of dissolution is stymied by a logjam of complacency.

Situation three is The Game Players. They have been described in both *The Dance-Away Lover* (Goldstine, Larner, Zuckerman, & Goldstine, 1977)—"The Tough-Fragile/The Prizewinner"—and *The Mirages of Marriage* (Lederer & Jackson, 1968)—"The Gruesome Twosome," for example. They might be described by the phrase "you and me against the world," or, at another level, "the role-reversers magnificent." From session to session, the therapist may not be sure who is the one wanting out and who wants to keep the relationship together, if anyone. The therapist may be confronted from time to time with joint statements such as, "What do you mean, one of us wants out of the relationship?"

Triangulation may indeed be a very great risk here. This type also reminds me of the old Abbott and Costello routine of "Who's on first?" They often leave the therapist, at least temporarily, out in left field.

A fourth couple type might be labeled The Emotional Divorcé(e)s. These couples have been splitting up for quite some time. The commitment level of one member is usually much less than that of the other, but both members recognize the futility of the ongoing relationship. Both members can probably give a date when they recognized that the marriage was coming to an end. The spouses do not necessarily agree on the date, the event associated with it, or the details surrounding the event—but they are able to say when. In a day and age of "living-together arrangements," this couple adds still another meaning for the term. The emotional divorce may have been going on since before the marriage date, or it may have been of relatively recent advent. Whatever the case may be, the emotional distancing is obvious even though the individuals remain together. Words and phrases like "withdrawn," "self-centered," "living parallel lives," and "dull and boring" often describe the individuals and/or the relationship.

The final couple type I include in the "one wants out . . ." relationship schema are *The Realists.* The degree of realism may vary between the partners; in fact it most often does to a significant level. Usually the parting process is traceable to an event—frequently an accident, illness, or crisis—which causes exaggerated strain on both members as well as on the relationship. I saw a number of such cases when I worked in a rehabilitation setting and dealt with spouses and families, as well as individuals, attempting to cope with the effects of traumatic spinal injury. The chances of couples remaining married for more than a year after being afflicted by paraplegia or quadraplegia were small. Few spouses were able to cope with the many sources of strain. Many couples decided it would be best to split simply because of an individual couple member's inability and/or unwillingness to cope with the situation. Nevertheless, the situation often became one in which the labels "betrayer" and "betrayed" were used. Perhaps the Vietnam era popular song *Ruby* gave some hint of the dynamics experienced in this type of relationship. In the song it is apparent that the male has been disabled and that the female is needing some attention from someone other than her husband, even though she has attempted to be "a good wife." The refrain pleadingly asks over and over again, "Don't take your love to town."

ASSESSMENT

So much for types! Undoubtedly there are others. Perhaps your list is even longer than mine. But what about identifying the clients we might see as "one wants out . . ." types? How and why do we do the identifying? The answer to the latter is so we can make some hypotheses and come up with some treatment plans; this is dealt with in more depth later on in this chapter. How we do the assessment depends in some measure on our own theoretical perspectives.

As I look back at my training and try to categorize my current approach, I keep thinking of Jay Haley's classic article, "Whither family therapy?" (1962), and find myself in a school of therapy not unlike some of his—"The chuck-it-and-run school," "The stonewall school," "The great mother school"—which I might name "the fly-by-the-seat-of-your-pants" approach. (Note: before you stop reading because of that statement, please give some thought to the idea that therapists who have been in the field awhile are more similar in approach, no matter what their professional backgrounds, than are the newly trained with specific identities to defend. Also, please keep in mind that the experienced therapist may be more likely to draw from a variety of approaches and techniques to best fit the treatment to the problem.) My approach includes elements of psychoanalysis, social learning theory, and behaviorism mixed in with systems thinking. Eclectic is the more usual label given to this approach. It is a blending of perspectives on human development and interaction that values individuals and their relationships, and it is optimistic about helping those individuals attain the realistic goals they have for their relationships. Within such a framework, assessment can take on many forms.

Sometimes I rely on clinical intuition and experience to accomplish the screening. Other times I am inclined to use a paper-and-pencil test or some computerized version of the same in the assessment process. Yet other times I go through a standardized, semistructured interview format with a formal, diagnostic statement as its end product. On other occasions, observation in the home or in a simulated problem-solving situation might be the tactic used to gather the information deemed necessary. Then, too, a combination of these efforts may well be "just what the doctor ordered."

From my point of view, the first assessment task at hand is attempting to decide whether or not a case exists: Is it something I think I can handle? Is it something I want to try and handle? Then, if there seems to be some evidence that a case exists for me to work with, I attempt to answer the question, "What is or who are the client(s)?" Most typically, the initial assessment phase of potential marital therapy covers two sessions. During the first, I spend an hour interacting with the couple members jointly, attempting to answer those questions. A second interview is then scheduled which is structured in such a way that I spend 15–20 minutes with each of spouses separately, and then conclude with a joint session.

If, during the first session, I feel that the couple could benefit from my intervention, I might request that the couple members take some paper-and-pencil tests. My purpose in so doing in the "when one wants out . . ." situation is to look for couple discrepancies that might show up using a "crisscross" technique. In this approach I ask each spouse to fill out the instrument(s) for herself or himself, and then to fill it (them) out as he or she thinks the other spouse would. Some examples of instruments to use are the Dyadic Adjustment Scale (Spanier, 1976), the Taylor-Johnson Temperament Analysis (Taylor & Morrison, 1984), the Family Inventory of Life Events (McCubbin, Patterson, & Wilson, 1981), or the Interpersonal Checklist (LaForge & Suczek, 1955). I have the couple do this task before seeing them for the second interview. This gives me time to score and interpret the materials and integrate those results with my observations from the first session. At the second session I give the spouses feedback on the results and ask them, as individuals, to give me their interpretation of the results.

I look for both similarities and differences in the "test" results and use them to help round out my initial impressions. Large discrepancies between spousal impressions, especially if unique to just one member of the couple, *may* be indicative of significant motivation differences for therapy and significant differences in the commitment to the marriage. Sometimes the data show very obvious discrepancies. For example, on the Dyadic Adjustment Scale, if Mrs. Jones indicates that she is very dissatisfied with the relationship yet rates her husband as above average in adjustment, and Mr. Jones rates both of them as being above average, the discrepancy may be a fruitful point of discussion in both the individual and couple sessions.

If other testing data are available (Taylor-Johnson results, for example), the similarities and differences in perceptions of personality attributes may assist the therapist and the couple in seeing and understanding differences not acknowledged in the couple members' day-to-day functioning. This *may* be of assistance to the therapist in recognizing couple member discrepancies not readily seen in treatment at this early stage of the process, including those related to commitment to the marriage and the therapeutic endeavor.

Friedman (1982) has commented on a similar, yet less empirically formulated, procedure. Couple members are asked to individually, on a scale from 1–10, rate six aspects of their feelings for one another. Discrepancies between the spouse's rating and self-rating are seen as communication problems in the specific areas. Low scores for one member combined with significant discrepancy scores between members may prove diagnostic of unresolvable marital problems.

If the results of the initial sessions indicate significant differences in motivation to stay in the marriage, as well as in motivation to pursue therapy, I confront the situation head on, asking the couple to come to a decision as to whether or not treatment should be pursued. Options might include: individual marital sessions; referral for legal consultation related to separation and divorce procedures; or individual sessions related to the dissolution process.

In another scenario, the couple might not return for subsequent sessions since their differences may have painfully surfaced in this initial assessment. The interview situations may have provided sufficient permission for the couple members to acknowledge their problems and pursue resolution of the situation through processes other than therapy.

The assessment process at this stage of therapy is aimed at establishing whether or not a case can be made for therapy, whatever format or formats the procedure might take. If, after discussing the results of the process with couple members, both they and I feel that a continuation of therapy is appropriate, the assessment techniques used are likely to be helpful in pinpointing specific sets of values, communication issues, content problems, and behaviors that might warrant therapeutic attention, including the gulf between them created by the "when one wants out . . ." situation.

TREATMENT

"Can this marriage be saved?" "Does the marriage have persons involved who are sufficiently motivated to work at therapy?" "Why do these people persist in staying together?" These are just a few of the questions the "when one wants out . . ." marriage will raise for the therapist, the clients, and those persons living in close proximity to the marriage, including family members and friends.

If the couple members find themselves in a truly dissolving marital situation that is distinctly one-sided (*The Realists*, for example), it may be that the result of the treatment will be a divorce. Since I do not see "marriage saving" for the sake of saving as a primary goal of treatment, helping the members work through the grieving process and become more adequately functioning individuals is a considerable part of what the treatment focuses upon. Therapy is oriented toward current reality and the future. "What is this going to mean to both of you,

the kids, the extended family, work relationships?" are questions
to which answers may provide the foundation for some information giving and/or an intensive, individual therapeutic series.
The therapist may become a mediator—literally and/or figur-
atively—actively seeking to help the members work through
their emotional pain and cope with the exigencies of a new,
separated status. Successful early diagnosis should facilitate this
situation.

Divorce counseling (coming to grips with the decision to divorce or not), divorce mediation (working through the details
in as objective a manner as is possible), and divorce therapy
(treatment of the individual(s) and the broken relationship after
the breakup has been initiated) are all part of the process in
dissolving marital situations that are distinctly one-sided. It is
likely that more than one "counselor"—including the primary
therapist, an attorney or attorneys, and a mediator—will be
involved. Thus it is essential that solid communication and cooperation be promoted—ironically so, because productive communication and cooperation may not have been likely if the
marriage had continued "as is."

But what about the couples who do not want to split up or
who are so bogged down by inertia that they do not in general
perform well at home, work, school, or anywhere? How do you
take the "one wants out . . ." situation and turn it into a
relatively positive outcome? Here I am thinking of *The Attention
Getters* and *The Lazys*. With these couples, motivation to work
on the relationship and motivation to seek and be involved in
treatment are likely to be the major tasks to be dealt with.
Frequently, it is the male in these couples who wants out. He
usually does not see the need for treatment at all, at least he
says this when his wife is present. Privately he may know that
much is wrong with the marriage but part of his game is to
deny this to his wife. If he does recognize a problem that deserves
intervention, he will identify it as his wife's—and once again
deny the need for his involvement in the counseling process.

Guillebeaux, Storm, and Demaris (1986) discussed the male
involvement process in an article entitled "Luring the Reluctant
Male." They found that threat of divorce by the wife, the male's

observing therapy, and men having nontraditional sex-role orientations were factors positively predictive of men becoming involved in the treatment process. The first two factors have significance for my treatment objectives in short- to moderate-term interventions.

A serious "I'm going to the lawyer's to file for a divorce" on the part of the wife *may* serve as more than just an attention-getting device. If the action is actually undertaken and evidence of it pierces the husband's emotional armor, behavior change may be initiated. This change may be sufficient for the husband to now be able to see the need for counseling in which he would be viewed as part of the problem as well as part of the solution. Once involved, he is more likely to participate in the process in a way that should help all involved to better define what needs to be worked on and how much each member of the couple is willing to invest in terms of time and effort.

An option that may help the reluctant male who has experienced the above situation, but has not come to view the condition as one for which he has any responsibility, could be involvement via observation of the therapy process of others. It is important that he observe situations where other men are participants in therapy. This observation might take on the task of viewing videotapes, sitting on the "other side" of the one-way mirror, or, perhaps, watching a couples group in process. It is vital for him to have the opportunity for feedback on the viewed process as it is ongoing or immediately after it has occurred. This feedback preferably comes from the individual with whom he might be undertaking treatment. An additional form of "observation" might come from direct contact with a male, or perhaps several males, who are currently involved in couples treatment, and who would be willing to share their experiences with him under guidelines set by the prospective therapist.

In either situation, I consider an individual, "transition-to-couples-treatment" session to be essential for the husband's potential involvement. It is also important that as the husband is undergoing this modification in his behavior, the wife is guided or coached in ways of encouraging her husband's commitment to the process, yet not overwhelming him or scaring him off.

And it is vital to help the wife work through issues related to having a positively participating spouse both in therapy and at home. The latter situation has therapeutic significance in that it is aimed at minimizing a return to old patterns of behavior. Helping the clients achieve small, observable, positive relationship changes is a key in this treatment sequence.

In the wife's focus in treatment, attention is paid to behaviors that will increase her self-esteem—perhaps taking some classes "she has always wanted to," for example—and activities that will reduce her identification with the second part of the "when one wants out and the other doesn't" label. She might be asked to keep track of the situations in which the couple finds itself in "the old routine," and record both members' behaviors. After a week of this recording, the therapist can discuss with her the reactions she has to both spouses' behaviors. Then the therapist asks her to come up with alternate possible responses and to make use of them, first in a therapeutic role play and then, the following week, at home. The subsequent treatment session with her focuses on an evaluation of the week's interactions and modification of responses, if necessary, to maximize future interactions.

Although both sets of interventions above might be viewed as linear, I see them as systemic in that they are helping to prepare the way for more couple-focused activities. Later sessions are joint and involve attention to the communication and cooperation aspects of the relationship. Reinforcement of positive experiences in the treatment sessions and at home are facilitated by assignments tracking specific behaviors between treatment sessions. Assuming the motivation issue has been resolved and both partners are now willing to work at therapy, issues of joint goals and objectives for the relationship are addressed, and means of achieving them are developed.

Treatment of *The Emotional Divorcé(e)s* may be less therapy than giving of permission to coexist and specific suggestions of how that coexistence might be made more tolerable. Since it is unlikely that these couples will legally divorce, the most likely direction of treatment is one that attempts to make the ongoing relationship livable as well as tolerable for both members. Many of these couples do not seek help for the relationship. They just "grin and bear it." With some of these couples, individuals seek treatment for personal or health-related difficulties. Partner-absent marital therapy may become an option, not so much because the partner is unwilling, but because the partner seeking treatment does not see this as a systemic issue. Also, he or she may not want the partner involved for fear of upsetting a balance that has existed for years—and it is thus less threatening to that individual and the relationship to leave it alone rather than risk change of any kind. This resignation may well be based in a reality that says, "Things aren't great this way, but they're tolerable. My material needs are taken care of quite well. And besides, getting out of the relationship may be both painful and risky—risky in the sense that I don't want to be alone, and a new relationship may be more problematical than it might be worth." For some the dialogue might even continue, "And maybe there's no one else out there who would have me as a partner."

Most often, the treatment method with persons in this type of relationship is one-on-one, individually focused counseling. Working through the meaning of the individual's acceptance of the situation and means of "making the best of it" are central issues. Insight into the problems may be of help. An understanding of the situation's meaning both currently and in the future is likely to be of value. Behavioral change, if any, is aimed at self-esteem issues without emphasizing marital restructuring. Although this may not appear to be marital treatment, it probably comes close to meeting the age-old counseling directive of "helping the client to help himself"—in this case the client being an individual, not a marriage, at least at the obvious level.

Treatment of *The Game Players* may well be the most frustrating of the "when one wants out . . ." couple types. These spouses may join together briefly to show therapists how incompetent the therapists are, and how skillful the clients are in their interpersonal manipulations. These are the individuals who come closest to making me want to require MMPI testing of all prospective clients. Generally, they score above T = 70 on scale 4 of the MMPI, indicating a great chance of psychopathy or sociopathy. They make great fools of persons "in authority" with their manipulative behavior. They are also clients who may go on forever in treatment, never quite resolving what it is (whatever that may be) that they came into treatment for. These individuals also delight in switching roles frequently, with great fluidity, in such a way that many therapists would have difficulty trying to diagnose let alone treat them. In the "when one wants out . . ." situation, it may be very difficult to detect which one it is, or if it is both or neither. More traditional approaches tend not to have much success with these individuals. These couples may even be quite effective in helping therapists down the path to seeking therapy.

The Game Players will often move out of treatment as quickly as they sought it out. They may seek help as a condition of some other problem: a judge or other law officer requires or suggests treatment as a condition of some other action; a financial counselor refers them for marital help in addition to his efforts to keep them out of bankruptcy; or a school counselor decides that one of their children's problems could be alleviated if the couple's marriage was functioning better. Sometimes, their involvement in marital treatment is simply to satisfy requirements set upon them by some other agent or agency. If the therapist is unaware of this, an assumption of positive motivation may be made, when in reality they are only looking for a "doctor's excuse" or a "note from Mom."

Although I have seen relatively few persons seeking marital help who fall into this category, I can personally attest to the fact that I have found working with them very frustrating. Early, accurate diagnosis of this type is a must if the therapist is to function in a reasonable manner. Perhaps some of the so-called "unconventional therapies" may have a measure of success with these people. Fortunately, they tend not to continue in treatment for long periods of time. Frequently their other problems—legal, financial, or school—may be more significant and require most of their energies. Then, too, they may move on to other therapists or locations. As is evident, my assessment of my success with *The Game Players* is low.

Confronting this couple type with an accurate diagnosis may lead to termination. Referral for in-depth or intensive treatment may be appropriate. Whatever the nature of the therapist's intervention, chances are it will not be seen as successful by either the therapist or the clients.

CONCLUSION

Polarized couples, where one wants out of the marriage and the other doesn't, come in many varieties. Diagnosis and treatment are necessarily unique to the individual couples and couple members as they may present themselves and their problems for treatment. The assessment process is especially important with this group because some of the types presented may well not be appropriate, or legitimate, candidates for marital therapy. Decisions about appropriateness of therapy, made with some of the ideas presented above in mind, will help clients and therapists save both time and effort in the treatment of couples and individuals with this presenting complaint. As with most other presenting problems, it is essential that the therapist establish the following: whether or not a case exists that he or she is willing and able to treat; who or what is the client; and what methods of treatment are likely to produce positive results. Treatment based on this assessment process increases the likelihood of productive outcomes.

Although some of the "when one wants out . . ." couple types may seem to offer little in the way of optimism for positive marital outcomes, others provide a brighter picture. Tailoring therapist personality, style, methods, and skills to client problems is the overall task on the road to helping such couples to be better able to help themselves.

REFERENCES

Bohannon, P. (1970). The six stations of divorce. In P. Bohannon (Ed.), *Divorce and after* (pp. 29–55). Garden City, NY: Doubleday.

Cuber, J. F., & Harroff, P. B. (1966). *Sex and the significant Americans.* Baltimore: Penguin Books.

Friedman, L. J. (1982). A simple marital assessment test. In A. Gurman (Ed.), *Questions and answers in the practice of family therapy, Vol. 2* (pp. 35–37). New York: Brunner/Mazel.

Goldstine, D., Larner, K., Zuckerman, S., & Goldstine, H. (1977). *The dance-away lover.* New York: Ballantine Books.

Guillebeaux, F., Storm, C. L., & Demaris, A. (1986). Luring the reluctant male: A study of males participating in marriage and family therapy. *Family Therapy, 13,* 214–225.

Haley, J. (1962). Whither family therapy? *Family Process, 1,* 69–100.

LaForge, R., & Suczek, R. (1955). An Interpersonal Checklist. *Journal of Personality, 24*(1), 94–112.

Lederer, W. J., & Jackson, D. D. (1968). *The mirages of marriage.* New York: W. W. Norton.

McCubbin, H. I., Patterson, J. M., & Wilson, L. R. (1981). Family Inventory of Life Events. In H. I. McCubbin & J. M. Patterson (Eds.), *Systematic assessment of family stress, resources and coping* (pp. 21–39). St. Paul, MN: Family Social Science, University of Minnesota.

Spanier, G. B. (1976). Measuring dyadic adjustment: New scales for assessing the quality of marriage and similar dyads. *Journal of Marriage and the Family, 38,* 15–38.

Taylor, R. M., & Morrison, L. P. (1984). *Taylor-Johnson temperament analysis manual: 1984 revision.* Los Angeles: Psychological Publications.

12

I Don't Love You Anymore (or At Least I Don't Think I Do)

Eleanor D. Macklin

Just now I went to my files and pulled out 15 completed cases in which at the first session one of the partners had said she or he wanted a divorce and the other had hoped there would be a change of mind. I was curious to see if I could figure out what determined the outcome.

When I can help people to postpone their decision regarding the divorce and agree to work in therapy for a while, it's my favorite kind of case—a real challenge. It's as though I've been called into surgery, and it's life or death, and only my skill and the patient's willpower can pull us through. Sometimes it's clear that the time has come to let the marriage die, and the kindest thing I can do, after a quick check of the vital signs, is to let death come as peacefully as possible.

Sometimes all that's needed is temporary life support—rest, some nutrition, and a lot of TLC—and the system will rally of its own accord. But often we're going to have to scrub down for a major operation, with a lot of painful incision and scraping and cleansing and suturing and a slow, carefully monitored recovery.

Which of the above is called for seems to depend upon how healthy the body was to begin with and how much damage has already been done. I think I tell this by listening to the heart. It is a rather intuitive process. The best way to tell about it is to describe some cases.

WHEN A "QUICK DEATH" IS THE KINDEST ANSWER

Three of the 15 cases fall in this category. Maybe more did and I didn't have the wisdom to see that and so prolonged life longer than was humane. But, when life is at risk, I know I tend to err on the side of life. Our emotional well-being seems so connected to the well-being of our intimate relationships that when family relationships are severed, this can take a heavy toll. So the decision to divorce seems a weighty one, to be made only after careful deliberation and hopefully in such a way as to preserve at least the broader family ties.

Perhaps it will be helpful for the reader to know that it took me 12 years to finalize a divorce from my own husband, to whom I had been married for 20 years. These were 12 years of evolution, of sifting and sorting and understanding and rising above and finishing and continuing and separating and building and redefining. I'm glad we took this long. It is a long story and I mention it only to illustrate my proclivities and perhaps explain why there are only three cases in the "quick death" category.

The cases are essentially all the same. The husband (or wife) calls to tell me that his wife has said she's leaving and he can't stop her. He had known there were perhaps some problems but hadn't thought they were this bad. He is relieved that she has agreed to come in for this one session and hopes that maybe I can change her mind. (It could as easily have been the case that she called and asked me to see them so that I could convince her husband she was serious about leaving.)

I see the couple in my usual format for such "heavy-duty" cases: an hour with her, an hour with him, and an hour with them together, letting the intensity of the session match the urgency of what we are about. The hour with her is to establish some rapport (since she was not the one who called), to determine how serious she is about leaving, to see what hope there may be for reconciliation now or later, to ask questions about her family of origin and relationship history that may give her some insight into her own patterns, and to identify any areas where I may be of help to her. At the end of the hour, I leave her in another room to sit quietly and reflect on our session, and to determine what she wishes to say to him or ask of him when we later have our joint session.

The content of my hour with him depends largely on how things went with her. If she has seemed adamant and there appears to be no wisdom in trying to resuscitate or sustain the relationship, I will try indirectly to prepare him for the hard message she later will deliver to him. Always I seek to help him ventilate his own feelings, identify his needs and concerns, reflect on his own relationship history, and find the strength to deal constructively with the evolving situation.

When it is time to see them together, I have them sit in chairs facing each other to emphasize the fact that they need to talk to one another. I sit close by, between them and to one side, for comfort and for control. I usually begin by asking the wife to share with her husband some of what we talked about, focusing on the ideas or points that were most meaningful to her. I exert a lot of subtle direction at this point: I do not allow debate, I help things to get stated as "I" messages rather than "you" messages, I focus on ensuring that each person hears accurately what the other has to say, and I reframe the messages as constructively as possible (e.g., when she talks about her anger, I help her talk about her pain). I interject frequently with my own restatements of what I hear her saying, and may remind her of important points that I think need to be made.

After she has spoken (maybe 10–15 minutes), and I have reframed and paraphrased, I ask him to summarize what he has heard her say and, in turn, to share with her the essence of what he and I discussed. After each has been heard, I ask if there are any questions that they wish to ask of each other. If either becomes too emotional to continue talking constructively, I seek to empathize as powerfully as possible and allow time for the tears or anger. If this expression of emotion appears to be new and I sense that the listening spouse is surprised, touched, or even possibly thawed by its presence, we stop and process the reaction and may even change course. Normally, however, the feelings have been heard many times, there is little to be gained from further ventilation in this session, and the grief work will have to be done later in individual therapy.

When there is little likelihood that the leaving spouse will agree to return for another session, and, hence, any couple work which is to be done must be done in this session, I try to stick as much as possible to the task of articulating the issues and helping them determine their future direction. The emphasis is on blocking patterns of blaming, beginning a process of taking responsibility for one's role in the marital failure, exploring how one's own expectations and behaviors may interfere with relationship success, and understanding how things look from the perspective of the other. Hopefully, if each feels heard rather than argued with, discounted, or blamed, there is a chance that at a later point they may elect to come again. At least they may have experienced a way of being together that will allow them to risk dialoguing in the future.

The following case demonstrates how the above works in more detail. On the phone, I had learned from the husband a lot of the specifics. (I prefer a rather detailed phone intake—15–20 minutes—for it allows me to make better decisions about whom to see when, what to be prepared for, and how best to operate. Time is short and precious when they come, the crisis is intense, and I want to make the best possible judgments about how to proceed and what needs to be discussed.) In this case, the husband had been married for 12 years to his present wife who was 10 years his junior; he had three adult daughters from a previous marriage; and he had left his first wife during an affair with the present wife. Two weeks ago he had learned from his current wife that she was having an affair with a man 10 years younger than she, and last week she had moved out to be with him. (Twelve of the 15 cases had had therapy precipitated by the disclosure of an affair.) He was dramatic about his pain: "She's ripped out my heart. Every day another piece of me is gone. I hurt so much I have to know if she sees any possibility of our making it again." He had already been to a counselor, who told him to wait and give it a little time, but he couldn't stand the uncertainty.

I didn't have a lot of hope. She sounded so definite, and he so desperate and full of self-pity. Their marriage had had a lot of strikes against it from the start—an affair, a stepfamily, teenage stepdaughters, and the new wife only eight years older than the eldest daughter. I wondered about her reasons for having become involved with him, what it had been like to be married to him, why they had had no children of their own, her attraction to the new relationship, the significance of the repeated age differences, his relationship to his daughters. I sensed that the most I could perhaps do was help them gain some insight into past patterns so that these might not be repeated in future relationships. It was definitely a plus that she was willing to commit to a joint session. She obviously wanted some resolution also.

She was reserved and hostile when she arrived, but as we talked she relaxed, apparently relieved to have someone to listen to her. I asked her to tell me about her relationship with her husband, to go back in time and begin with how she met him. (I would listen to see if she had ever loved him, what had attracted her to him, what expectations she had had of the relationship.) The answers came clearly; the issues were evident from her first words. "I never really wanted to be married. I never loved him. He was the first man I ever dated," she said. "I was 21 and had finally managed to leave home. He was married. It felt safe. I hadn't wanted a serious relationship, but it got out of hand. We had a two-year affair. It wore me out— no fun. Suddenly one day he appeared on my doorstep with his things and moved in without my asking. His wife had kicked him out. I felt so guilty, I had to take him in. Then soon after we were married, his two oldest daughters got thrown out by their mother and also moved in. I felt totally out of control."

"And your own parents?" I asked. "Tell me about them." The themes of guilt and codependency and suffocation began to build as she talked: "My dad was an alcoholic. My mom left when I was very young, and I became the built-in babysitter for my little sister. I have had to care for others all my life. I am so tired of apologizing for what I want to do for me. I don't ever want to be married again. Children are hard for me. They tie you down. *(a pause)* I am in my second affair."

"Tell me about your second affair," I suggested. She answered quickly, "He's independent. Not like my husband who puts people on pedestals and then relies on them, who was out of work for a whole year. I lost all respect for him. He became repulsive to me. I didn't even like to kiss him." (She needed to talk more about her husband than about her affair. I let her.) "We're so different. He's not interested in bettering himself or his home. Just like his dad who got on disability and then just sat and waited to die. I'm working to have a good job, to make something of myself. I've always felt like a paycheck to him. I deserve my money's worth in return." "Your money's worth?" I asked, curious as to what a good return on her investment might be. She clarified, "Someone who's interested in me and what I do and not just in my income. My husband doesn't want to take responsibility for anyone."

"Like your dad?" I asked. "I gave up on my dad when I was 21," she replied. "I'd had enough. I finally said, 'We're done.' My stepmother called recently and told me I'm a bad daughter but I don't care. At least my husband doesn't drink. He's more like my mother—just interested in herself—I can't respect either of them." "It must hurt not to have ever found anyone you can depend on," I said. She denied any hurt: "I don't care. I used to be angry at my parents, but I just don't care anymore. When I left my husband it felt like such a weight off my shoulders. I can still feel the relief as I drove down the road. He says he'll change, that he'll do it for me, but he has to do it for himself. I just want him to leave me alone—no phone calls, sell the house, move on. I'm so scared I'll be dragged back in. I'm so susceptible to guilt. If I came back it would be because I gave in and I would hate him for it."

I empathized with her—with how hard it had been, with how it felt to once again be on the brink of freedom. She cried. They felt like tears of relief rather than sadness. I imagined myself in the role of the "good mother," the mother she never had, to whom she could unburden herself, who understood and was strong enough to help her do what she needed to do for herself. (I like being "the good mother.") We talked about what it felt like to cry and what she wanted to tell her husband. I told her that I would try to help him hear her. As I walked her to the waiting room, I felt that the kindest thing I could do for this woman was to help her break free.

Her husband took her chair. "How are you feeling?" I asked. He was amazingly articulate. Scared and angry was the theme. Very scared and very angry. (I needed to hear a lot more about this. Scared of what? What did he do when he was angry? I explored these issues as he talked.) He told me about his first marriage: His parents fought all the time and were constantly splitting up. He got married at 17 and vowed never to fight, but was married for 15 years and fought all the time. "Fifteen years of hell—she got pregnant right away—I never wanted kids—she complained that I wouldn't fight with her, that I withdrew when I got upset. I'm scared of being alone, but I don't ever want to be hurt again. I grew up to be a 'tough soldier'—don't even know if I can love."

"And your second marriage? What was that like?", I asked. "She was everything to me. It meant a lot to me that she was a virgin when I met her. I was determined we would never fight about anything. I would just stay out of the way. It probably would have been better if I'd been more verbal, showed more emotion. I didn't want to hear about it when she was unhappy. I don't have a lot of self-esteem. They eliminated my job at the print shop and I was out of work for a year and to get another job I'd have had to take a drop in pay. I enjoyed being out of work, like on sabbatical. Besides I didn't want any more rejection."

I asked him more about his own parents: "Sometimes, you know, even though we don't want to, we end up repeating the same patterns we saw in our parents. Do you think that's been true for you?" He grabbed at the thought: "My dad made Mom the strong one. Mom was full of life, active. Dad got to feeling terribly sorry for himself. My wife says I'm doing what my dad did to my mom. She's tired of being the strong one. But I've tried not to dominate."

I inquired what his ideal marriage would be like. "Like it was when we met. We didn't fight, did a lot together, I was happy and content, she was everything I wanted." (I thought: not a very mature image of marriage, but that's understandable.) I asked about their sex life, because sometimes if the sex is still good, or was once good, it's a good sign. There may be some chemistry there to work with. He said the frequency of sex had been declining for a year and was nonexistent for the past six months, except for a month ago when they had a weekend like old times. (I wondered: Was that when she first met her present lover?)

"What do you think it would take for this marriage to work?" I asked. (I was pressing to see how realistic he was.) "We'd have to leave our jobs and move away. I'd be too embarrassed to stay, what with everyone knowing she once left me." I asked what he would do with all that anger. "Stuff it, like always. I'm very good at being the 'nice guy.' " "Ever let it out?" I inquired. He described an episode of shooting a pet rabbit with such glee that it alarmed me. I asked directly: "Ever think about shooting her or her lover?" "Yes," he said, but assured me he'd never do it. (I made a mental note to bring this up when we were in joint session so that she would be sure to know the full extent of his anger.)

I noted out loud that it sounded as though he had always felt out of control in his life and didn't know how to change that without losing his temper and fighting and ruining everything. I asked what he thought it would take for him to feel good about himself. He answered quickly: "Lose 20 pounds, get a job with higher pay, and live in a peaceful house." I planted a seed: "Do you think you might finally find the peace you've been looking for by living alone for awhile?" He looked thoughtful and acknowledged that that might in fact be true. (Was he just being the "good guy" with me, too?)

I invited his wife to join us. They sat facing each other. The agenda seemed very clear to me. They had a lot of individual growth to do and there was not sufficient love, attraction, or motivation to do this within the context of their present relationship. I hoped that in the hour we had left they would be able to listen to one another, own their own issues, forgive each other, feel some increased respect for themselves and each other, and gain some hope that they could each find a way of creating a life that would work for them. I felt very hopeful. Maybe my hope would help them.

I began the joint session with a spontaneous playful thought. I asked the husband if he could think of a metaphor that described him, a symbol or an animal that represented him in his relationship to date with his wife. My intuition was on target, for he responded immediately: "Yeh, like a turtle, lying on a log, soaking up the sun." I added, "Or a sponge soaking up love." We all laughed. It broke the ice and cut through to the heart of what needed to be said. It was also a measure of his openness to change, and I was relieved that he could acknowledge his passivity and even laugh about it. The image became our theme for the rest of the session.

She talked about images of feeling trapped and weighed down, and shared with him, with a bit of coaching, the pattern of her life to date: she was abandoned at a young age by her mother and had to care for a dependent father and a younger sister; just as she was finally able to move out of her father's house and give up the role of caretaker, she suddenly found herself with a lover who needed someone to take care of him and his children. She stated forcefully, "I don't want to ever be responsible for someone else. I am afraid to even be your friend because I am so scared that you'll stay dependent on me." He heard her in a way he apparently never had before and told her so.

To help them focus on feelings (they had both been so good for so long at denying the existence of any emotion), I diagramed for them the characteristic feelings associated with loss. I pointed out how the pattern can differ for the leaver and the leavee (leaver: denial, anger, pain, resolution; leavee: denial, pain, anger, resolution). I noted that the wife had yet to let herself really grieve for the losses and injustices of her life, that up until now she couldn't afford to do so because she had to be strong, that now she needed to find a safe place where she could afford to relax and get in touch not just with her anger, but also with her many years of pain. He, on the other hand, needed someone to help him work through his many years of anger at having to always be careful to not "rock any boats."

And then to lighten what had become very heavy, I turned to him and asked: "I don't think you're going to be willing to always be a turtle. What kind of animal would you like to be?" He laughed: "A teddy bear." I noted, "But teddy bears, lovable as they are, are still sitting there waiting to be loved. I think you will slowly find yourself just as eager to give as to receive love. At least, that is my goal for you." And then we talked about the image of the sun shining so strongly within himself that he radiated its warmth outward to all those about him whom he loved. He tried to imagine that.

And then I directed the wife: "My wish for you is that you allow yourself two years to just think about yourself, to just focus on what you want and how you feel." I urged her to not even contemplate pursuing a relationship until she had done that. And I told her about adult children of alcoholics and wondered if she might have some of those issues. Perhaps it even fit for him.

I ended with the question: "And now, how do you want to relate to each other after you walk out of here today? What do you want to do about your marriage?" She stated firmly that she wanted a divorce as soon as possible and then didn't want to see him for a while. He agreed to go and see a lawyer with her. I asked them how they were feeling now compared to when they walked in a few hours ago. They both said, "A lot of relief." I urged them to seek counseling on an individual basis closer to home and assured them I'd be glad to share this session with their therapists if they so requested. As they left the office, I went back to the room, pulled the sheets up over the dead body, took a deep breath, and went upstairs to my partner for a good, long hug.

WHEN A LOT OF TLC MAY DO THE TRICK

Actually, that's probably deceiving. It takes a bit more than just TLC. But there do seem to be couples who do most of the work themselves. All I have to do is believe in them, care about them, and provide a warm safe place where they can be open with one another.

I am thinking of one couple who healed not only their own relationship but also their relationships with their parents, siblings, and children—and all within six months. That's a lot of healing. It all started for me with a call from the wife who indicated that after 25 years of marriage she'd been to see an attorney about a divorce. Since the attorney recommended that she not make a final decision until they'd given it one more chance, she was giving me a call. She reported that the youngest of their five children was a freshman in college, and she didn't like not having anyone left at home. She was currently involved with a man whom she'd met at work ("I needed someone"), and indicated that she would already have left her marriage if she'd thought he'd make a commitment to her. She said that her husband was pressing her for a decision regarding their relationship and wanted to come in for therapy.

Already I had positive vibes: The partner who had contemplated leaving was the one asking for help in assessing the marriage; she was involved with another man but seemed reasonably rational about its potential; the husband already knew about the affair and yet wanted to work on the marriage. The fact that the last child had just left home suggested we were dealing with a classic "empty-nest-throws-spousal-system-into-chaos" phenomenon.

As usual, I scheduled a three-hour block and, having already talked to the wife on the phone, saw the husband first. Again, the vibes were good. He began by recounting how a month ago she'd announced that she was seeing another man and wanted a divorce. When he had pressed her about why, she had talked about feeling hollow inside and unloved. When he asked her if she still loved him (her husband), she said yes, that she didn't think she was in love with the other man but just really enjoyed his attention. He talked a lot about how he had neglected his wife. For years she'd resented his many activities and pleaded with him not to always leave her alone. He acknowledged that he couldn't say no to anyone but his wife, and constantly over-committed himself to community, athletic, and civic projects.

When I asked if this had been true all his life, he launched into how hard it had been growing up. He talked about harboring resentment toward his father for years because of his harsh discipline ("I was so afraid of him I would hide when he came home"), about his humiliation at having to wear ugly hand-me-downs to school, and about the fact that the kids made fun of him because of his thick glasses. He said he learned to be a comedian to make people laugh ("my wife was often the brunt of my jokes") and always tried hard to make everyone like him—everyone, that is, except his wife, whom he had taken for granted until the last few months when she stopped cooking and cleaning and washing his clothes ("she hasn't felt like doing anything for me lately"). He talked passionately about how he knew he could change and that he could understand why she'd look for someone else ("I drove her out of the house"). He knew he needed to do things differently and stated that he had already started on this.

As I listened I felt so much potential, so much readiness on his part to be vulnerable and to give. I reflected this to him, and guessed that this was exactly what his wife had always yearned for. I asked him to wait while I talked to her.

"Tell me how things are for you," I said to her. She began, "He (the other man) was just someone to lean on. I had no one else left in my life." She said that her parents had never been there for her, had never wanted to know about her problems, had always preferred her sister, and had always needed her to have her life together. She said that she worried about everything and had a lot of health problems—migraines, backache, colitis, and severe asthma (it was obvious that this was a serious case of somatization and repressed emotion). She had worshipped her husband, given him her whole life, but had never felt worthy of him or appreciated by him: "He's such a free spirit—everyone loves him." One night a few months ago he went out drinking with the boys and didn't come home until very late. She went to bed crying and it was a month later she told him she wanted a divorce. Since then she had had no more headaches or stomach pains.

She reported that the attention from the other man had done wonders for her self-esteem. She didn't think he would be a good partner for her ("very independent and definitely a work-aholic"), but he made her feel like a million dollars. "My husband is stagnant, complacent. He has to change or I can't stand living with him. There must be more to life than this." I asked my bottom-line question: "How are things sexually?" She answered quickly, "Good. Couldn't be better. But I'm so afraid it won't last. He's making such an effort. I'm so afraid he'll pay me back for making him change. Is he staying just because he's afraid to be alone?"

I noted to myself how similar they were: each having never felt sufficient love and acceptance, neither secure in their love-ableness, each having worked so hard to win love—she as a wife and mother, he as a friend to the whole world. I would share that observation with them when I saw them together. It would help with the bonding and allow them to feel safer with each other. I empathized with her new-found sense of power and noted that this had facilitated the necessary crisis in their lives: By pressing the issues in their marriage so forcefully, she was taking care not only of herself but of the relationship as well. She was relieved that I did not judge her. Her friends thought she was crazy and accused her of trying to smother him.

When I saw them together, their sharing was direct and loving. When I asked him to tell her where he was regarding their relationship, he was beautifully articulate: "I was always rejected by girls in high school, and I feared for years that you wouldn't want me either. I've been defending against that all these years. I've been afraid to show you I needed you. I've kept busy so in case you left I'd have something. I want to be the friend you find in him. You need to tell me what you need. Don't be afraid to confront me. Don't confuse change with smothering. I want to be close to you." She was persistent: "But it never did me any good to tell you. You were out enjoying life and I was home. It didn't feel fair. I don't want to be as resentful of you at 60 as Mom is of Dad." I let them talk without interference. They had obviously done a lot of talking in the month since they had started this process. They were clear and constructive. There was no discussion of the outside relationship. It was clearly not the real issue. I did not mention it either.

I ended the session by asking them each to list on a sheet of paper three specific things they needed from the other in the next week. She asked him to share responsibility for the housework, to take more interest in the house, and to do something fun with her. He asked her to tell him what she needed from him at the time she needed it, to help him work on the outside of the house, and to be willing to do some of the things he liked to do ("and I don't want to hear your usual excuses"). I pressed them to be as specific and behaviorally oriented as possible in their contract for the next week. He promised to do the dishes with her every night; she agreed to rake the lawn as he cut it; and they decided to go out the next Friday night. We all committed to work together weekly for the next several months.

The next week I saw them for two hours, giving them each some individual time with me so that the wife could talk freely about any feelings she might be having about the outside relationship. Predictably, she had talked to him several times that week. He had seemed cooler, and she was mourning the loss of that relationship. Her husband was giving her a lot of attention and she loved it, but now she was complaining of being smothered herself. Moreover, she felt guilty when his friends complained that they never saw him anymore. She felt like an emotional yo-yo: on a high one day, crying the next, having terrible headaches and stomach aches, and taking four tranquillizers and one sleeping pill a day. She assured me that she would see her doctor the next day.

When I saw her husband it was clear that he was holding steadily on course. He was enjoying her company more than ever before. They had even joined a theater production group. In fact, he said, he agonized when he couldn't be with her. He reported having had a difficult time one night when she went out to the movies with the girls, saying it hurt when she didn't ask him to go along. He wondered if this was how it used to feel to her when she was alone at home without him. He wanted her to quit worrying about coming between him and his friends— he was with her because he wanted to be. He felt badly that she wasn't initiating sex or affection, but they'd had good sex on Saturday. He felt things were a little better every day, but knew she was still dealing with her feelings about the other man.

When I saw them together I asked them to talk with each other about how the week had gone. I suggested that they start by reviewing the contract from the last session and thanking each other for any efforts they had made. They were able to sit facing each other and say, "I really appreciated it when you. . . ." It was a very frank discussion. She talked about her need for him to be at ease about being at home without her, and tried to help him see that she didn't want to have to rush home just to comfort him. She poignantly described her need to learn to do more things on her own and her fear of losing his new-found affection in the process. He talked about his hope that she'd be more spontaneously affectionate. She hoped he'd understand that it would take a while for her to trust that it was safe to do so. They both laughingly told me about letting the phone ring while they made love on Saturday afternoon. For the first time they mentioned their children and their concerns about them, and the fact that they were going to Alabama in a month to visit her parents.

I ended the session by noting the strengths I had seen: their openness; their ability to hear each other; their courage to tackle the issues directly; their enjoyment of each other's company; her willingness to become more independent and he more dependent; and their willingness to not let others' expectations determine how they would relate as a couple. I summarized what I saw as their central issues, normalized these as common for couples in their life stage, and sowed the seeds for starting to work to ensure that the dysfunctional patterns in their own families were not perpetuated in their children. I suggested that we might start by planning for the visit to her parents so that they could use that time to begin some healing in that relationship. For homework, we decided to try a nongenital massage exercise to help them grow closer in their physical relationship, and I urged them to spend 20 minutes a day actively listening to each other's feelings, whatever they might be. The emphasis was to be on open expression of themselves and their feelings to each other and to their families, both positive feelings and negative feelings.

It was clear to me by the end of the session that this couple would make it. Their love was still strong, stronger in fact than they had even realized. The passion was still there, also probably stronger than they had yet realized. Their interpersonal skills were good. Their motivation was high. They needed to clean up some important unfinished business from their childhoods, to learn to trust that it was safe to be themselves, to more easily and consistently express their thoughts and feelings to their family members and to each other, to break a family pattern of denying one's own needs in order to be loved, and to work out between them a mutually acceptable degree of closeness. Those became our goals for the next 12 sessions.

Coincidentally, or not so coincidentally, crises related to parental illness occurred in both their families of origin within the next several months. Given the new strength in their relationship, and their awareness of the importance of differentiation, we were able to utilize these opportunities to help them and their families move toward the above goals.

WHEN MAJOR SURGERY AND INTENSIVE CARE ARE CALLED FOR

Cases that fall into this category are long-term (a year or more) and, for the first few months, sessions often last for two hours. It is common for there to be emergency sessions and phone calls between sessions to help one or the other partner reduce his or her panic and to reinforce productive ways of dealing with stress.

The challenge is to help each partner find the courage to hang in there and deal with the inevitable pain directly rather than resorting to old defenses (e.g., running away to another relationship or alcohol or suicide or lawyers, withdrawal in sullen self-righteousness or self-protection, lashing out in hysteria or violence or retaliation). Often there are long-term intrapsychic issues, such as fear of intimacy, lack of trust, fear of abandonment, or feelings of personal inadequacy, that must be dealt with. Traditional marital conflicts regarding power, commitment, communication, and lack of sexual satisfaction are common. Always therapy involves exploring patterns brought from families of origin, developing more effective ways of expressing and meeting needs, learning ways of nurturing the spousal unit and appreciating the importance of doing so, and working to achieve differentiation and more bonding. Sometimes there is sufficient motivation to do the hard work, sometimes there isn't.

These cases take a great deal of energy on the part of everyone. Emotionality is high, there is no certainty that therapy will work, and at the beginning I must be the one who carries the faith in our therapeutic process. The couple have usually had no experience to convince them that going through the pain is better than avoiding it, that talking about one's feelings and increasing one's vulnerability can actually increase intimacy and emotional security. For some time I need to be the committed one—calm, clear, confident, and caring.

When I sense at the end of the first three-hour session that a case will fall into this category, I am usually very frank. It is not unusual for me to say something like: "You no longer have a marriage, and I'm not sure if you ever did. The challenge for us will be to help you decide whether you would like to be married to each other." Or, "It feels to me as though you have a 50–50 chance of saving this marriage. I'm willing to give it my all if you are, but I can't promise you how we will end up. At the very least I will try to help you make a good decision and to respect yourselves and each other for having done so." The reality is that about 50% of these couples end up getting a divorce, but if they do not terminate prematurely it is usually fairly amiable. (Whether the variables that predispose them to "hang in" during therapy are the same variables responsible for the amicability at separation, and hence the therapy itself is at best only partially responsible for this outcome, is beyond the scope of this chapter.)

I often ask these couples to postpone making a decision about their marriage for at least six months, and to make a commitment to at least 10 sessions of therapy. This is important because we have a lot of work to do, it may take some time before we will see any clear-cut results, and the stress may, in fact, get worse before it gets better. I explain to them my surgery metaphor, pointing out that for a while it may feel like they are undergoing a serious operation and they may hurt a lot, but surgery is necessary and I will stand by them. They usually understand, within a few sessions if not immediately, and during the course of therapy we may come back to this surgery image. For instance, one day I may say, "Well, I think we've finally made it out of intensive care," and they are relieved to know that the therapist thinks they have progressed that far.

If couples in which one partner has threatened divorce do not elect to go into therapy, with its implicit honesty, intensity, pain, and hard work, then by definition they have already made a decision about their marriage and essentially fall into a category of cases that might best be called "death by default." For even if they do decide to stay together, their marriage will be no more alive than it was to begin with and so might as well be considered dead.

In the above cases, I say to the couple loud and clear: "So you have decided that the marriage is over and that you have all the information you need with which to make that decision. You feel sure that you have made the best decision and you don't anticipate ever saying to yourself, 'I wonder what would have happened if we had tried harder.' " Or, "So you're willing to settle for the status quo. The cost of staying in a relationship which does not meet your needs is less than the cost of trying to make that relationship better." Sometimes I suggest that they go home and "sleep on it" and come back in a week and decide.

The following case is a good example of a couple who needed surgery and a great deal of intensive care. They had been married for four years with no children, were in their late twenties/early thirties, and were both successful young professionals. The wife called to say that her husband had been having a lot of doubts about their marriage and, in fact, had become so depressed that he'd taken a week off from work to go away to sort things out. She felt they had to get some outside help.

He came into our first session looking very distressed, with 12 pages of carefully thought-out introspection and reflection. He was, in fact, so primed to talk to her that I decided (as it turned out, unwisely) to forego seeing them separately. We spent the whole three hours together, talking intensely about their expectations of marriage, what was missing in their own marriage, and their fears and anxieties.

He stated that he felt loved by his wife and secure in their relationship, but did not know if he loved her. He felt no physical attraction to her and no passion ("no desire to hold hands, to put my arms around her, to kiss her, to sit on the sofa together, to neck"), and he yearned for those things. On the other hand, a long-time friend had told him that the most important thing in marriage was commitment, and that financial security and getting along well together were more important than sex. He wondered if he was being unrealistic in his expectations and felt terrible guilt about hurting his wife. He confessed that he had always had doubts about his feelings for her, but it had felt so good to be loved and everyone in his family had thought they were such a great match that he had accepted the marriage as a good idea.

As they talked, the pain in the room was so intense one could almost taste it—the burning of old dreams, old images, old fantasies. As he spoke of not having been in love with her on their wedding day, it felt as though he seared her very heart. She said she'd loved him from the moment she met him and couldn't imagine living without him. As she talked of her love for him, the guilt broke out in beads on his forehead. There was no flow of tears, just hot pain and cold sweat.

The first task was to help the wife find some emotional distance, some power, some sense that she could survive whatever happened, and some conviction that she was a lovable woman even if her husband did not love her. We talked about where she could find support. It could not be her husband. Right now he needed to know that he could leave and she would be all right, that he could have needs and be honest about them and not be seen as a bad person for having them. The only salvation I could see for the relationship appeared to be in equalizing the power by helping her get out of the roles of pursuer, co-conspirator to the lie, and accommodator. We listed all the alternatives available to them. They decided to come back in a week, ready to discuss these.

The week proved to be difficult. When they came in, they reported that they had bickered together, cried together, been painfully silent together. The wife felt stronger and could easily list a whole host of personal qualities of which she was proud. She had talked to her family and to her friends, and had rallied a tight support network. In fact, in her effort to gain some power, she was about to triangle-in the whole universe (i.e., she would attempt to get anybody or everybody to be on her side and to see things her way), and her husband was quickly becoming the bad guy, the outcast. I sought to rein things in a bit by pointing out these dynamics, and wondered out loud if she had to turn everyone against him in order to get the support she needed.

They decided that they would try a trial separation. It was too hard for him to get perspective on the relationship while living at home—too many memories, too aware of her pain. And she needed to have him away so she could focus on her own growth and work on feeling good about herself. Her anger had finally been kindled. She could tell him clearly that she needed him to go and that she resented the fact that he had not been honest with her about his feelings before he married her. She began to get in touch with her anger at her own father for having been unloving to her mother and at her mother for having been so compliant.

Her anger was at fever pitch the next time I saw them. She had learned what I would have learned if I had not been seduced out of my normal individual sessions at our first meeting: Her husband was having an affair with a married woman and was deeply involved in that relationship. She had found hotel receipts and gone to confront him with them. The husband had called me to tell me, so I was prepared. I saw them separately and then together.

When I was alone with the husband, he talked a lot about his need to exert control in his life, to protect himself by not telling others the whole truth. It was a technique he had learned by dealing with an overly demanding, overly controlling, overly critical mother. What she didn't know he didn't have to hear about. It was clear to him that being honest meant giving up control, and yet he sought the peace of mind, the self-respect, the freedom from guilt that he realized would come from greater honesty.

He was high from the feeling of being in love and his first experience of real sexual passion. He could not imagine ever experiencing this same excitement with his wife, yet couldn't imagine not having her as a friend and a member of his family. It was so hard for him to leave a woman who had done nothing to deserve that leaving. He was still wearing his wedding ring but had moved out of the house four days before. He wanted time to experience the outside relationship before deciding about his marriage.

The wife was feeling a lot stronger. Somehow it was easier, knowing that he had left her because of another woman. It allowed her to be really good and angry. Still, she did not want to give up hope for the relationship. She was trying to find a way of talking to her friends and family about the situation and still be supportive of her husband. She knew that he was very confused. I played for time: "Is there any way you could work on what you need to do for you while leaving the option open for things to work out with your husband?" We talked about what kind of relationship she wanted with him in the next few weeks. Almost as a paradoxical injunction, I warned her not to give up her anger too soon since she might need it in order to stay strong. Her goal was to stay married, but she knew it would have to be a more equal relationship. She was clear that he would have to work to win her back if the marriage was ever to work.

In the joint session, she told him how angry she was about his dishonesty: He had said he would be completely honest with her. He had said that no one else was involved. Why had he lied? Why hadn't he used his feelings for the other woman simply as a sign that things were not right in their own marriage and come to her earlier? He did his best to tell her of his internal struggles, of his fear of losing her, of his fear of making her cry, of his love for her but his inability to make himself feel in love with her, of how good it was to realize he could feel passion for someone. They made a date to talk more that night about what had happened, where they were now, and how they saw the future.

I saw them for three hours the next day. He was consistent: He cared about her, he wanted good things for her, he wanted to be friends and to be able to talk together without animosity, but he did not want to be married to her—at least, not now. He begged her not to be vindictive and asked her not to press for an official separation. She said she would try to find the strength to wait for three or four months. They both talked about how confused and scared they felt.

The rest of the session was devoted to reviewing the history of their own relationship. I asked each of them to draw a marriage time line, starting with when they met and noting the crucial events, and they talked about their differing perceptions of these events. They both realized that they had married for the wrong reasons: She had been in love with a fantasy, and he had wanted the unconditional love he had never felt from his mother. They both agreed that their relationship was better than it had ever been: "We have talked more in the last two weeks than in the whole time we have known each other, and for the first time about feelings." She cried. I asked if she'd like him to hold her. She sobbed in his arms, he stroked her hair. Through her tears, she sighed, "I wish I could stay angry with you. It would make it so much easier to leave you. But I know deep down I will always love you."

The following week we had another two-hour session. They worked further on exploring and expressing their angers and disappointments about the relationship. The husband realized that soon after their marriage he had felt trapped and that her happiness had only made him feel more so. He had expressed this by withdrawing and by snapping at her. They both acknowledged their tendencies to sweep problems under the table and vowed to help each other try to confront the truth. She pressed him to do this with his own family.

For the next several months I saw them in individual sessions. The husband worked on his relationships with his parents and his many siblings, and pondered his relationship with "the other woman" who had by now left her own husband. The wife scheduled two sessions with her own parents, followed by one conjoint session. She lost some weight, got reinvolved in sports, began to date and develop a sexual relationship with another man, and saw her husband from time to time.

In about three months, he asked her if he could move back into the house. He had decided he couldn't work on a second relationship until he was sure that he could not learn to love his wife. She agreed, but they both wanted to go slowly, careful not to set themselves up for further disappointment. For some time they even hesitated to share the same bed. On occasion they would catch themselves falling back into old patterns, with the husband withdrawing and the wife allowing it to happen. Sometimes they made great love, but he was often skeptical, wondering if it might just be that they were "horny." Most of the time they were enjoying being together, and they were feeling much better about themselves as individuals.

I went away on vacation, concerned about leaving them at such a tenuous time. When I returned, they reported that they had decided to stay together and that they did not feel the need for any more therapy at this time. I urged them to remember their patterns of denial that had gotten them into so much trouble before, and invited them to come back if they should feel the need. I crossed my fingers and hoped they would. They had made so much progress; I wondered if it had been enough.

CONCLUSION

The conclusion is obvious: The fact that one person wants a divorce is no sign that the marriage is over. A lot depends on why that person wants the divorce and how much the other desires to save the marriage. If one is leaving because she or he feels unloved or unappreciated, discounted or not listened to, bored, frustrated, or attracted to another, the desire to leave may evaporate if the partner rallies quickly, consistently, and definitively to the cause. This is especially true if the couple were once in love and there is still a flicker of that love, as in the case of our second couple. The one's ambivalence about leaving and the other's strong determination to create a more mutually satisfying relationship gives the therapist a lot of resources with which to work.

The situation is more complicated and more challenging when both are ambivalent, when a long history of hurt and anger has buried much of the old attraction and caring, and when the individuals bring into the relationship a lot of personal issues related to control and intimacy. If there is little apparent benefit to staying in the marriage, a lot of pulls to leave, and not much love to begin with (as in our first case), therapy for the relationship may not stand a chance. Something has to motivate the individuals to want to make the necessary changes in the relationship before couple therapy can be successful.

Often the first thing a therapist must do is help each partner assess his or her own motivation for working on the marriage. Before marital therapy can begin in earnest, "limbo therapy" is often necessary in order to help the individuals sort out for themselves how important it is to them to try to improve their relationship. (This was clearly the situation during our third case.) Hopefully a lot of this exploration can occur with both persons present in the room, for the very process of clarifying thoughts and feelings—necessary before one can assess one's motivation—fosters an increase in differentiation and helps the couple learn new self-disclosure/listening skills and grow in openness and honesty with each other. This phase may take as long as six months to a year, sometimes longer, and may involve periods of living apart or even dating others, before the couple can resolve whether they are ready for divorce therapy or marital therapy. But even though they may not yet be ready to commit themselves to improving their level of marital intimacy, the process of decision making may do much to improve their general relationship. It is not unusual for couples to proclaim, after sorting out whether or not to divorce, that they have become better friends than ever before, even if they decide to separate.

It is particularly with the latter cases—the limbo cases—where the therapist's skill as a healer is truly tested. Can the therapist encourage the couple to put the decision about the marital relationship on hold in order to give themselves time to explore together whether they wish to be married? Can the therapist create an atmosphere in which each feels safe enough to be vulnerable in the presence of the other—to examine their own individual issues, explore the patterns learned in their former families, experience their pain, express their fears, assert their needs? Can the therapist help the committed partner to use the other's uncertainty as a time in which to grow in his or her own capacity to love—to learn how to be less emotionally reactive, to let the partner be free to do what is needed for his or her well-being, to focus efforts for a while on personal growth? Can the therapist help the couple brainstorm creative solutions to their own particular combination of individual and relationship needs, to expand their options, and to see new possibilities for their relationship? Can the therapist help them come to trust in the process of dialogue, in the possibility that change can be permanent, and in themselves and each other?

It is not an easy process—for client or therapist. It is not easy for clients to risk opening themselves up for more hurt or for the therapist to stand beside individuals who are in intense anguish and anxiety. The therapist withstands the pain more easily because experience has taught him or her to understand and believe in the healing process. It is precisely this belief that will provide the conflicted couple the hope, the strength, and the safety they need in order to face the surgery necessary for the survival of their relationship. The secret to success lies in the therapist's commitment to this healing process, the individuals' desire to change, and everyone's willingness to "hang in there" and work. If this can be achieved, the result will almost certainly be a new, different, and far healthier relationship, whatever external legal form it may assume.

Afterword

VALIDATION OF ONE'S OWN THEORY AND METHOD

Some—I hope many—will experience these 12 therapy accounts to be validating and confirming. I hope the reader will experience a feeling that "my own work is pretty much on target" (defining "on target" as the type or methodology of therapy advocated and demonstrated by the various authors). The fact of validation and confirmation does not mean that the reader has failed to learn anything new! Nor does it mean that the reader is satisfied with himself or herself and his or her own theory and methodology! It does mean that by reading the 12 accounts we may feel good about how we have been handling similar cases.

DIFFERENCES AND SIMILARITIES AMONG THE AUTHORS

There are some notable differences between and among the authors. Several chapters are more systemic and contextual than others. One chapter is primarily based on object relations theory, and several chapters are more theoretical than others. One would have to be pollyannish or glibly reductionistic if one did not see these differences. Certainly we do not want to force the 12 accounts into a Procrustean bed by making them fit into a common mold. On the other hand, the differences need to be placed in perspective.

249

We do not have a dyed-in-the-wool structuralist going head on against an equally adamant strategist, Bowenian, or experientialist. Nor do we have any serious clashes between those who stress aesthetics and those who stress pragmatics.

The differences are more in terms of emphasis than in terms of basic theory. Some of the authors have chosen to emphasize assessment more than others. Several authors allow their theoretical perspective to show through their approach, while others are simply more pragmatic.

The similarities include a goodly amount of attention to careful assessment, a focus upon clarity in the establishment of a therapeutic contract or agreement, and an emphasis on slowing down the partner who expresses the desire to end the marriage. Another similarity—taking seriously the threat to divorce but not necessarily accepting it at face value—will be discussed shortly.

On a more integrative level I see a rejection of monotheory, be it structural, strategic, extended, behaviorist, analytic, or experientialist. I do not see anyone copying anyone! I do not see anyone modeling themselves after a circuit-star or a mentor. Nor do I see anyone feeling or thinking that true integration means taking an equal little bit from every one of the stars or every one of the theories!

LET THE READER EXTRAPOLATE, CLASSIFY, AND INTEGRATE

As I stated in the Introduction, I would like the reader to write his or her own Afterword. I would like to challenge the reader to create his or her own taxonomy wherein each of the accounts is placed on a continuum. The question is which continuum? The continuum of single theory to multitheory to integrated theory to minimal theory to nontheory is one possibility. Another possibility for an overall taxonomic classification would be a continuum extending from manifest practicality at one end to a superimposure of a forced theoretical frame at the other end. A third type of classification might be based on assessment at intake and prognosis for staying together versus uncoupling.

Surely there is consensus that some marriages should be terminated. Likewise, there is surely consensus that in many marriages one partner or the other or both give up too quickly, thus shutting the door on the possibility of change, growth and rebuilding, a type III error (Crosby, 1985).

WHEN ONE WANTS OUT . . .

The therapist is at risk whenever she or he takes at face value statements such as, "I want a divorce," "I think I want a divorce," "I want out," or "I don't love you anymore." These statements and similar ones are always to be taken seriously but not necessarily as final, irrevocable, or the last word! The very fact that the couple or only one of the partners is sitting with the therapist in a therapy session is mandate enough for the therapist to accept such declarations of intended divorce with a healthy degree of skepticism.

The following list is an extrapolation of points and comments made in the 12 chapters, together with several that I have added, relating to the basic theme of "some wanting out."

Some don't really want out, they just threaten!—a power ploy, often a part of the couple's dance.

Some really do want out, until they have a chance to ventilate years of pent-up anger.

Some want out and they want the therapist to help him or her get out.

Some really feel that love has died, but as they deal with their negative feelings they are surprised that positive feelings begin to reassert themselves.

Some want desperately to be overruled by an impartial therapist.

Some want concessions from a stymied partner: "Talk me out of this. Show me how we can stay together."

Some don't want out but they feel helpless in otherwise dislodging themselves from impasse.

Some don't want out but they feel themselves growing stagnant, losing all vitality and aliveness.

Some don't want out but they feel they must punish their mate for an infidelity.

Some don't want out but they must redress verbal, emotional, or even physical abuse.

Some want out and they go into therapy in order to attempt to manipulate the therapist into doing rescue therapy for the one who doesn't want out.

Some want out and they also want to appear to others and themselves as having left no stone unturned in their effort to save the marriage; nevertheless, their performance is pro forma.

Some don't want out but they feel they have never been taken seriously and hence they play their trump card, actually filing for divorce.

Some—even many—think they want out, but when systemic patterns are discovered (including intergenerational repetition), the partners are able to see that they have been scapegoating their marriage.

Some want out because they have found someone more attractive, more desirable, and/or more attentive to their needs, but in therapy they discover their own dependency patterns and the illicit attraction soon subsides.

Some want out because their new lover has demanded they divorce. These persons often secretly hope that their marriage will improve so that they don't have to marry the illicit lover.

Some want out and they will get out no matter what the therapist says or does.

Some don't want out and they really should get out! They stay married for the wrong reasons, a type II error (Crosby, 1985).

Some should have ended the marriage years ago; both partners need help in uncoupling.

Some people don't need a therapist! They know what they want and they know what they're doing.

THE POSSIBILITY OF DIVORCE

When we begin to move out of the preambivalent stage into the ambivalent stage of marriage, we face the concrete possibility of divorce (Nichols & Everett, 1986). Although knowledge about divorce has always been part of our reality, the intimate and immediate coming to terms with the possibility of divorce "for me" may be a crisis point.

Whether our journey leads us to postambivalence resulting in divorce or to postambivalence resulting in a renewal of our marriage, facing the possibility of divorce is often the necessary prerequisite for our continuing growth. As such, it is good for us to face who we are and where we are in our life together. Otherwise our preambivalent homeostasis may regress into a pseudomutuality, which frequently becomes lethal for both partners. Sometimes we just can't proceed to rebuild until we first come to terms with the possibility that there may be nothing left to build upon, that maybe the relationship really is over! Paradoxically, once we come to grips with this possibility, we may find ourselves motivated and committed to the task of rebuilding.

DIVORCE THE FAMILIES OF ORIGIN
AND SAVE THE MARRIAGE

I believe the major extrinsic reason for scapegoating marriage that needs to be factored out before focusing on intrinsic issues is the ever-present and unrecognized influence of one's family of origin. Systems theory has highlighted this dimension in a profoundly significant way. My own bias is that when systems theory is pragmatically integrated with a "liberated" theory of object relations we will be on the brink of discovering the major set of causes, patterns, beliefs, and values that underlie marital discord and failure.*

In spite of what the romanticists say, we do marry the family. The more we can help our clients free themselves from their families of origin, or at least understand their families of origin, the greater the possibility for rebuilding the marriage.

In metaphorical terms, we need to divorce our family of origin (Berne, 1964). Paradoxically, in divorcing our family of origin we perhaps have the first real opportunity to reconceive, recon-

---

* By liberated, I mean released from the classical theory of personality structure with its emphasis on libido, ego, and superego, as well as from the classical theory of human development (i.e., the oral, anal, phallic, latent, and genital stages).

struct, and rebuild our marriage. Further, for the first time in our life we may have an opportunity to become truly adult-equals with our parents. In short, the minimization of enmeshment and the maximization of differentiation, combined with the minimization of transference and the maximization of autonomy, are the sine qua non for genuine intimacy, closeness, and a meaningful sharing of life together.

John F. Crosby, Ph.D.

REFERENCES

Berne, E. (1964). *Games people play* (pp. 182–183). New York: Grove Press.

Crosby, J. F. (1985). *Illusion and disillusion: The self in love and marriage* (3rd Ed.) (pp. 299–300). Belmont, CA: Wadsworth Publishing Co.

Nichols, W. C., & Everett, C. A. (1986). *Systemic family therapy: An integrative approach* (pp. 287–290). New York: The Guilford Press.

Index

255